P9-AOO-841

Keeping the World On Two Wheels

How J&P Cycles Changed the American Motorcycle Industry

By Ed Youngblood

Published by Motohistory
for J&P Cycles®

Design by Kim Barlag, Nicole Ridge & Brett Medema.
Main cover photograph by Michael Lichter.
Back cover photograph by Mike Farabaugh.
Photos of the John Parham collection, pages 96 through 133, by Doug Mitchel.
Photos of "Chaos" custom motorcycle, pages 142 and 143, by Pam Proctor.
All other photos from the J&P Cycles archives unless identified otherwise.

Books are available in single copies or quantity from
J&P Cycles
13225 Circle Drive / P.O. Box 138
Anamosa, IA, USA 52205
Phone: 1-800-397-4844
Worldwide Fax: 319-462-4283
Web site: http://**WWW.JPCYCLES.COM**

ISBN 978-0-9788817-2-6

54321

Printed in the United States

(photo by Michael Lichter)

Shoeless Joe Jackson:
"Is this heaven?"

Ray Kinsella:
"No, this is Iowa."

— *Field of Dreams*
1989

Table of Contents

(photo by Arlen Ness Enterprises)

Foreword

In the mid-1980s, the American Big Twin began to come into its own. After 25 years of domination by imported motorcycles, the classic American motorcycle was suddenly popular again; so popular that soon all the leading foreign brands would begin to imitate it. This new interest in traditional American motorcycles, plus the uniquely American art form that some people call "Kustom Kulture," set loose an exciting era of custom motorcycle design that has grown into a large and important niche in the worldwide motorcycle market.

As one of the pioneers of motorcycle customizing in America, I was invited in 1993 to be a special guest at the European Super Rally in Italy. This is a major international annual event that moves around Europe, from country to country, and that year it was in Elba. I wasn't real certain what to expect from the Super Rally, but I saw something that I never would have guessed in my wildest dreams. There was John Parham, from the little town of Anamosa, Iowa, standing in his booth, handing out J&P Cycles catalogs.

I knew who John was, and had seen him at many shows and rallies in the United States, but his presence in Italy left a really strong impression on me. Here was a guy who would go the extra mile to build his business, who would cross an ocean to see if he could find a new opportunity to sell custom motorcycle accessories and promote J&P Cycles. You talk about your Midwestern American work ethic; this is it!

Since then, I have gotten to know John and his wife Jill pretty well, and what they have accomplished never ceases to amaze me. For example, I was surprised again when I was invited to attend their open house at J&P Cycles in 2005. I couldn't believe my eyes. Here, in a small town in Iowa farm country, there were more than 10,000 bikers gathered for a one-day event! I have no idea where they all came from, but it became clear to me that J&P knows how to make its customers happy, how to build a following, and how to earn their loyalty. It is widely known throughout the industry that J&P does this through a very high standard of customer service.

Over the years, John and Jill Parham, and their dedicated employees, have pioneered new ways to sell products and promote motorcycling. They were the first in the American motorcycle industry to learn how to augment their point-of-sale business with catalog and mail-order sales, and they've kept their customers coming back by providing prompt service, accurate fulfillment, and technical support. At the same time, they have not only maintained, but have expanded their Iowa retail business by opening a store in Florida, at Destination Daytona, that is surely an industry benchmark for merchandising and presentation. They've been named one of America's Top 100 motorcycle retailers many times, and twice have been named top independent retailer in the nation!

J&P Cycles is not a business that has just passively ridden the wave of Big Twin popularity over the last decade. To the contrary, J&P Cycles has been an important contributor to the growth of custom motorcycling in America. Their catalog makes best-brand products available to motorcycle builders and owners everywhere, even in little towns that don't have a dealership. They have contributed measurably to the sales of the leading suppliers, and there are some smaller suppliers who will unashamedly tell you that it has been J&P Cycles that put them in business and kept them in business. And J&P has built a brand that is as strong as many of the leading brands in the industry.

There are some people in the motorcycle industry who have recently started talking about J&P Cycles being an overnight success. I guess they intend that as a compliment, but it is far from the truth. If they had been with me and seen John standing all alone in a booth in Italy about 15 years ago, or selling his wares from a table at Sturgis nearly a decade before that, they would know that J&P is anything but an overnight success. Rather, it has earned success through years and years of struggle and hard work, by John, by Jill, and by hundreds of loyal, hard-working employees.

John Parham likes to talk about the fact that the inspirational motion picture "Field of Dreams" was filmed on a farm near Dyersville, Iowa, just 35 miles north of his hometown of Anamosa. To John, that movie is about a man who had unwavering faith in a vision, even when others thought he was crazy. John's dream, even as a teenager, was to find success in the motorcycle industry, and there is no doubt he has done this, with the constant support of his wife and family. But John has not kept success to himself. Rather, he has shared it with the National Motorcycle Museum, one of the leading motorcycle museums in America. As someone else in the motorcycle industry has pointed out, what we have in Dyersville is just a movie set. For motorcyclists, the real Field of Dreams is in Anamosa, Iowa.

On the occasion of J&P Cycles' 30th anniversary, I am glad to see that there is a book that reveals what it took to follow a dream and build the most successful retail motorcycle accessory business in America. Ed Youngblood has placed this story of J&P Cycles, and John Parham's many other enterprises, in historical context, describing not only what went on inside the company, but identifying the external forces that have changed and influenced our industry over the years. I think you will find it a fascinating and inspirational story about a company that all of us can be proud of, that has brought higher standards of service and professionalism to our industry, and that has become a kind of a Field of Dreams that shows us what any of us can accomplish through hard work and belief in a vision.

—Arlen Ness

Introduction and Acknowledgment

In 1954, the same year that both John and Jill Parham were born, the motion picture "The Wild One" hit the big screen. It was a movie that had far more cultural influence than its doubtful historical accuracy or cinematic quality would justify. Playing Johnny Strabler, a stylized motorcycling rebel and social misfit, Marlon Brando shrugged and mumbled his way through a performance that established the archetype for the American outlaw biker. "The Wild One," subsequent B-movies, and a spate of sensationalized "news stories" taught Americans how to think about people who rode motorcycles. They were slothful, destructive, and a threat to the order of a decent society.

In spite of—or possibly because of—this movie, there were those of us who still devoted our lives to motorcycles. John Parham is such a person, defying the gentle urgings of his parents and community to redirect his interests toward making a decent living, or should I say making a living decently. This was exactly what I thought I would find when I accepted John's proposal to write a history of J&P Cycles on the occasion of its 30th anniversary. It is something I could easily understand because I too had at one time consciously abandoned a "respectable" career path because I simply could not quit thinking about motorcycles. Guys like us just followed our obsession and sneered at those looking down their noses until one day we woke up to find that motorcycles had become fabulously fashionable in America, regarded as toys of the rich and rolling art.

All of that was old news to me. I've written about it before, and maybe it is why I keep writing about motorcycles, because I never cease to be fascinated by America's love and hate for the machine. But as my research for this project unfolded, I found something I did not expect. Rather than "How J&P Cycles Changed the Motorcycle Industry," I could have just as easily sub-titled this book "A Love Story." In this case, I am not thinking of John's love for motorcycles, but rather John and Jill Parham's love for each other. All of the things you will read about hard work, risk-taking, good customer service, and entrepreneurial spirit are quite important to the phenomenal success of J&P Cycles, but the real engine behind the company's achievement has been a teenage love affair that matured into a powerful partnership that both maintained a marriage and built a business empire. I am quite convinced that one half of the Parhams could not have done it without the other. I have enjoyed studying and learning to understand this rare but simple relationship, and I only hope I have written about it sufficiently that readers can grasp how essential it is to the J&P story.

I had a lot of help in developing this book. First, I want to thank the entire good-natured crew at J&P Cycles that, collectively, I shall refer to as The Work Ethic Express. They are a gang of hard-chargers who believe in their company, its leadership, and their mission, yet they never failed to interrupt their work to respond to my many requests for interviews or research. Without diminishing any of these, I need to single out a few people. First, there was John's father, John, who always arrived at our meetings with pages of hand-written notes and bags of family photos and newspaper clippings. He always diligently did his homework, even when I had not asked him to. The fact that he took this project so seriously helped me understand early on how important putting this story on paper was to many of those near and dear to John and Jill. I want to thank Nicole Ridge for the many, many hours she spent going through the photo files and digging out old company newsletters, Brad Mrstik for compiling statistical and financial summaries, Suzy Gilkerson for reading the manuscript (more than once), and Jeff Carstensen for coordinating a photo shoot that defied all reasonable deadlines. Especially, I must thank Heidi Meeks and Jill for their skill in helping me obtain pieces of that rarest of all commodities at J&P Cycles, John's time.

I hope you will enjoy this love story that helped keep the world on two wheels. A lot of good people had a hand in its development.

—Ed Youngblood

August, 2008

Chapter One:
The Road to Monticello

It was spring, 1971, and John Parham was aboard his little 65cc Honda, heading north on Highway 151 toward Monticello. His parents allowed him the motorcycle to ride around town, but he was not supposed to go onto the highway. This morning he had ridden off as usual, venturing from the streets of Anamosa onto county roads, casually working his way northward across Jones County. Finally, well outside of town, he left county roads and entered the highway, speeding up to the 45 miles per hour that the small bike could comfortably produce. On either side, eastern Iowa's rolling hills spread outward toward the horizon, scarred by tractor-pulled plows at planting time, making large geometric patterns that looked like a huge quilt made to cover hectares, tossed across the land like a giant Grant Wood painting. The air felt cool, but the sun was invigoratingly bright, enhancing the contrast between the brown patterns of plowed soil against the green of virgin fields. John could smell the springtime. He could detect the aroma of the broken earth as he traveled past areas that were already plowed, smelling the contrast so strongly that he was certain he could picture the landscape through closed eyes. Excitement and joy became palpable

John, on the bicycle, and sister Luann with neighborhood friends.

Right: John at age six.

John with younger siblings Luann and Mark, posing for the family Christmas card.

Below: John's mother Anna teaches pre-schoolers at the Sunshine Pre-School. John is to Anna's immediate left.

as he made his way to visit Jill Hessing, the girl he had met on a cold night last January 11 at a steamy teen hop at the youth center in Monticello.

Interrupted from his reverie, John suddenly saw the grille of a huge 18-wheeler in his left mirror, overtaking him at least 25, maybe 30 miles per hour faster than his little Honda could go. As the big truck swung out and around him, John looked over to see a spinning chrome wheel that stood at least as high as his shoulders, its ten big lug nuts turning like a monstrous rendering machine built to pulverize flesh and bone. Wheel after wheel thundered past him as he hunkered down and squeezed the hand grips until his knuckles went white. The thunder of diesel engine and howl of huge tires drowned out the small sound of the motorcycle. When the truck completed its pass and swung back into John's lane, he suddenly felt himself pulled forward into the vacuum created in its wake, his dark, collar-length hair parting up the back of his head and flapping forward into his eyes as his little Honda gained speed against its will, pulled along ever faster with its engine screaming and its speedometer needle touching 60. Gradually the Honda settled back to its normal speed as the truck pulled away, then its wake began to whip John back and forth as if he were riding the tail of a big, invisible snake, pulled along by the truck as it sped into the distance. As eddies of air and swirling grit subsided, John spied with some relief the exit to Monticello.

John was rattled by his confrontation with the truck, but also strangely exhilarated. This too contributed to his joy. Vulnerable, exposed to the elements, riding where he shouldn't have been, taking a chance, living by his wits, making his way in the world aboard a motorcycle, which was still considered by most of John's elders a dangerous and forbidden vehicle, good for nothing except transporting countless young Americans down a path to juvenile delinquency. The young Anamosan had embarked on two lifelong and inseparable love affairs, one with Jill and one with motorcycles.

John W. Parham was born September 14, 1954, in Shelby, Iowa, where his father, John William Parham, was a vocational agriculture teacher. His mother, Anna, had a degree in education with a specialty in childhood development and ran the Sunshine Pre-School business in their home. John had two siblings, Luann, two years younger, and Mark, his junior by six years. In 1956, when John was two, his family moved to Anamosa where his father had taken a job with the Rural Electric Cooperative. Thus, Anamosa is really the only home John has ever known.

John grew up in a respectable middleclass family in a green-shingled, one-story house on Webster Street, a tidy neighborhood with tree-lined streets and groomed lawns. He was a Cub Scout, played halfback on his high school football team, and was a member of a highly-competitive swimming squad with classmates David Hahn, Steve George, and Dean Legg. From the ages of 10 to 19, the four swam together for almost a decade, winning most of their meets and placing sixth for Anamosa in the Junior Olympics. About this generation, John's elementary school principal Dale Hackett recalls, "There was a group of 10 or 12 kids John's age who were real achievers. They were not the kind of boys who got into trouble." John's younger brother Mark recalls, "John was a popular guy in high school. He did football and swimming, and he has always been a people person." Academically, John was an average student, but he went to Boys' State in Des Moines his senior year and was good enough at football to be offered athletic scholarships to two Iowa colleges.

About the swimming experience, John says, "The relay team taught me about teamwork, but it still required individual excellence. Trying to win, whether individually or as a member of the team, taught me how to set goals and challenge myself." John was industrious and demonstrated early-on an entrepreneurial spirit and an interest in earning money, announcing to his father while he was still in kindergarten that someday he intended to be a millionaire. On trips to visit his grandmother Shaver in Missouri, John would haul home cases of soda bottles because they were worth five cents in Iowa and only two cents in Missouri. By 12, he had a savings account and was always looking for odd jobs. About his upbringing, John says, "I was taught to be polite, courteous to my elders, and that hard work is a virtue."

His father's job with the electric cooperative required him to travel around the Iowa countryside, and John would go along, looking for derelict bicycles he could bring home to rebuild and sell. John's father recalls, "Sometimes he would buy them by the pile, then strip them all and mix and match parts to build as many complete bicycles as he could." He mowed lawns in the summers and shoveled snow in the winters, sometimes bartering his work for goods that he thought might have more value than the money he could earn. On one occasion he traded lawn-mowing services for a huge pile of lumber, which he and his best friends Dean Legg and Denny Conrad used to build a three-story tree house. Eventually, property ownership would become one of John's successful businesses, and whether it was cash or barter, he was always looking out for the best value he could get for his time and trouble. Denny Conrad recalls, "One winter we had a heavy snow, and John and I spent several hours digging out the walks for a woman in the neighborhood. When she asked us what she owed, I named a figure. Then John quickly interrupted and corrected me, naming a higher figure. John prevailed, and the lady paid the higher amount." Conrad adds with a chuckle, "But I'm not sure she invited us back."

John Parham, Sr., with John in the winter of 1955.

Below: Mark, John, and Luann with pet rabbits.

Jill, as she looked when John met her at a dance in Monticello in 1971.

Below: Jill on the left, with infant brother Doug and older sister Sue, 1958.

In his pre-teen years, John also developed a fascination for snakes. There was a ravine not far from his home that was teaming with them, mostly garter snakes of non-poisonous varieties. John put a 55-gallon drum containing two and a half feet of dirt in his back yard and made it his own private snake farm, going to the ravine to catch snakes then turning them loose to live in the drum. On more than one occasion he was bitten, and once by one of the largest snakes he ever captured, which was better than an inch in girth. John recalls, "It bit down on my hand and could not release. Its teeth were hooked into the flesh between my finger and thumb, and Dean Legg had to hold both its upper and lower jaws and pry its mouth open wide enough to get the teeth out of my skin." As with most things John did, there was a mercantile aspect to the Parham Snake Farm. He explains, "If some kid decided he needed a nice snake, I would sell him one for a quarter."

ௐ

When it came time to forget about snakes and think about girls, there wasn't a lot for a high school boy to do in Anamosa, especially in the winter. So sometimes John and friends would drive to Monticello to attend a dance, despite the fact that Anamosa boys were not always welcome. With the nearest cities of Cedar Rapids and Dubuque about 30-miles distance in opposite directions, Anamosa and Monticello—each with a population of about 5,000—are little towns surrounded by farm land. They only have each other, and in a situation like this, it is only natural that they would become rivals. Teens were not welcomed on the neighboring turf, and young people from one town rarely dated those from the other. These conventions didn't faze John where Jill was concerned. He spotted her at the dance that night in January and went after her. Jill was a junior and John only a sophomore. She recalls, "He was cocky and really self-confident. His attitude was, 'How could you not want to dance with me?'" She was not sure this was the kind of person she wanted to be with. Jill, who was a thin, attractive young woman, then slightly taller than John, continues, "John and his friends acted like wild boys; they acted like punks. Sometimes they had liquor in the glove box of their car, and I was really pretty prudish."

About John's pursuit of Jill, his childhood best friend Dean Legg says, "John was a risk taker. It seems silly now, but our world then was small and very well defined. People were not expected to look outside of Anamosa for a friend, and the idea of dating someone from another town, or even going to another town for friendship or recreation really took guts. It was a very adventurous thing to do." Legg adds, "It also indicated how determined and single-minded John can be. When he decides he wants something, he really goes after it, regardless of the odds or what anyone else might think. And we thought Jill was exciting, just because she was a girl from another town."

Though there were only 10 miles between Anamosa and Monticello, there was a world of difference between the life experiences of John and Jill. John's family was not rich, but they were comfortable. His father was well-known and respected throughout the community, and his mother was a high achiever. She had earned the Silver Beaver, the highest award an adult volunteer can earn from the Boy Scouts of America, and she had served as chairperson of Anamosa's

bicentennial celebration, which was not only successful but profitable for the community. And she was trusted among other families who utilized her day-care and pre-school services.

Jill's father, on the other hand, was an active alcoholic, and she was raised in near-poverty. Born on August 13, 1954, Jill was the middle of three siblings, which included Sue, about a year older, and Doug, four years her junior. Both Jill and Sue went to a Catholic school and did well, earning As and Bs. By the time Doug came along, the family situation had become too grim, and he suffered its effects, dropping out of school in order to work, exaggerating his age to get a job at the Mid-Continent Bottling Company in Cedar Rapids. Eventually, Doug would return to earn his GED. Sue explains, "Our father drove a truck for a propane distributor. One night he made an emergency delivery out in the county and the grateful farmer offered him a drink. He accepted it, his boss found out, and he got fired. Our home life was rough before that, but it went downhill from there." Jill recalls, "We rarely had a vehicle that ran, so we kids walked everywhere or rode our bicycles." She adds, "We were a hard-working family. Doug did not leave school because he was a delinquent. He did it because he had to work to help the family get by." After high school, Sue got a scholarship and escaped to Mount St. Clair College in Clinton, Iowa, where she earned a degree as a medical transcriptionist.

Jill reacted to her difficult home situation by seeking work and accepting responsibility. Realizing she had to get out and make her own way in the world, she had already been taking regular baby-sitting jobs by the time she was 12. Sue recalls, "Jill was always outgoing and personable. She was mature and able to fit in and get along with others." Jill's first part-time job was as an after-school car hop at the Dairy Mart in Monticello, but she was quickly promoted to counter work inside the store. This is where John, one Sunday afternoon in December, began to learn the consequences of his aggressive behavior when he turned up with some of his friends to see Jill. As Anamosa guys, they were not welcome, which was noted openly by a booth full of beefy Monticello football players. One of them made a remark to John, and John mouthed back on his way out the door. John recalls, "I got out the door and turned around, and for a split-second all I saw was this big fist coming at me." The parking lot was a sheet of glare ice, and John went down. He got up and hit back, but recalls, "I couldn't even make a dent in the guy." John was knocked down again. Jill says, "It was really embarrassing for John, getting beat up in front of all these other kids."

John and his friends got in the car and left, but it did not end there. The Monticello boys began to come to Anamosa and prowl the streets for John. This was not a rivalry over Jill. None of the Monticello boys was pursuing her; they just had it in for John and wanted to let him know he could not come to Monticello to chase women

Jill (on the left) and Sue Hessing with grandmother and grandfather Norton.

Below: John with his Christmas sled, 1955.

Jill aboard her Christmas tricycle, 1958.

Below: Jill's father Don, aboard his Harley-Davidson in July, 1954. On the back is his father-in-law, Leonard Norton.

and behave as if he belonged there. With the climate of rivalry between the two towns, perhaps John's popularity in Anamosa contributed to his unwelcome status in Monticello. Whatever the reason, it came to a head one night that winter at an Anamosa/Monticello basketball game in Anamosa. Jill came to the game to sit on the Anamosa side with John. A group of eight Monticello guys glared at John across the gym throughout the evening, then came after him as soon as the game was over, chasing him home and even coming onto his porch to kick on the door. One, Ronnie Craig, known to his friends as Poncho, seemed to be the fighter designated to deal with John. Craig recalls, "John had mouthed off at me sometime before that, and I had it in for him. It infuriated me, and I had been looking for an opportunity to teach him to keep his mouth shut."

It was clear by now that a bad situation was not going to blow over, and John knew what he had to do to settle it. John recalls, "I weighed all of 140 and Poncho was about 230. I told him I would fight him if that would end it.

I said, 'If I have to take a beating I will, but is that going to put an end to this?'" John wanted to be assured he could see Jill with no further harassment. Poncho agreed, and later that spring at a basketball game they set out to fight. Craig recalls, "John had a couple of guys with him and a couple of my friends came along.

It was looking like there was going to be a little gang war on school property, so John's buddies backed off and walked away. So did my guys, and John and I agreed to go to a deserted country road just off Highway 151 outside Anamosa." The boys must have realized the fight was largely ceremonial, because they actually traveled together to the site in Poncho's car. Craig continues, "We got out and stood around looking at each other, kind of squared off, but not doing anything. Then I took a swing and hit him in the eye, then John came at me. It was really stupid. We scuffled around a bit and then decided it was over. We shook hands and went back to town."

As far as honor was concerned, John had his beating, because he had to go to school with a tremendous shiner that stayed with him a couple of weeks. Craig adds, "I always felt bad about that. I was not a big fighter. I probably had two fights in my entire life, and I always felt bad about hitting John. After that we were not really friends, but we were no longer enemies. We said 'hi' to each other and were cordial, but kind of kept our distance." Today, Ronnie Craig is a principal in Duffy's Collectible Cars in Cedar Rapids, a nationally-known brokerage for rare and valuable automobiles. He says, "About 20 years later, I saw John one day. It was still eating at me, so I walked over and told him that I still regretted fighting with him, and that I wanted to apologize." For John, it was a long-finished chapter. He accepted Craig's apology and the two have remained friends and sometimes business associates, since they have found opportunities over the years to conduct co-promotions for Duffy's and the National Motorcycle Museum in Anamosa.

With John's ostracism in Monticello behind them,

his and Jill's relationship could flourish. Jill's sister Sue recalls, "They couldn't get enough of each other. They would talk on the phone late into the evening, then when they finally had to go to bed they would leave their phones off the hook so they could secretly get back on the line at 4 a.m. to talk some more." She also remembers how John was well-regarded after the Monticello boys accepted him into their community. She says, "He was a pretty cool guy because he had a motorcycle. We other kids wanted to go for rides with him." Soon, John traded his little Honda for a 250cc twin-cylinder Kawasaki, then later set his sights on a used 1971 650cc BSA. By aspiring to that big BSA, John Parham threatened to cross a cultural boundary into what adult society regarded dangerous territory. For her part, Jill was certainly not unfamiliar with motorcycles. Her father once owned a Harley-Davidson and, in fact, was part of the generation who gave motorcycles their post-war reputation for reckless adventure and danger. Jill recalls, "Dad was known for how wild he was on that motorcycle."

ᘓ

In the year John was born, Hollywood released a movie starring Marlon Brando entitled "The Wild One," based on an alleged riot by hoodlum motorcyclists that took place in Hollister, California, in 1947. A great deal of the press coverage of the so-called Hollister riot was overblown and downright contrived, spearheaded by a photo in *Life* magazine of a drunken lout on a Harley-Davidson, surrounded by beer bottles, that had admittedly been staged days after the incident. But the movie gave the legend convincing imagery, and "The Wild One" triggered a decade of low-budget films about motorcycle madness, debauchery, mayhem, and rebellion against authority.

To many young people, the images of free-wheeling bikers on the silver screen were exciting and appealing, beckoning them to break loose from the strictures of their up-tight teachers, parents, and clergy. These films were just one aspect of a post-war social upheaval that led to a schism in values, rending the fabric of the American middle class along generational lines and resulting in the so-called Generation Gap, defined by differing tastes in music, dress, and sexual behavior, and culminating in political activism and the Peace Movement of the 1960s. It was utterly baffling to the adult establishment to witness flower children, hippies, and peaceniks fraternizing and smoking weed with Hell's Angels—otherwise known for their violence—at open-air love-ins and concerts in San Francisco.

For many adults, youngsters who rode motorcycles became an underclass in America, regarded as thugs and wastrels, and a dichotomy emerged in the popular attitude toward two-wheeled transportation. The traditional brands—Harley-Davidson, Indian, Triumph, BSA, and others—became associated with young punks with greasy hair and cigarette packs rolled up in their T-shirt sleeves, decked out in heavy engineer's boots and black leather jackets decorated with chains and macabre and demonic symbols. Honda and the other Japanese brands, which at that time built only small motorcycles, succeeded in bucking this trend by presenting themselves as the joyful transportation of youthful, harmless suburbanites and preppies. The Beach Boys, wearing white chinos and candy-striped shirts, rode onto stage at their concerts aboard little Hondas, and American

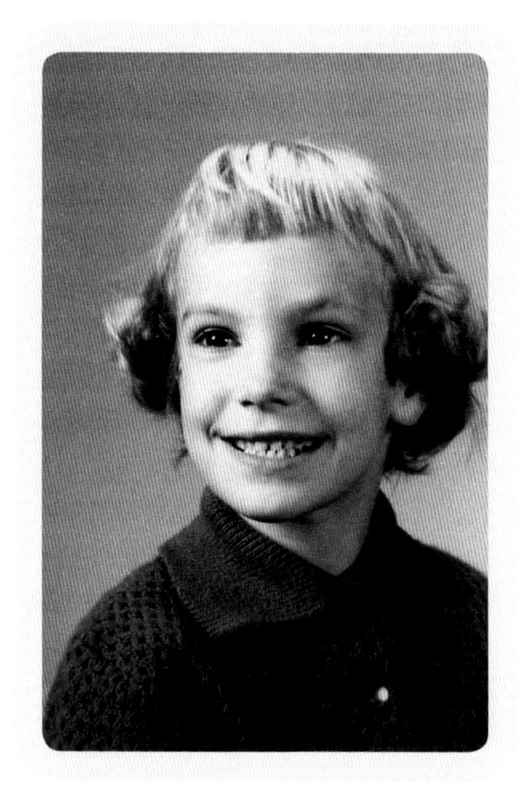

Jill in the first grade.

Below: John, age five.

Jill and John at the high school prom time, 1971.

mothers were heard to remark, "I don't mind if my son rides a Honda, but I'll never let him own a motorcycle."

John's parents apparently felt the same way, because they told him they did not want him to buy the BSA. John rebelled by running away from home. Actually, all he did was spend a couple of nights at the home of Don Brown, his high school science teacher, who also was a fan of motorcycles. This was no consolation for the Parhams. They did not much like Mr. Brown, and, in fact, they were not at all happy with the direction their son seemed to be heading. His academic work was mediocre, he showed no interest in a higher education, and Anna did not like his dating an "older woman" from Monticello. In fact, Jill was only one month older, but John was one year behind her in school. This was a situation of Anna's own making, because she had held him back a year in the beginning, believing he was not physically developed and mature enough to enter public school at the time of his sixth birthday. Concerning John's dedication to motorcycles and Jill, today his father admits, "We did not forbid John to do what he wanted, but we didn't provide any support either."

It was in this period of tension with his parents that a defiant John bought his big BSA, then spent the winter chopping it, extending its forks, installing Z-bars, TT pipes, a fiberglass gas tank, a special seat and sissy bar, laying on a custom paint job, and installing a side-mount taillight and the other bits of chrome accessories that would make it look as much as possible like the machines of the outlaw bikers seen in the movies. Because his parents so despised the motorcycle, he kept it in the hallway of Jill's apartment house. The BSA proved to be a learning experience, and not always a pleasant one. John discovered that, like many British motorcycles of the era, the BSA was plagued with electrical problems. He sought out Ron Payne, a local metal worker and mechanic who was six years his senior and had more experience with motorcycles. Ron recalls, "I really did not want to work on it. I was trying to get away from fixing other people's junk. But John kept coming around. He was persistent, and eventually I helped him with it, although we never got it right." As a result, Payne and Parham became friends. Payne continues, "We did a lot of running around together, and I took John and Jill to their first motorcycle swap meet." This would prove an eventful experience for John, who would some years later become the biggest motorcycle swap meet promoter in America. Furthermore, Payne would figure in John's early business growth, and though they are no longer professionally connected, the Paynes and the Parhams remain friends even today.

☙

Jill's parents divorced in the spring of 1972, the same year she graduated from high school. She got a job at Energy Manufacturing in Monticello, left home, and got an apartment in Anamosa where she could be closer to John, who had his last year of high school to complete. Jill started in the mail room at Energy, running a printing press, then in a year was promoted to the data processing department where she began to learn about business systems, accounting, and information management. It was the dawn of computerized information technology, and Jill learned about the IBM 360, that great gray box that was as big as a car and put off heat like a furnace. With the company's transition to the IBM System 3—a tidy blue main frame no larger than a refrigerator—the era of computer miniaturization began, and Jill continued to learn about the infrastructure, information management, and business systems that would one day make her a critical asset at J&P Cycles. In the evenings, she spent time with John and helped him with his school work. In fact, John could have graduated at mid-year, except for lacking one credit, so while taking a light class load he took a job as a welder at a factory in Monticello. He says, "I quickly learned that welding was one of the things I didn't want to do." During that year, John took a class in business administration, which was much more to his liking. It interested and motivated him more than anything else he had studied in high school.

John graduated in 1973 and got a job at Pamida, a department store chain with over 200 locations in the central United States, mostly in small towns like Anamosa, where he advanced to the position of assistant manager. He had a boss named Gene Lanfeer who became a mentor. John says, "It was a very good learning experience for me. Pamida had very good customer service, pricing, and return policies. Gene provided good guidance, and I learned many of the high standards of performance and customer service that we would later apply so successfully at J&P Cycles." He adds, "I would have stayed longer if there had been any kind of money in it, but they just didn't pay very well." John did not follow up on the athletic scholarships he had been offered. Rather, he attended Kirkwood College in Cedar Rapids for a year, but did not return for a second year. Other than a course in retail marketing and merchandising, which he found interesting and motivational, John felt he was not learning much and that college was not a good use of his time.

☙

During this time, John and Jill discussed marriage, but nothing was decided. Then, one day in the spring of 1974, John drove to Monticello to pick up Jill after work. On the way home, he pulled over to the side of Highway 151 and took out an engagement ring. He had purchased the ring just that day for $170, amounting to a full month of his earnings, and he asked Jill to marry him. Jill recalls, "It was a big surprise. Though we had talked, I didn't think it would happen this soon." She adds, "We were only 19 years old."

It would seem that the road to Monticello had become the path to John's destiny. It was where he had paid his dues to Poncho for the right to visit Jill, and three springs before he proposed to Jill, he had taken frequent motorcycle trips on this highway to visit her, surely not realizing then that he was embarking on a love story that would contain his struggles, triumphs, disappointments, and eventually his success with a partner who would complement his skills and fill the gaps where he might be found lacking. Jill and John, two people with very different histories and personalities, would become a Yin and a Yang, composing a whole that would prove to be greater than the sum of its parts in their adventure to build a successful business, a family, and a life together.

John's 1955 Harley-Davidson, restored in dark brown before it was later returned to its original yellow.

Barney the Wonder Dog was a fixture at J&P Cycles in the early 1990's. He was bought as a watch dog, but also became a pet to all the J&P employees.

John is shown here in the Anamosa Eureka newspaper with his swim relay team: Left to right: Dean Legg, Dave Hahn, John and Steve George. The team placed 6th in the freestyle competition at the Iowa Junior Olympics in Iowa Falls in July 1969.

John during Sturgis 1994 next to the J&P Store / National Motorcycle Museum on Junction Ave in Sturgis, South Dakota.

Robert Peiffer was a very early loyal J&P customer. Every Saturday he would come from Washington, IA (about 85 miles) and be parked out front waiting for John & Jill to open the doors. He built his entire bike through parts from J&P. Robert and his wife Joyce became longtime friends of John and Jill.

John, Jill and the gang getting ready to go to Muscatine, IA for Riverboat Days with friends in 1979.

Chapter Two:
The Adventure Begins

John graduated from high school in the spring of 1973 and began to work full-time at Pamida. He continued living at home, but spent most of his time with Jill. She had an apartment in Anamosa and was commuting to her job in Monticello in an old green 1965 Volkswagen. John did not want to go away to a college where he would have to leave Jill, so in the winter of 1973 he enrolled for business classes at Kirkwood College in Cedar Rapids, which was an easy commute. He liked retail merchandising, and he did well in that area of study, earning As and high Bs. Still, he did not think school was a very good use of his time, and even when he received football scholarship offers to Upper Iowa University and Grinnell, two small colleges in the area, he did not follow up. Rather than make plans to continue college in 1974, he proposed to Jill on the road to Monticello, and they set a date of September 14, which was John's 20th birthday.

John and Jill began their life together with no money and very little outside support. John's parents would have preferred to see him continue school, and while they did not create obstacles, they also did not offer encouragement.

Jill and John, high school sweethearts, at Jill's sister's wedding.

Right: John and Jill, 1973.

John and Jill were married on John's 20th birthday, September 14, 1974.

Below: Jill with her Sister Sue and mother on her wedding day.

Jill could not afford a wedding dress, so she borrowed one from her sister. Jill recalls, "I was taller than Sue, and her dress was too short for me, so I wore flats so the dress would come a little closer to the floor." For their honeymoon, the couple didn't have a car reliable enough to travel out of state, so they borrowed John's parents' Chevy Vega and went to St. Louis. Jill laughs, "We didn't have money for the trip, and as we drove out of town, we were opening the wedding gift envelopes, looking for cash." John says, "We were on a wing and a prayer, but we were having fun. I didn't even know how to read a map, and we were yelling at each other all the time in St. Louis because we were always lost." Jill says, "We had no idea what we were doing. The drinking age in Iowa was 19, so we went into a bar in St. Louis, and when they carded us we proudly produced our IDs, not realizing that the drinking age in Missouri was 21."

Upon returning to Anamosa, the couple took up housekeeping in Jill's apartment, and John changed jobs. He explains, "Even with the title of assistant manager at Pamida, it was still a minimum wage job. I was earning $2.35 an hour, and they were talking about making me a manager, which would have required us to move to another town. Jill had a good job, earning more than I was, and it just didn't make sense." John quit Pamida and took a job as a foreman at Doehr Electric in Anamosa, a company that manufactured electric motors. Over the next few years, John would change jobs several times, looking for better earnings. After Doehr, he took a second-shift job as a machinist at Energy Manufacturing, where Jill worked, in Monticello. During a lay-off at Energy, he went to LeFebure, a company in Cedar Rapids that made bank vaults, working second shift on a metal stamping press. After a year at LeFebure, he went to P & H Harnishfeger, a company that made cranes, where he worked as a machinist. He says, "I thought it was a dream job. I quickly went from $6 to $12 an hour, and I worked third shift and could go to swap meets on the weekends." Jill says, "Sometimes we cut it so close that we would arrive back in town just in time to drop John off at his job." This, however, was not what he ultimately envisioned for his future. John wanted to be his own boss. He wanted to run his own business, and there was no reason he should not look for that opportunity with what he loved most, which was motorcycles. When Harnishfeger laid him off in 1982, John said, "This is it. Now's the time to start running my own business."

By now the troublesome BSA had stranded John and Jill several times on the road, and John decided it was time to get something else. His choice was a used 750cc four-cylinder Honda. He recalls, "It was pretty ratty-looking, but it ran well." Considering "ratty-looking" an understatement, Jill says, "I was so upset when he brought that motorcycle home. He paid $600 that we didn't have. It looked awful. The gas tank was smashed in, and we had to ride it around that way for awhile because we didn't have any money to fix it." But soon John set out to rebuild the Honda into a custom, from the ground up. He installed the engine in an Amen brand aftermarket frame with Smith Brothers girder front forks. He bought a Prismic custom fuel tank and Corbin-Gentry seat, repainted the bike, and rebuilt it with chrome accessories. He says, "It was a really pretty bike, a show bike. It had a gold-leaf and pin-striped paint job."

Actually, John rebuilt the Honda twice, thanks to a near-catastrophe that took place that summer. John explains, "We were in Cedar Rapids, and I had just gotten gas. We pulled onto the street and were sitting at a red light next to a McDonalds." John continues, "The float bowl on one of the carbs was stuck, and while I was sitting at the light, it began to overflow. The electrics caught the gas on fire, and I looked down and there it was, blazing beneath the carburetors with fuel continuing to feed the fire." There was a fountain outside the McDonalds, and John leaped off the bike, tore off his jacket, and ran over to the fountain, using his jacket like a bucket to scoop up water, which he carried back to throw on the bike. John says, "I didn't know that you don't put water on a gasoline fire, so it kept getting worse, and I kept running back to the fountain to get more water. A total disaster was averted when a McDonalds employee came running out with a fire extinguisher to put out the fire.

During this time, John began to understand the special mystique of the Harley-Davidson. Jill and John would often ride the Honda to Cedar Rapids to cruise the drive-ins where there were lots of young people with hot cars and customized motorcycles. John recalls, "I had turned that Honda into a really special motorcycle. It was a beautiful machine, but some pretty ordinary Harleys would attract more attention. I told Jill, 'Someday we're going to get a Harley-Davidson.'"

Eventually, John would get his first Harley. He and Doug Hessing both built 90-cubic-inch strokers. They were hopped-up machines whose loud pipes could break windows. Jill laughs and says, "They would work on them at night and fire them up at all hours." Jill adds, "I'll bet our neighbors really hated us."

A lot of people were customizing bikes, just as John had done with his, and he decided to team up with his motorcycling friend and former high school teacher, Don Brown, with whom he opened D&J Cycles in Anamosa to provide service and accessories. It did not take Don and John long to begin to learn a few things about being partners and running a business, and not all of their experiences were positive. First, they learned that their interests in motorcycles were quite different. At this time, motocross had become very popular in America. All of the Japanese manufacturers were selling motocross bikes, and lots of young boys and girls were buying them, especially in rural areas like eastern Iowa. Don Brown was attracted to this hot and growing market, and he wanted to position their business toward off-road and competition motorcycles. John was interested in the street scene, and especially the vintage and custom Harley communities. He saw their future in providing accessories, repair, and services to owners of choppers and road bikes.

John's 750 Honda chopper was a true show bike, but he soon learned that any run-of-the-mill Harley-Davidson would get more attention.

Below: Jill aboard the Honda chopper. John's Honda had all the latest custom parts. Smith Brothers Girder front end, Amen hardtail frame, Corbin Gentry seat, prismic gas tank and a beautiful custom paint job with goldleaf and pin striping. ***But it still wasn't a Harley-Davidson.***

John and Jill began to spend much of their time on the road, attending rallies, shows, and swap meets. They are pictured here at Muscatine, Iowa, 1980.

Below: John's first Harley Shovelhead stroker, built in 1978 while he was still a partner in D&J Cycles.

Both began to understand that even in the midst of a national motorcycle sales boom, Anamosa was a very small town and the customer base was limited. Under the stress of insufficient income, the differences in opinion and ambition became a point of contention. Jill says, "I was never one to hold my tongue when I didn't agree with something, and Don Brown was also pretty vocal and opinionated."

ଔ

There is within the American motorcycling community a world of commerce and entertainment that most owners of new motorcycles don't even know exists. It is a world where the participants know their history, revere the past, honor traditions, and enjoy nostalgia. This is the world of motorcycle swap meets, which take place somewhere in America almost every weekend of the year. In the summer, the promoters of swap meets rent mall parking lots or county fairgrounds, and in the winter they move inside into pavilions and sports arenas. They use mailing lists to reach their clientele and advertise in specialized motorcycle magazines. Today, the internet has become a basic tool of the trade, where swap meets are promoted through websites and e-mail messages. Essentially, swap meet organizers contract to use a large facility for a day or two, mark it off in ten-by-ten-foot sections, then rent those spaces to vendors who want to sell their wares. These vendors may be one-time sellers wishing to clear the excess motorcycles and parts out of their garages, or they may be people who attend swap meets regularly, making their living or supplementing their income buying and selling parts and memorabilia. Some swap meets are as small as 20 or 30 vendors, but some of the larger include more than a thousand booths where buyers can spend days prowling the aisles for that special part or unexpected treasure. The public is charged a modest fee to visit the swap meet and look for parts, or just enjoy the carnival-like atmosphere.

At first glance, motorcycle swap meets look like the bottom rung of commerce where people buy and sell useless junk, and their style defies all conventional rules of merchandising. Except for the few vendors who may be selling reproduced and packaged parts, swap meet vendors never clean or make an effort to make their wares more presentable. They arrive with trucks and trailers piled with old motorcycles and parts. Usually, these are rusty, dirty, or greasy, just as they were when dragged out of the shop or barn where they may have lain for years. Items for sale are stacked on tables, laid out on tarps, or just tossed on the ground. Yet there is a kind of merchandising integrity here that K-Mart shoppers would never understand. If a swap meet vendor were ever to clean up his wares, make the chrome shine, and create a tidy and professional-looking display, the buyers probably wouldn't trust him. "What's wrong with it? Why did you clean it up? Is there something you're trying to hide?" As a result, the typical swap meet looks like a junk yard. There are motorcycles so old, derelict, and obscure that you can't imagine a single person on earth would want to own them. There are boxes and piles of parts so rusted and damaged that it seems they should have been sent to the foundry decades ago. But swap meets thrive on the old axiom that one man's trash is another's treasure, and this is reinforced even through an amusing terminology. For example, an old, rusted motorcycle, covered with pigeon dung, sitting on tires that went flat from dry rot years ago, with a seat gutted and turned into a happy home for mice would never be called "junk." Rather, it is characterized as "barn fresh." More often than not, the people who participate in the swap meet economy are colorful characters. They may have beards and unkempt hair, and wear dirty bib overalls. They may be balding men with long pony tails, but buyers are mistaken to take them for fools. They are intelligent, often well-educated and well-read, and usually in those bibs are large rolls of cash. They know how to make a buck at this business, or they wouldn't continue to do it. Rikki Battistini, a designer of custom accessories who originally met John Parham at a meet in Europe, says, "These guys are hungry for a deal, and they are good with people. John is a true swap meet guy. This is probably where he learned a lot of his basic skills in knowing how to spot a deal, negotiate, and make a deal." John's brother Mark, however, suspects that John always had the skills to get along well in the world of swap-meeters. He says, "John always knew how to put himself on the same level with others. It seems like there was never anyone he could not sit down with and talk to, and make a deal." Both men are probably correct. No doubt, becoming a swap meet vendor and eventually an organizer helped develop John's inherent interpersonal skills.

Sometimes, swap-meeters buy by the "pile," acquiring a great mound of rusty motorcycles and parts when perhaps there are only one or two items therein that they desire. They will take big risks because they have confidence in their ability to wheel and deal. Recently at a swap meet in Davenport, Iowa, Dale Walksler, a collector and long-time friend of John Parham, bought a huge mound of parts and a half-dozen motorcycles because it contained a single motorcycle he wanted. He said, "Wednesday night I was sweating. I had spent every penny I had and borrowed money from four or five guys. I didn't even have enough cash to get home. But by Friday afternoon I had sold most of the stuff, paid off my lenders, and made a good profit." Lonnie Isam, another longtime friend of John's, once learned of a fleet of 88 ex-police Harley-Davidson three-wheelers. Acquiring them for $500 each, he sold them off one at a time for an average price of $1,500 each. He says, "It tapped me out to swing the deal, but in the end I made a killing."

Sometimes, elaborate transactions will include four or five parties and take days, months, or even years to negotiate. Somer Hooker, a classic bike dealer and broker who stays in touch with the market by attending most of the leading swap meets and auctions, has sometimes spent five or more years finding and acquiring just the right bike for a client, and leads will take him to Argentina or Japan just as easily as a neighboring state. For those who understand the market, stay in touch with the subtle shifts in demand that can affect value, and keep their ear to the ground for what another guy needs, there is good money to be made, not to mention fun to be had. For the serious and professional participants, the swap meet never ends. It just moves from one location to another, week after week, and in the meantime negotiations continue on the telephone or through e-mail.

Swap meets are closely connected with a second sub-set of the motorcycle community, and this is

John in overalls, the official dress of a professional swap-meeter, at a Detroit, Michigan, swap meet.

Below: In addition to attending shows and swap meets, John began to promote events. He is seen here at a hill climb at Anamosa in 1976.

the world of restoring and collecting. Many of the people who trade at swap meets are also highly-skilled craftsmen. They are welders, hot metal workers, painters, and fabricators. Some are quite ingenious, and through their skills they transform hopeless-looking junk into rare and priceless historical vehicles. An example of the close connection between the lowly world of swapping and the rarified society of collecting is a 1926 four-cylinder Cleveland Fowler motorcycle once owned by actor Steve McQueen. This motorcycle cost $375 when new, and less than ten were built because it was not a reliable machine, and in its day, one could purchase a Model T for the same money or less. McQueen bought one that would not run for $7,500. After the actor's death, the motorcycle was given to McQueen's friend and famous competition rider Bud Ekins for helping the family sort out the McQueen collection. Ekins restored it and later sold it to wealthy collector Otis Chandler. After Chandler's death it sold at auction in 2006 for $104,500! In the 80 years since it was manufactured, this Cleveland Fowler increased in value more than 250 times its initial cost, but only after it had taken a circuitous journey through the world of swap-meeters, collectors, and restorers. The importance of swap meets to the world of restoring and collecting is articulated by Dave Leitner, a historian and restoration expert who has helped John Parham obtain some of his valuable collectibles. Surveying his surroundings at the recent meet in Davenport, Leitner said with a smile, "This stuff isn't junk. We're recyclers. If it were not for us, all of this would be wasting space in some landfill." Indeed, swap meets are the first step toward protecting and honoring motorcycling's great heritage.

Below: John Parham's dream machine, his 1955 Harley-Davidson Panhead, after it was restored to its original yellow.

Over time, as his fortunes improved, John Parham would become one of the top motorcycle collectors in America. His first collectible was a yellow 1955 Harley-Davidson FLH, known to enthusiasts as a "Panhead," that he saw at a swap meet in Indiana in 1978. Although it was approaching antique status by then, John had no intentions of placing it on a pedestal. It was going to be his and Jill's rider. John had no idea where he was going to get money to buy the bike, but he wanted it so badly he committed to the owner to purchase it. Shortly thereafter, the IRS saved the day when a refund check for $2,200 arrived. John understood the price to be $2,500, so he and Jill took off for Indiana with money in hand to retrieve the motorcycle, sleeping in the van because they could not afford a motel. Upon arriving, they learned there was a misunderstanding, and the owner wanted $2,900. John was distraught, because he could not pay the price. However, the owner of the bike trusted him and told him to take the Panhead back to Iowa, and send the money within a month. Through a series of circumstances over the ensuing year, the Panhead would become John's most sentimental motorcycle possession. It would come to represent his struggles and eventually his success.

ɷ

After Ron Payne and John Parham became friends while struggling to make useful transportation out of John's BSA, Ron introduced John and Jill to their first motorcycle swap meet, which was a small event in Des Moines, Iowa. By 1976, when John was discovering that motorcycle service and accessory sales were disappointingly limited in a town the size of Anamosa, it was only natural that he would go to a swap meet in search of more customers. In September that year, John and Jill attended their first swap meet as vendors, borrowing a Chevy Suburban from Charlie Baker, a friend of Ron's, because they did not own a vehicle that would make the trip. At a meet in Des Moines they set up a single card table to display some pins and patches. Jill recalls, "We sold about $300 worth that day, and we thought we were rich. We thought we had struck gold." John spent some of the money they earned on parts he thought were going for a good price, figuring he could resell them for a profit. This made Don Brown unhappy. He didn't like the idea that his partner spent some of their income to drag some old Harley parts back to the store. John says, "Don just didn't get it. He would freak out because I would take away new stuff to sell and come back to the shop with old stuff." The gulf between John and Don's commercial visions was becoming more apparent. John not only thought that speculating on new and used parts at swap meets was good business, he felt it was exciting. His eyes had been opened to a whole new world in motorcycling, including new business opportunities.

For John, swap meets were exhilarating. They were not like standing behind a counter and waiting for customers to come through the door to buy packaged parts. They were rich with characters, wheeler-dealers, hagglers, and fascinating people. They offered a surprise or an exciting opportunity at every turn, and it reminded him of his youth when he would look for and find profit in a pile of old bicycles. It was a world that thrilled and excited him at several levels. Not only were meets an opportunity to buy and sell, take risks and make money as a vendor, but he also got the idea that it might be fun and profitable to become a swap meet promoter. Attending swap meets became a weekly occurrence for John and Jill, and Jill's brother Doug often came along to help. They discovered that even in the winter there were major indoor motorcycle swap meets all over the nation. The first winter after they started vending, they attended a major meet at the Minneapolis Armory and made nearly $5,000. Jill says, "We went crazy. All the way home we played Pink Floyd's 'Money' on the tape deck in the van."

Doug Hessing recalls, "We started attending every meet we could find, and that winter we went to a meet at the Chicago Amphitheater. It was one of the biggest motorcycle swap meets in the nation. We walked in and I was overwhelmed with the size of it. But John just looked around and said, 'You know, we could do this!'" Eventually, John created J&P Promotions, and eventually they did

John's Shovelhead stroker, a bike that Jill says frequently let them down, pictured at the Dickeyville, Wisconsin, hill climb in 1977

Below: Jill parties with brother Doug at the Anamosa hill climb, late 1970s.

After ending his partnership with Don Brown, John learned that breaking away with his own shop was not an easy task.

Below: J&P employee Terry Heady at the Anamosa hill climb in June, 1984, with John's Triumph hill climber sponsored by J&P Cycles.

run meets in Chicago, at both the Amphitheater and McCormick Place, which they developed into the world's largest indoor swap meet and bike show, but first John and Jill started small. In 1977, they promoted their first meet at the fairgrounds in nearby Monticello, and within three years were attracting 5,000 people. In 1980, they started a meet at a larger facility in Cedar Rapids, then the following year opened an indoor winter meet in Davenport.

ℛ

Neither John nor Jill was afraid of hard work. She had her full-time day job in Monticello and helped at the shop in the evenings. John worked the shop during the day and went to his regular job in the evening. When there was a swap meet or a motorcycle show within 300 miles, they would take off for the weekend, often sleeping in their van to keep expenses down, or because they would not have had time to make much use of a motel room even if they could afford one. Doug Hessing, who often traveled with them, reminisces, "We had an old van that was so cold in the winter, we would scrape the ice off the inside of the windshield. The engine cover on those Ford vans was not air tight, and snow would blow in and pile up inside the van." John concurs, "There were times I actually drove in a sleeping bag, pushing on the accelerator and brake with my feet inside the bag." But the travel and long hours were paying off, and in 1978 John and Jill decided to buy a house and move out of Jill's apartment, though they were stretched thin to make the deal. John sold his customized Honda chopper for $2,700 to make the down payment, and they moved to a yellow, split-level home at 402 East Hickory Street in Anamosa.

Swap meets remained a world that Don Brown was not interested in, and as John began to speculate more on used Harley parts with what was essentially company money in a market that Brown did not understand, the partnership became even more strained. Brown explains, "John got more interested in the Harley-Davidson aftermarket, and I was more interested in the Japanese machines. We disagreed on which way the business should go, and finally we agreed to end the partnership." Brown took sole ownership of D&J Cycles, and as he moved toward the motocross market he eventually renamed his business MotoX Plus. John says, "I agreed to let Don keep the name D&J Cycles and stay in the store in downtown Anamosa. He kept all of the Japanese and competition-oriented inventory, and I took the used Harley stuff and moved out to start over." He adds, "It was a lot harder than I thought it would be to start a new motorcycle shop."

At first, the Parhams put a business phone in the basement of their house and rented a dirt-floor garage a half-block down the street so they could have a business address in order to qualify for an Iowa business license. Jill laughs, "The UPS man still brought his deliveries right to our house." She adds, "I don't think our neighbors liked it. We had motorcycle guys there all the time, sometimes working on their bikes out front in the street."

John later bought a building with a dirt floor at the corner of E34 and Forest Chapel Road on the outskirts of Anamosa. It belonged to Ron Payne's mother-in-law, and she carried the mortgage contract on the sale. The all-wood building, which was heated with a wood stove, did not even have running water. There was no toilet either. John explains, "We had a hose and funnel through the wall so we could pee, and if someone had to do number two, he had to run over to Ron's mother-in-law's house a block away." To make the public area more presentable, John, Doug, and Ron poured a concrete floor in about half the building. John named his new shop J&P Cycles. "J" and "P" were simply the initials to his name, but he included the "&" with the hope of keeping some continuity with his prior business, and because he thought it sounded more business-like. But he discovered that breaking out on his own was rough going. "I did not account for the fact that people are creatures of habit," he says. "Customers kept going to the business they knew, and that was D&J Cycles. If they were looking for Harley stuff, I suspect Don did not bother to send them my way." John also discovered that suppliers he had a good relationship with at D&J were not so anxious to support him at his new store. Because Brown was the senior partner at D&J, suppliers likely thought he was the controlling and stable side of the partnership. John–now 25–was just a kid and had gone off and set up a shop in a place with a dirt floor. How serious could this venture be? John says, "I know that Don left the impression with suppliers that D&J was the 'real' cycle shop in town, and that I didn't know what I was doing and probably wouldn't last very long."

But John and Jill's venture did survive, and it was an old bike show buddy who helped J&P Cycles eventually achieve a distinct and dominant image in its field. At a custom car and motorcycle show in Monticello in 1976, John and Jill met Kenny John, a fellow enthusiast who became a lifelong friend and a creative asset to their business. Kenny John recalls, "I first saw John and Jill standing behind a card table with a few pins and patches spread out on it." He laughs and says, "They had these lonely expressions like, 'Will someone please talk to us; please buy something from us?'" Kenny is a commercial artist, a sign painter, and an illustrator. He did a lot of work pin-striping customized cars and motorcycles, and he and the Parhams became good friends. He promoted summer outdoor bike shows on the riverfront in Muscatine, Iowa, and John and Jill would ride down from Anamosa with their friends to put their bikes on display. Parham explains, "It was a really big deal. It was a big show, and sometimes there were so many of us the police would meet us on the outskirts of Muscatine and escort us in a big parade through town." Later, when the Parhams broke away with their own motorcycle business, Kenny John designed a logo for J&P Cycles, helped with the graphics for early J&P catalogs, and came up with the slogan "Keeping America on 2 Wheels," which was later changed to "Keeping the World on 2 Wheels." That early logo was a bit complex and busy, reminiscent of biker T-shirt graphics of the era. But later, Kenny John would create the crisp yellow J&P lettering over stylized blue wings that would help J&P Cycles become a recognizable brand throughout an international motorcycle market, an achievement that cannot be claimed by any other retailer in the business.

John and Jill's friend M.K. John designed J&P Cycles' early logos and created the slogan "Keeping America on Two Wheels" (above). Eventually the slogan was changed to "Keeping the World on Two Wheels" as J&P Cycles started selling parts to customers in Europe and the rest of the world (below).

T-shirt art for "The Pub," one of John's non-motorcycling business ventures, also designed by M. K. John.

Below: John and Jill's close friend M. K. John. Kenny created many of J&P Cycles logos, artwork and t-shirt designs.

Struggling with his own motorcycle shop, John Parham was determined to make it, and he began to look for other sources of income. He began to study real estate and learn how to acquire commercial property with no money down. Also, by the early 1980s, the electronic video game craze was taking hold, and John viewed this as a potentially good source of revenue. First came Pong, a simple game of video table tennis that got its name from the sound it made. Bar patrons–both male and female–took to this new form of entertainment with relish, and before it was displaced by more sophisticated designs, nearly 180,000 Pong machines were placed in saloons and arcades across America. Then came Pac Man, which was more complex, requiring more skill and creating an even more elaborate cacophony of electronic noises that fairly begged people to insert their quarters and play to the hypnotic wonka-wonka-wonka-wonka of the voracious little Pac Man, eating his way across the screen. Next came Donkey Kong, which took video gaming to a level of skill and sophistication as difficult and visually appealing as any conventional pinball machine. Seeing the growth in this new form of recreation, in 1981 John opened a video arcade in a small storefront he had acquired on Main Street in Anamosa. Only 20 feet wide and 65 feet deep, the store was ideal for lining up a row of machines. John recruited his younger brother Mark to run the arcade, which, in a sleepy town like Anamosa, became a very popular place for young people with little to do. Mark recalls, "I ran the arcade for about a year and a half, and during that time I was about the most popular guy in town." With the arcade doing well, John partnered with an accountant named Don Archer to create a video game distribution and service business in eastern Iowa.

Archer was 25 years John's senior, and functioned as financier while John did all the work. They established a territory within a 50-mile radius of Anamosa that included Dubuque and Cedar Rapids, and began to distribute and service jukeboxes, pinball machines, pool tables, and video games at bars and arcades. In 1982, John was laid off from his job, which left him free to devote his full energy to his motorcycle shop, swap meet promotions, and the extensive local travel required by the video game business.

The video game route also introduced John to a style of business he was not so comfortable with. In Cedar Rapids he began to have problems with a man that he describes as "a mafia type." The man used heavy tactics to try to get bar owners to use his machines and not John's. John says, "A guy could take a squirt gun filled with Coke or Pepsi, and squirt it into the machine's coin slot. It would destroy the electronics. The guy would threaten that something might happen to my machines, and it was pretty clear what he was getting at." When John would not be intimidated, the man tried to intimidate bar and arcade owners. In some cases, he simply bought whole businesses and replaced John's machines with his own. What's worse, the video game fad was wearing off, and it was becoming more difficult to support the expense of servicing the 1,000-square-mile territory. As the home video game market emerged, people could enjoy games that were far more versatile and sophisticated in the comfort of their living rooms. Arcades began to close, and bar owners began to dispose of the idle games that now only took up space.

John thought it was time to get out, and he tried to sell the business for $165,000 to the man in Cedar Rapids who was giving him problems. John says, "The whole business was going down hill, and he was as broke as we were. He couldn't pay that kind of money, but offered me two residential homes in trade for the business." Parham was already involved in real estate, and he wanted to make the deal. He says, "The houses were dumps, but they were right across the street from Mercy Hospital. There was pretty good potential that the area would develop in the future." However, Don Archer didn't agree. What would he do with part ownership of houses in Cedar Rapids? Archer was not doing any of the work to support the video game route, he had already amortized his expense of the game machines, and he was willing to let the business play out and collapse as John traveled to earn less and less money. Time would prove John's instincts correct, since the area where the old houses once stood is now a large medical complex. Jill says, "By now we had learned something about partners. We were figuring out that you can't exercise control over a business when you have a partner."

In the end, John and Jill decided to take a $25,000 loss to get out of the business, and John converted their video game arcade in Anamosa into a bar they called The Pub. John explains, "There was no place in Anamosa for young people to gather, and we opened The Pub to attract a younger clientele." He would learn that running a bar, especially for young drinkers, was not always fun. He explains, "It was lucrative, but it was very time-consuming and often very aggravating. It was about like being a high school principal when all of your students were drinking. There was always some kind of a hassle." A case in point was opening night, when a wall-to-wall crowd turned out to enjoy the new establishment. Then there was a fight. John says, "I was really disillusioned. That really spoiled the evening. I went home that night very discouraged." John Parham is a man who does not especially like confrontation, and dealing with drunks and disciplinary problems was not something he enjoyed. Jill was equally disenchanted with the bar business. She says, "Drunks who got turned out would actually come to our house to harass us and complain."

With John out of work, having sold the video game business at a loss, and struggling to establish the motorcycle shop, he and Jill were working even harder to make ends meet. By 1984, they were promoting a dozen swap meets a year and attending 25 as a vendor. Promoting swap meets could generate large chunks of revenue, but for reliable cash flow they were terrible. They were always risky, especially since weather was a factor, and the facilities for the meets often had to be reserved with deposits six to nine months in advance. This tied up a lot of money in deposit fees for meets that were yet months away. To complicate matters, on the day they opened their bar in Anamosa, Jill discovered she was pregnant.

John loved customized motorcycles and catered to like-minded enthusiasts through his fledgling aftermarket business. His customized Shovelhead stroker went through many changes during the time he owned it. Here it is with a stretched frame, prismic tank and an M.K. John paint job.

Above and below (right): These are actual photos sent by John to Custom Chrome to be signed up as a dealer to sell their product retail. You had to provide proof that your business was in a separate building from your house (1979). Notice the D&J is taken off the side of the white store van. This truly is the building J&P Cycles started out in after John split his partnership with Don Brown and D&J Cycles.

Jill and John in their vendor booth at the Chicago Amphitheater swap meet in 1982.

Chapter Three: John the Risk Taker

When John arrived at his motorcycle shop at 3 a.m. on the morning of May 18, 1984, smoke was boiling out of every crack and corner. Fire had not yet broken through the walls and roof of the structure, but the flames were visible inside the building. One fire truck was already on the scene, and another was on the way. There was no electrical power, it was pitch dark, and the firemen were worried about the location of welding tanks and combustible liquids inside. John put on a fireman's coat and helmet and led them into the building. It was a procedure that firemen would likely never follow today, but Anamosa was a small town and everyone knew everyone else. John knew the floor plan and contents of the structure, and it only seemed logical that he would help. Jill arrived, but because she was more than seven months pregnant, she was ordered to leave the acrid atmosphere of the smoke-filled site and return home.

John says, "The fire—later determined to be an electrical fire—had started in the shop area. All of the new parts inventory in the showroom, which adjoined the shop area, was destroyed. There was a storage room with lots of used engine parts, and the fire did not reach there, but everything was all smoke and water damaged. Everything not burned up was covered with rust and a gray coating." There were also three

In May 1984, John and Jill lost everything to a fire that destroyed J&P Cycles. But they were not to be defeated. After moving to a temporary facility on Main Street in Anamosa, in July, 1984 John acquired a former farm equipment dealership on Highway 151, just north of town. It would become the permanent home of J&P Cycles.

Zachary Parham arrived on July 23, 1984.

Below: Zach at age one on the saddle of a Simplex motorbike.

motorcycles in the building. These were John's beloved 1955 Panhead, Doug Hessing's Harley-Davidson Super Glide, and a 1947 Indian. Doug's Super Glide was parked closest to the source of the fire, and got the worst of it. John's Panhead was farther away, but was still badly damaged. The Indian, parked across the building against the far wall, was not too badly damaged. As the sun rose the next morning, it became clear that the building was totally destroyed. In the front of the burned-out structure was a gaping hole with a curled, half-burned J&P Cycles sign drooping sadly over it. John says, "We had a new baby on the way, just a month before we had lost $25,000 in the closure of our video game business, and now this."

John and Jill had $20,000 insurance coverage on the building, on which they still owed $10,000. On the contents, of which about $40,000 of new parts inventory was destroyed, they were woefully under-insured with only $25,000 in coverage. In addition, there were about $20,000 in used parts, which were not insured. The next day, John, Doug, Ron, and a number of friends began to dig through the mess, looking for anything they could salvage. John says, "In the storage area were lots of used metal parts, such as engine cases and front ends and frames, that were okay, but they were covered with rust and residue from the smoke and water, and everything smelled terrible." Knowing he had about $10,000 coming from the building insurance, John went out that day and signed a rental agreement for a vacant storefront in Anamosa. Jill was in tears: "Taking a risk like that scared me to death. I would get so upset when John would risk everything we had like that." John didn't see an alternative. He explains, "I didn't see any other option. I had no intention of going out of the motorcycle business. We still had parts to sell, and there was nothing to do but find a place where we could start again." John, Doug, Ron, and sympathetic friends sat out back in the alley for days, scrubbing damaged engine parts. John laughs, "We saved a lot of good stuff. I'm sure I was still selling smoke-damaged engine parts years later."

By June, J&P Cycles was again open for business in its temporary store on Main Street. John was renting month to month, hoping he could find a more suitable permanent facility. Then, on July 23, 1984, Zachary John Parham was born. John looks back on the hectic period and says, "We had a lot going on. With the failure of the video game business, then the cycle shop fire all within a 60-day period, I expect I was not a very good father-to-be when it came to being supportive of Jill. There was just so much on my mind." In retrospect, Jill says, "I am glad I let John follow his dream. It was such a frightening time. I could have said, 'That's enough! We've got to stop this. You need to settle down and get a regular job so we can have some security.' But I didn't do that. I let him chase his dream instead." It must have taken extreme fortitude for Jill to make this choice. She was a woman who had known grinding poverty most of her life. And now they had a son to raise.

Again, from John's point of view it seemed there was no alternative. Parham is a man with supreme confidence in his ability to succeed when he decides on something he really wants to do. He had dabbled in day jobs, a bar, and video games to make ends meet, but his true vision had always been fixed on a place in the motorcycle industry. Motorcycles were his love, and making a living with them was his dream. Today, looking back, he talks as if there was no other way his life could have gone. With straightforward simplicity he says, "People talk about risk, but if you really want something, you know there is no way you are not going to get it. One path may not work, but if that is the case, you just need to stick with it and find another path. If you keep believing in your dream, you can't help but succeed."

Perhaps it is significant that the path to John's dream lay on the road to Monticello, which he once traveled so often to visit Jill and fight for his right to be with her. About a mile north of Anamosa on Highway 151 was a 6,000-square-foot building left vacant by an Allis-Chalmers tractor dealership that had gone bankrupt. It had become known around Anamosa as the Cow Palace, because an auctioneer named Mike McGovern used the empty building for cattle auctions. It was full of straw and manure and smelled terrible, which might have seemed a suitable home for the remaining J&P parts inventory that still stank of smoke and water damage. Ron Payne recalls, "The place was a mess. It had cow crap on the walls. I couldn't imagine why John wanted the place, but he could see something there that I couldn't." John raised enough to buy the building and three acres of land for $77,000. After John, Ron, and their friends cleaned the building, John's artist friend Kenny John recalls that John surveyed the scene and said, "What the hell am I going to do with all this space?" Setting up shop in only the front half of the building, he rented out the rest as storage for cars and boats, to help pay the mortgage. Over time, J&P Cycles would outgrow that space, and John would acquire adjoining land, giving the business room to eventually sprawl with the company's extraordinary growth and success. Today it is a huge 165,000-square-foot complex that generates over $75 million in sales per year. Although most of that revenue comes from mail-order sales fulfilled through J&P's mechanized warehouse operation, significant traffic flows through a showroom that is still located in the defunct tractor dealership that Parham acquired in 1984.

The early J&P Cycles showroom. This is the same parts counter they used for the tractor dealership that was in the building before John bought it for J&P (January 1988).

Below: The early J&P parts room shelves behind the front counter. J&P Cycles sold new and used parts at this time.

However, success did not come just because J&P Cycles had a nice, new home. Trouble continued in 1985, the company almost had to declare bankruptcy, and its insurance coverage was canceled. There was not enough service work to justify Ron Payne's position, so John was faced with either finding another solution or laying off his best friend. John says, "I offered to rent some shop space to Ron so he could continue to service motorcycles on an independent basis, but he chose not to go that route. So I was faced with laying off a good friend and the most dedicated employee I had." Then he adds, "It was an awful time, but in the long run it all worked out for Ron, and he has done well and remained a good friend." Later, Payne opened his own repair shop.

ര

Undoubtedly, 1984 began one of the most challenging periods in the life of John and Jill Parham. But something else was going on in the American motorcycle industry in 1984 that no

In 1984, the same year that J&P Cycles found its permanent home, Harley-Davidson introduced its Evolution engine, which would reverse the Motor Company's fortunes. John had taken a risk on Harley-Davidson when many in the industry had written it off as the next casualty of the onslaught of Japanese motorcycles. The risk paid off as J&P's reputation grew among Harley owners.

Below: John, in front of his new store on Highway 151.

one—not John, not Jill, not the Harley-Davidson engineers and executives involved—could imagine would be so fortuitous and beneficial to all concerned. That year, the Motor Company introduced yet another version of its ancient V-twin engine, which it called the Evolution. The Evolution-powered Harley-Davidson would launch a revolution in the landscape of American motorcycling, in turn creating enormous opportunities for J&P Cycles and others.

If one were to look at John Parham's life in terms of risks taken, smart money would never have backed him when he walked away from D&J Cycles to focus on the Harley-Davidson aftermarket in 1979. Smart money would have backed Don Brown all the way, because by then the Japanese manufacturers had become a collective juggernaut rolling over everything in its path. By the early 1970s, the once-mighty British motorcycle industry was nearly extinct, due to its inability or unwillingness to compete with the quality and engineering of the Japanese manufacturers, and it appeared that Harley-Davidson was not far behind on the road to oblivion. Furthermore, motocross had become so wildly popular, anyone with half a brain would have bet on Don Brown as the man with the correct vision for motorcycle retailing in America. In fact, in 1979, when John Parham made his commitment to the Harley-Davidson market, his horse looked like a sway-back nag in comparison to the quick and agile Japanese. The Motor Company was close to an all-time low point in its history.

With the exception of its Model K and subsequent Model XL, introduced in 1952 and 1957 respectively, the Harley-Davidson Motor Company had built nothing new since it introduced its Model EL—aka the Knucklehead—in 1936. With the Japanese introducing exciting new technical features almost every year since the late 1950s, Harley-Davidson made snail-like progress with its chassis and engine improvements. Twelve years after its introduction, the Knucklehead finally gave way to the Panhead in 1948, then another 18 years later came the Shovelhead in 1966. At best, these iterations represented minor improvements to the Knucklehead by comparison to the advances taking place elsewhere in the industry. Steadily losing ground to the Japanese, and lacking capital to compete in the new import-dominated era, the Motor Company—still largely family owned—allowed itself to be acquired in 1969 by American Machine and Foundry. AMF gifted the brand with capital and a much larger manufacturing capacity, and began to increase production in a drive for greater market share. Although by 1971 the styling genius of Willie G. Davidson had begun to turn the company in a nostalgic direction that would eventually pay off in sales, AMFs higher production quotas also contributed to lower quality. Consequently, by the late 1970s more than 40 percent of the motorcycles coming off the assembly line could not pass inspection sufficient to be crated and shipped to dealers, and those that could gave the Shovelhead models a reputation as some of the worst and most unreliable motorcycles ever built.

By 1981, AMF had lost interest in the venture, and sold the company to a group of 13 executive employees who still believed in the marque and the product. Burdened by crushing debt, the new owners launched a desperate program to improve reputation and quality before they could be overtaken by bankruptcy. Although the company was approaching a declaration of bankruptcy in 1985, and saved only by recapitalization by going public with an IPO in 1986, in terms of production quality, a corner had already been turned with the introduction of the Evolution engine in 1984. Many aspects of quality had undergone significant improvement—including fit and finish—since the departure of AMF, but it was the Evolution engine that became the symbol of a new-era Harley-Davidson that was more than capable of competing with the Japanese. It took a few more years for a skeptical marketplace to become a believer, and in the late-1980s the Motor Company began an astonishing upward trend in sales, revenue, profits, and reputation that would continue unabated for the next 20 years.

The nag that John Parham bet on when he left D&J Cycles in 1979 turned out to be one of the greatest thoroughbred brands ever, not just in motorcycling, but in the whole history of American manufacturing and cultural influence. J&P Cycles, along with many aftermarket companies that remained faithful to a struggling Harley-Davidson, found themselves well-positioned to hang on for a stratospheric ride that would eventually find even the powerful and innovative Japanese brands shamelessly aping their American competitor in order to grab a piece of its market.

ଔ

But in the year that John's shop burned down, no one could have predicted these events, and it would be several years before J&P Cycles or anyone else would benefit from the economic trickle-down created by the resurgence of Harley-Davidson. In the meantime, J&P Cycles had to find a way to survive. John knew he had to reach beyond the tiny Anamosa market, and in 1985 he began to take a one-page product flyer to swap meets, in addition to parts to sell on the spot. Ed Ahlf, who later served as both a contractor and in-house employee for J&P, recalls his first meeting with John. Ahlf, who was representing ABATE of Iowa, a non-profit motorcyclists rights advocacy organization, at the time, says, "John had given us a free booth space at a swap meet in Monticello. I think at that time he still envisioned only eastern Iowa as his potential market, and though Monticello was just a small town, it was located midway between Cedar Rapids and Dubuque. He had on his table a little mimeographed flyer about his shop and some of the parts you could order through the mail." The strategy worked, and J&P Cycles started getting phone calls from people in outlying areas wanting to buy parts. With orders starting to come in, John started a mailing list for broader circulation of his promotional flyer. Jill explains, "J&P could not afford a computer, so I got permission to store our mailing list on the computer at Energy Manufacturing, so long as I updated or downloaded it only on my own time, after hours."

J&P Cycles also made its first trek to Sturgis in 1985. John had planned to go in 1984, but there was just too much happening. When Sturgis rolled around in August that year, he had a new son and was too busy trying to clean up and relocate into his new shop on Highway 151. Sturgis, located in the Black Hills of South Dakota, is the mecca of American biker culture. The event dates back to 1936 when the Jackpine Gypsies,

In 1985, John began to take a one-page product flyer to swap meets. By 1987 it had grown into a full-fledged catalog, helping J&P Cycles expand its sales beyond its small local market in eastern Iowa.

Below: The 1990 catalog. The first year J&P used the slogan Keeping America on 2 Wheels.

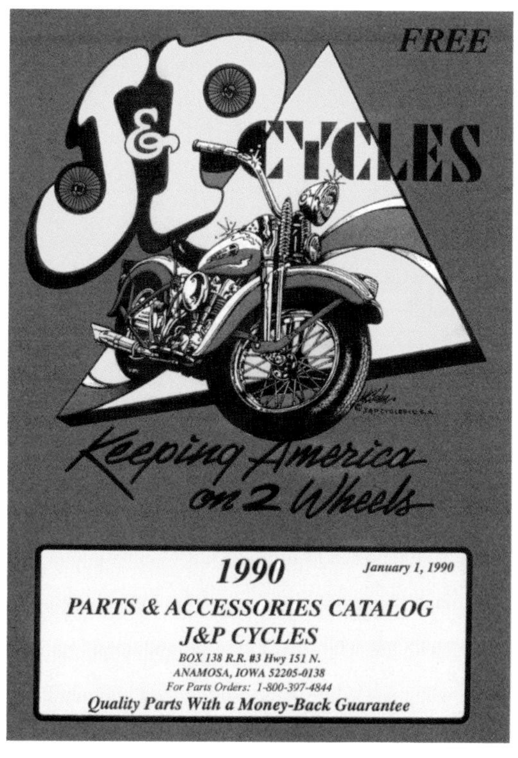

Above and below: The 1867 Colonial on Ford Street. Acquiring it nearly left the family homeless and cost John his business.

a local motorcycle club, teamed up with local businessmen to stage a motorcycle race in the hope of bringing tourism and revenue to the Depression-strapped community. The first race, called the Black Hills Classic, took place in 1937, and in 1938 the club applied for a sanction from the American Motorcyclist Association. As an AMA-sanctioned race, the event began to attract national caliber riders, and as attendance improved, the organizers next applied for an AMA Gypsy Tour. Gypsy Tours were the most prestigious rallies for touring riders because the AMA would sanction only one per state per year.

Over time, Sturgis became such a popular motorcycle touring destination that the races became only a minor feature. By the time J&P Cycles began to exhibit at Sturgis, it was attracting tens of thousands of riders. Harley-Davidson was beginning its resurgence in the market, and a keen interest was emerging toward personally customizing one's motorcycle. Sturgis provided a vast customer base of just the type John Parham was looking for, and even the Japanese manufacturers had begun to exhibit there in an effort to understand the sea change that was taking place in the American motorcycle market as their customers began to return to Harley-Davidsons. It was a crucible of learning for trends in what touring riders liked and wanted to buy. Sturgis would not only figure prominently in J&P's growth, but it would become one of John's best annual opportunities to stay in touch with his customers. As his employees and suppliers will tell you, John Parham's unique genius lies in his ability to identify trends and understand where the market is going. As a senior staff member said, "When it comes to the motorcycle industry, John Parham can see around corners."

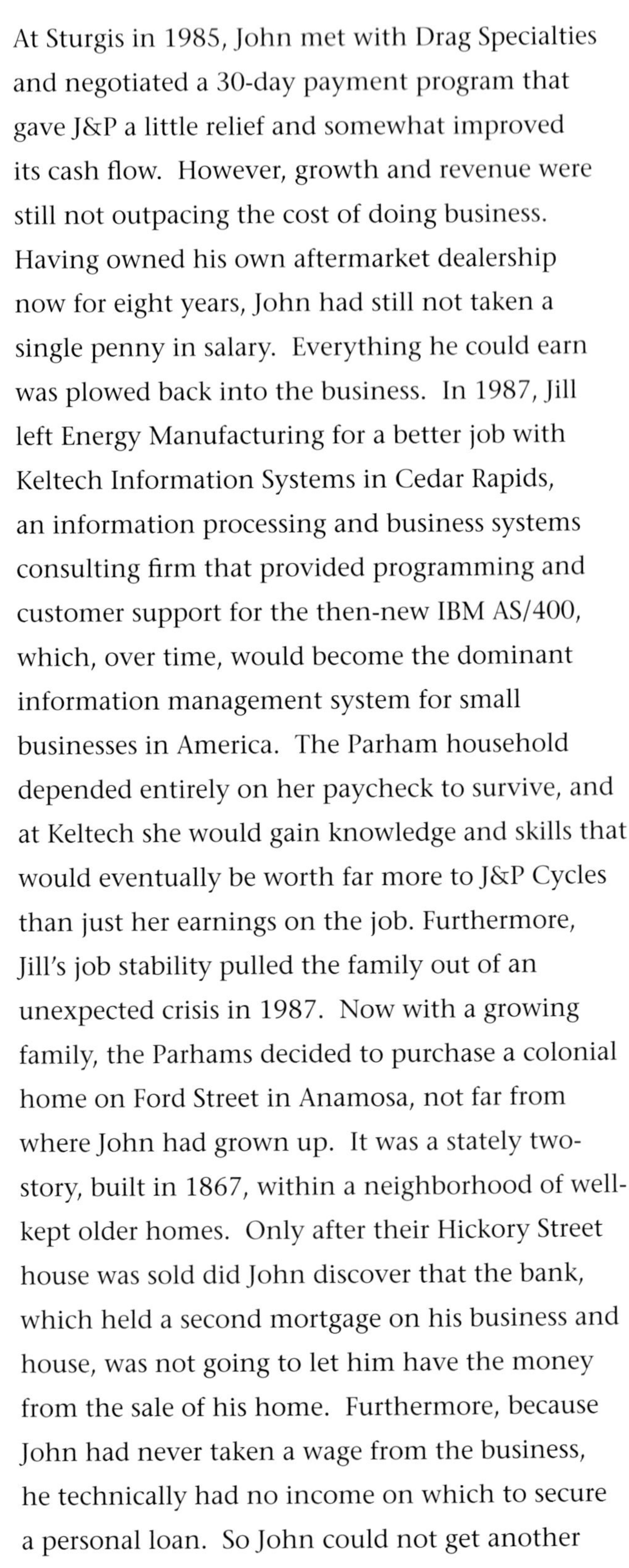

At Sturgis in 1985, John met with Drag Specialties and negotiated a 30-day payment program that gave J&P a little relief and somewhat improved its cash flow. However, growth and revenue were still not outpacing the cost of doing business. Having owned his own aftermarket dealership now for eight years, John had still not taken a single penny in salary. Everything he could earn was plowed back into the business. In 1987, Jill left Energy Manufacturing for a better job with Keltech Information Systems in Cedar Rapids, an information processing and business systems consulting firm that provided programming and customer support for the then-new IBM AS/400, which, over time, would become the dominant information management system for small businesses in America. The Parham household depended entirely on her paycheck to survive, and at Keltech she would gain knowledge and skills that would eventually be worth far more to J&P Cycles than just her earnings on the job. Furthermore, Jill's job stability pulled the family out of an unexpected crisis in 1987. Now with a growing family, the Parhams decided to purchase a colonial home on Ford Street in Anamosa, not far from where John had grown up. It was a stately two-story, built in 1867, within a neighborhood of well-kept older homes. Only after their Hickory Street house was sold did John discover that the bank, which held a second mortgage on his business and house, was not going to let him have the money from the sale of his home. Furthermore, because John had never taken a wage from the business, he technically had no income on which to secure a personal loan. So John could not get another loan, and on top of that had no money from the sale of his house to roll over as a down-payment for the new house. The Parhams were practically out on the street, and the purchase of the Ford Street property was completed only after Jill was able to negotiate a personal loan, based on her earnings. She also had to cash in her retirement from her job at Energy to come up with a down payment. It was a shocking experience that taught John something about the small town bankers he had been dealing with. John recalls, "It was a devastating experience. They just about bankrupted us. We look back now and wonder how we ever got through it."

At the time, most of the banks in Anamosa and surrounding towns were small, privately-owned institutions that had built their business on farming. They were accustomed to dealing with individuals, not businesses, to which they made small, relatively short-term loans backed by hard collateral, such as farm equipment, buildings, or land. John says, "To them I was John Parham. It did not matter that there were several J&P corporations, including J&P Cycles and J&P Promotions. They would loan only a certain amount to a customer, and regardless of how the loan agreements read, they figured they were dealing with John Parham. If one company owed them money, they were not about to loan money to another if it exceeded their limit, and they even kept our money from a personal mortgage because I also owed money through my corporations." This was an old-school, agrarian banking mentality that would never support J&P's growth, and it had already begun to threaten the survival of Parham's business interests. Vic Hamre, a banker with whom John works today, moved to Anamosa in 1987, and he recalls what it was like then and how banking has changed. He says, "They didn't have a clue what J&P was doing. They were used to financing annual crop production, not a growing mail-order business. They wanted to see hard assets they could lay their hands on. The idea that income depended on your assets flying out the door and onto the UPS truck as quickly as possible was something they just couldn't get their minds around." John's progressive vision, ambition, and business model had collided headlong with the conservative policies of his sole source of growth capital, and he knew his banking relationship had to change. Not only did it stifle business success, but it had nearly made the Parhams homeless.

At his core, John Parham is a very sentimental person. His favorite Christmas movie is "It's a Wonderful Life," and for him Christmas is one of the most important times of year. When he was a child, John and his siblings dressed up as angels and posed to be photographed for the Parham family Christmas card. Christmas was a season of tenderness and giving, but by 1985 he had begun to dread its arrival. John says, "It was such a hard time of year, I began to hate Christmas. No, I didn't hate Christmas, but I hated the fact that we were so broke. For us, December was the worst month of the year. The motorcycle business was dead, and any money we had was tied up in deposits for shows and swap meets for the coming year." He continues, "I could easily relate to George Bailey in 'It's a Wonderful Life.' I understood his anger and his despair. We were worse than broke that time of year, and we had

Jill, John, and Zachary at Christmas, 1985. Christmas had always been an important family event for the Parhams. By 1985 it had become a bitter-sweet season because money was so tight.

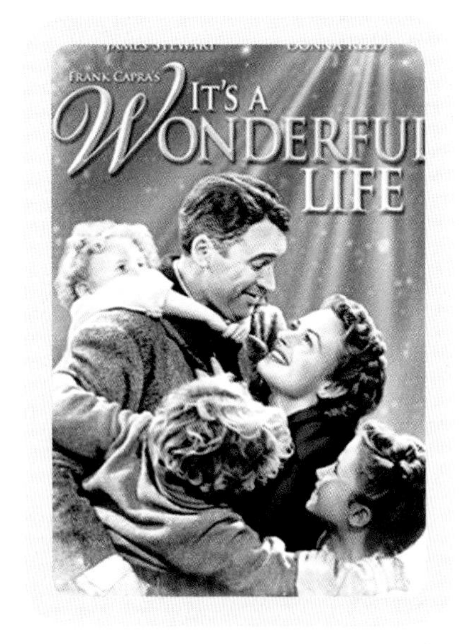

John, Jill and Zach with John's beloved 1955 Harley Panhead (1990). (Photo by Mike Farabaugh).

Below: John's Panhead has been used more than once on a J&P Cycles catalog cover.

no idea how we were going to make payroll or pay our bills. The movie always made me feel better because it all came out for the better." The 1987 winter was especially bitter for John because in order to make payroll he had to sell his beloved 1955 Harley Panhead, plus another 1939 Harley and a trailer full of parts to Larry Averitt, a motorcycle specialty shop owner in Whitestown, Indiana, just north of Indianapolis. Averitt had known the Parhams since the early eighties, and he promised not to sell the 1955 Panhead without notifying John and giving him first right of refusal.

Ed Ahlf remembers the J&P employees Christmas party that year. He says, "We all got together in a little hall downtown. All of us knew what John had done, and we got a picture of the Panhead and blew it up into a big poster that we presented to him for Christmas. He broke down and had to leave the room." Fortunately, two years later John was in a position to buy the Pan back from Averitt. The bike, which was originally yellow, had been fully restored in a color called Root Beer after the fire, and while this was a beautiful metallic brown paint, John felt it never sat right on the Pan. After re-acquiring the motorcycle, Parham restored it again and had it done in its brilliant Canary Yellow by Elmer Ehnes, a restoration expert in the Twin Cities. Today it sits at a focal point in the National Motorcycle Museum in Anamosa, and John still nearly chokes up when he talks about it. It was his first collectible motorcycle and the first bike on which he and Jill could tour in comfort. It was almost destroyed by fire, then nearly lost to financial adversity, and today John never retells its story without asserting with conviction, "And it's never going away again!" For John, his Pan is a reminder that no matter how hard things get, it's still a wonderful life.

For 1988, the J&P Cycles catalog was doubled to 48 pages, then in 1989 it doubled again to 96 pages. By 1990, the Harley-Davidson market had returned with a vengeance. Well-funded Baby Boomers were indulging their nostalgic memories, returning to motorcycling after successfully building businesses and raising families, and their bike of choice was the classically-styled Harley-Davidson. Harley dealers were oversold and the Motor Company could not produce enough to meet demand. And while the rush to own a Harley-Davidson seemed almost a herd mentality, each of these Harley owners wanted his or her motorcycle to be unique and special. This desire to customize drove an explosive accessory aftermarket. The dream on which John Parham took his big risk back in 1979 when he left Don Brown and founded J&P Cycles had finally arrived. Enjoying extraordinary growth in sales, J&P took over the whole of its building and added staff to serve its larger customer base. Sales grew by over 50 percent in 1989, then exploded with an additional 80 percent growth in 1990, exceeding $1 million in revenue. But at the end of his best year ever, John discovered he was broke. After more than a decade, he still had not taken a single penny of salary out of the business, and despite recent enormous growth in sales and a million-dollar year, the Parhams were still living on Jill's salary at Keltech. Money was flowing out as fast as it was coming in. Taking a risk was no longer an occasional event. It seemed more like a constant state of affairs, and the risks were getting bigger. John knew what it was like to be broke, but now he was learning how to be broke on a large scale. How, he wondered, could the dream, once arrived, have turned into a nightmare?

Chapter Four:
J&P Promotions, The Load-Out

John and Jill Parham organized their first swap meet at the fairgrounds in Monticello, Iowa, in 1977. John was first attracted to swap meets because they offered an opportunity to expand the sales reach of D&J Cycles, the motorcycle accessory store he owned with Don Brown in Anamosa. But John was further attracted to swap meets because of the excitement. It was fun to prowl the aisles, meet people, look for parts, and talk with like-minded enthusiasts. Though John's early interest in motorcycles tended toward customs and choppers, at the swap meets he began to learn about and appreciate classic and antique motorcycles as well. Typically, he was not willing to be just a vendor, just as he had not been willing to be a custom bike owner if he could be in the business of selling custom bike parts as well. Why, he thought, not have a shot at swap meet promotion and earn money while he was vending on behalf of D&J Cycles? As the D&J partnership broke up and John went off on his own with J&P Cycles in 1979, swap meets became even more important, since the shop in Anamosa was earning very little money. John and Jill—and sometimes Doug Hessing, Ron Payne, and other friends of the Parhams—began to travel to swap

John and Doug Hessing in McCormick Place on the night before a show. Within hours it will be transformed into a noisy, vibrant room filled with excitement and hundreds of motorcycle enthusiasts. (George Barnard photo)

The J&P Promotions crew at Road America in Elkhart Lake, Wisconsin, 1995.

Below: Just an empty hall hours earlier, a typical J&P Promotions Super Series Show set a new standard for indoor motorcycle commerce and entertainment.

meets almost every weekend, and John began to look for vacancies in the schedule of Midwestern venues where he could organize and promote his own meets. At some of these, especially at the winter indoor venues, he began to include bike shows where owners of custom motorcycles were invited to put their bikes on display in competition for trophies and cash prizes. The array of unusual, glittering motorcycles was one more attraction to bring more people, both participants and spectators, to the event. Bike show swap meets were an opportunity to create a happening, to include music, biker fashion shows, and beauty contests where local young women could vie to be crowned queen of the show.

John liked not just the earning potential of shows and swap meets, but they appealed to him on an emotional level. The organization and execution of shows, sometimes under difficult circumstances, the financial risk, the complexity, and the opportunities to attack and overcome problems excited him and made him feel productive and alive. One of his favorite songs is Jackson Browne's "The Load-Out," because it describes the experience John came to know and love in the promotion of swap meets and bike shows. Browne sings:

Now the seats are all empty
Let the roadies take the stage
Pack it up and tear it down
They're the first to come and last to leave
Working for that minimum wage
They'll set it up in another town
Tonight the people were so fine
They waited there in line
And when they got up on their feet they made the show
And that was sweet . . .
But I can hear the sound
Of slamming doors and folding chairs
And that's a sound they'll never know

Browne is singing about a concert, but the process of promotion, organization, and execution is the same. Being the first to come and last to leave gave John a sense of accomplishment and fulfillment that could never be experienced in the day-to-day running of a shop. Still today, when he describes it, he becomes visibly animated. He says, "You and the crew travel in a truck to a city where you've rented a hall. You have your banners and awards and everything you need. There's nothing there, and as you mark off booth spaces and decorate the stage and set up the hall, you begin to see it all come together. The bike owners and vendors arrive, and there are always problems to deal with and disputes to sort out. You've laid out a lot of money to get to this point, and you have no idea if it is going to work; if enough people are going to come. You're still working on last-minute details as show time arrives, and you look out and see all the people, lined up and waiting for the doors to open. Then the doors open and they come pouring in and the room comes alive. There's music being piped into the hall and with the people the sound level grows and grows until it is like constant thunder. It is very exciting. Everywhere you look, people are making deals, buying and selling parts. Then comes time for the special programs and awards, and your announcer takes the stage and gets everything under control. You present the awards for the winning motorcycles, and everyone is cheering and applauding. It all comes to this great crescendo that you've orchestrated, then suddenly it is over and the people begin to file out of the building. The hall becomes quiet, and there's nothing there but a few vendor stragglers, still clearing out their stuff, and your own crew is taking the equipment to the truck. You can hear the banging doors and folding chairs, just like in the Jackson Browne song, and finally there you are, in an empty hall, the last to leave. You feel good because the people have had a great time, but they'll never experience or understand what you have been through in the last 36 hours." He adds, "I loved to see it come together, explode into something big, then kind of melt away."

In late 1979, John organized a show at Hawkeye Downs in Cedar Rapids, Iowa, then in 1980 he went to the Mississippi Valley Fairgrounds in Davenport, Iowa, then later to the Davenport River Center downtown. In 1982, he launched shows at Mecca Arena in Milwaukee, the Dane County Expo Center in Madison, and the Will County Fairgrounds in Peotone, Illinois, southwest of Chicago, and in 1983 he went to the Civic Center in Omaha, Nebraska. In 1985, he opened a show at the Sports Arena in Toledo, Ohio, and started a show at Chicago's McCormick Place. To attempt to level out the seasonality of his motorcycle event promotions, in 1985 John also tried his hand at concert promotion, booking the Glenn Miller Band, Les Brown and his Band of Renown, and the Four Tops at various venues in Cedar Rapids. But John did not stick with the music concerts. He explains, "We hit a home run with the Glenn Miller Band, but the other two concerts lost money. I decided to focus on the motorcycle meets and shows, which I understood better."

The following year he went to Vets Memorial Auditorium in Columbus, Ohio, and to the Belle Clair County Fairgrounds in Belleville, Illinois, to reach the St. Louis market. In 1987, he set up in the St. Paul, Minnesota, Civic Center, the Indianapolis Convention Center, and the Amphitheater in Chicago. Clearly, with nearly a decade of development, swap meets and custom bike shows had become a great deal more than a sideline to his Anamosa motorcycle shop. They had become a significant profit center and a huge consumer of time and personnel, so in July, 1989, the Parhams formed J&P Promotions, a separate for-profit corporation for the purpose of running their show and swap meet business, and then they added a show at the Farm Show Center in Harrisburg, Pennsylvania. Their friend Kenny

J&P Promotions was formed as a separate corporation in 1989. As with all of John's new ventures, artist friend M.K. John designed a logo.

Below: Doug Hessing and his sister Jill Parham sell tickets at the Anamosa hill climb.

J&P Cycles advertised at J&P Promotions races and sponsored drag races organized by other promoters, such as the races conducted at Sturgis Dragway pictured above. (Larry Smith photo)

Below: When John Parham could not find adequate print media within his Midwestern market, he created his own, forming Zacharia Advertising and Publications in 1989.

John designed a clean, modern logo for the company that integrated the letters "J&P" into a single graphic with "Promotions" slanting to the right to suggest speed, progression, passion.

☙

John Parham would also find promotional opportunity in the world of motorcycle drag racing. America's love affair with high performance vehicles actually began during the Great Depression, when the rich had their Auburns and Duesenbergs and the kids from blue-collar families had their stripped-down Ford roadsters, compensating for a lack of class and luxury with big Cadillac and Lincoln engines. Then, young America's interest in hot rods exploded after the Second World War when speed and acceleration became an obsession, leading to the formation of car clubs and legal drag strips in communities all over the nation. Motorcycles also were significantly involved, and in the early days they were almost exclusively Harley-Davidsons. The occasional British Vincent could beat the Milwaukee brand, but they were few and far between in the late 1940s and early '50s, so most of the hot bikes were souped-up Harley Knuckleheads, and in the early days of the sport they could consistently beat the fastest cars in town. Then, in 1957, Harley-Davidson introduced its 883cc Sportster, a bike with a greater power-to-weight ratio than anything else on the street, and throughout the 1960s the fuel-burning Sportster reigned. Fans of British bikes got into the game also, but it usually took twin-engine Triumphs or Nortons to beat a top-performing single-engine Sportster. Japanese brands were not yet involved because they were still more than a decade away from building the kind of big-bore, high-performance models capable of competing with the Harley and the Brit bikes.

Local drag racing organizations, dominated by car people, did not always make the motorcyclists welcome, which remained the case with the formation of the National Hot Rod Association in 1951. As a result, organizations that sanctioned drag races exclusively for motorcycles sprang up around the country as early as the mid-1980s. These included the American Motorcycle Racing Association, the International Drag Bike Association, the All-Harley Drag Racing Association, Dragbike, Pro-Star, and others. Most were only regional in their scope. Because of his love of high-performance Harley-Davidsons, John Parham naturally found motorcycle drag racing appealing. In 1990, the year after he incorporated J&P Promotions, John approached AMRA founder Richard Wegner to promote drag races under his organization's sanction. Later he would work with the AHDRA, organizing races in East St. Louis, Xenia, Ohio, and Racine, Wisconsin.

In 1991, John came up with the idea of organizing the AHDRA Western Swing, a regional series designed to expand the organization's presence on the West Coast. It included races at Palmdale and Pomona, CA, Phoenix, AZ and Houston, TX. A race in Sacramento, not promoted by J&P, was also brought into the series. By 1992, J&P Promotions was organizing seven of the 15 events in the AHDRA schedule, and for some races where it was not the promoter, such as Sturgis, J&P Cycles became the event sponsor. J&P Promotions continued to promote drag races through most of the decade, but conducted its last drag racing event in 1997. John says, "It was glamorous and exciting. I loved the smell of the nitro-methane when the top fuel bikes came to the line. But it was also a lot of work, and there was a very high level of risk. There was a lot of cash flow, but you could easily find yourself only breaking even at the end of a season." He explains, "With a series of five or six races, you might have only one big pay day, but there was also likely to be at least one rain-out, and then you would lose your shirt. At best, it would all balance out and you would end up with very little to show for a summer of lots of travel and aggravation."

ꝏ

In the late 1950s, there were only two national motorcycle magazines and no local or regional publications of any significance. When the Baby Boomers reached their teens, concurrent with the introduction of inexpensive, good quality, easy-to-ride Japanese motorcycles, the market exploded, and the 1960s saw a huge growth in sales of both road and off-road motorcycles. Motorcycling became popular enough to support local publications, most of which took the form of tabloid newspapers, rather than glossy magazines. *Cycle News* appeared in Southern California in 1965, then launched an Eastern edition near Cleveland in 1968, followed by a Southern edition in Atlanta a few years later. New England had *Cycle Sport* and *The Motorcyclist's Post*, which appeared in 1967. *Michigan Motorcyclist* came along to serve that state's riders, and New York had *The Motorcyclist Mirror* while Kansas had *Checkered Flag News*. All focused on local news and offered calendars of events in their market areas. None did much good for John Parham's Iowa-based interests. *Cycle News East*, which was the largest of the Eastern tabloids, barely penetrated into Illinois and contained very little information about the street riding or custom motorcycle scene.

Parham's solution was to create his own publishing company, and in 1989 he formed Zacharia Advertising and Publications, named for his son, Zachary. While Zacharia served Parham's interests in many ways, the flagship of the publishing company was *The Motorcycle Dispatch*. Introduced in 1989, it was a colorful and attractively-designed bi-monthly tabloid. It contained stories of national interest, but focused mostly on local stories in the market areas where J&P Promotions was hosting swap meets and shows. It promoted J&P Cycles, but not to the detriment of other retailers. In fact, in a strategy to build good will, the paper highlighted a leading motorcycle retailer in every issue and readily published press releases provided

The Zacharia logo designed by M. K. John.. Zacharia Advertising was established in 1989. Zacharia Advertising and Publications produced: The Motorcycle Dispatch, the Motorcycle Event Guide, Asphalt Angels Magazine, AHDRA Rule book and Event programs and J&P Promotions Super Series Event Programs.

Below: The Motorcycle Dispatch was produced 6 times a year and circulated around the country free through motorcycle dealerships and J&P Promotions events.

MOTORCYCLE DISPATCH

Keeping America on 2 Wheels

March 1996

DAYTONA 96

photo by Charlie Brewton

Harley-Davidson drag racing is a popular event during Daytona Bike Week. The AHDRA will be in Bithlo at Orlando Speed World March 6-7.

Daytona Beach gears up for 55th Annual Bike Week

"The World's Largest Motorcycle Event" will celebrate its 55th anniversary March 1-10, 1996, when Bike Week '96 roars into Daytona Beach with races, shows, parties and much more!

The 10-day festival for motorcycle enthusiasts is expected to draw as many as 400,000 riders from across the United States and around the world.

"We're anticipating the biggest Bike Week ever," Suzanne Heddy, director of the Bike Week Task Force for the Chamber, Daytona Beach-Halifax Area, said. "The 55th anniversary will make this year's event that much more exciting."

The hub of Bike Week is world-famous Main Street – the place to see and be seen. Hundreds of customized machines will line the cobblestone street as bikers cruise Main Street's unique shops and restaurants. A Welcome Center will be open from 10 a.m. to 10 p.m. March 1-9 so visitors can find additional information on area activities.

Daytona International Speedway will be the center of motorcycle racing during Bike Week, highlighted by the Daytona 200 by Arai on Sunday, March 10. Two other races on Sunday – the 600cc Supersport and Harley-Davidson Twin Sports AMA Road Races – cap off nine days of activities at "The World Center of Racing."

Bike Week's unique events include the 12th anniversary BMW Bike Week Camp at the Bulow Resort Campground; coleslaw wres-

see *Daytona 1996*, p. 46

photo by Doug Mitchel

Beautiful bikes are a common site at Bike Week. Don't miss the Boardwalk Bike Show on March 8 and Rat's Hole Custom Chopper Show on March 9.

photo by Mark Poeppelmeier

Fun, sun, and sandy beaches can make you forget those winter blahs.

year's event that much more exciting."

The hub of Bike Week is world-famous Main Street – the place to see

area activities.

Daytona International Speedway will be the center of motorcycle racing during Bike Week, highlighted by the Daytona 200 by Arai on

Bike Week's unique events include the 12th anniversary BMW Bike Week Camp at the Bulow Resort Campground; coleslaw wres-

see *Daytona 1996*, p. 46

Asphalt Angels, produced in the late eighties, was one of the few early publications geared specifically towards women riders and was published by Zacharia Publications.

Below: In 1988, John began to promote nostalgic races at the Antique Motorcycle Club of America meet at Davenport, Iowa, becoming the first to offer a class for the classic pre-1920 board track racers.

by J&P's competitors. It was circulated free to motorcycle dealerships, eventually growing to a print run of over 20,000 copies per issue. While its main purpose was to promote the interests of J&P Promotions, it was in fact a legitimate and objective news medium run as a profit center through the sale of advertising. As the J&P Promotions schedule grew, as J&P Cycles expanded its operations with seasonal storefront outlets in Sturgis and Daytona Beach, and as the whole Harley scene gained momentum, by the mid-1990s *Motorcycle Dispatch* increased its frequency to eight issues a year and its size to more than 60 pages.

Zacharia Advertising and Publications also produced posters and programs for all of J&P's swap meets and shows, and as the corporation moved into the promotion of motorcycle drag races, Zacharia contracted to publish the programs for the AHDRA's full schedule of events. In 1997 it became the publisher of *Harley Women*, which was later renamed *Asphalt Angels*. At its peak, Zacharia had a staff of eight and more than 20 regular outside contributors. Its corporate lifespan was roughly concurrent with J&P Promotions, for which *Motorcycle Dispatch* was the primary marketing medium. Zacharia was later dissolved when J&P Cycles became so large and successful that all advertising and marketing functions were taken in-house.

ঔ

Drag racing was not the only form of motorcycle racing in which J&P Promotions became involved. For example, J&P teamed up with the management of Road America in Elkhart Lake, Wisconsin, to organize a ride-in, bike show, swap meet, motorcycle rodeo, and AMA-sanctioned short track race at the Sheboygan County Fairgrounds, in conjunction with their AMA national championship road race. Plus, J&P promoted two motorcycle hill climbs a year in Anamosa, just off Highway 151, not three miles from the headquarters of J&P Cycles. John also developed a program of vintage motorcycle races at the half-mile dirt track at Mississippi Valley Fair Grounds concurrent with the giant Antique Motorcycle Club of America meet at Davenport, Iowa. The crowd would roar when thundering, open-piped machines as old as 1915 rolled onto the track. John says, "At first it wasn't easy to get the guys to bring out their bikes that were so valuable and fragile. In the beginning I had to waive entry fees to get them to do it, but it really worked. They had a lot of fun, and it made the show." Other promoters around America had initiated races for vintage motorcycles as old as 1930s models, but John was the first to create a program for the rare factory racers from the board track era.

By 1993, J&P Promotions was organizing more than 30 events a year. In addition, J&P Cycles was still operating as a vendor at other swap meets all over the Midwest and as far away as the East Coast. It became a punishing schedule that less-motivated men than John would not have had the ability to maintain. Personnel were added, but both J&P corporations were still operating with skeleton crews, many of whom worked in the shop all week and went to swap meets or promotions on the weekend. Doug Hessing recalls, "At the peak, we attended as many as 50 events a year. It seems like all we ever did was stay on the road and load and unload the van." Often, the schedules were so tight that there was no point in worrying about motels. Most of the crew slept while others drove, or after setting up in the wee hours of the morning, they would sleep in the van or on the floor of a hall to get a few hours rest before the public began to arrive. Charlie St. Clair, the organizer of the Laconia Rally in New Hampshire, which J&P Cycles sponsors, says, "John Parham is the most driven, hard-working person I know. He has earned every single gray hair on his head."

This kind of relentless hard work brought success, but it was also John's attitude as a promoter that made the shows grow. Often, race and show promoters are illusive and shadowy characters who remain in the back office and work with their clients through middle men and underlings. John never outgrew being a swap meet guy, just like the people who continued to rent booth spaces from him. He was always out on the floor, dealing with his people and facing his problems head-on. Denny Tyson, who runs Eagle Leathers in Akron, Ohio, says, "We always liked working with John. He was always fair and helpful. I remember a little meet somewhere that went bust. For some reason, weather or whatever, it just didn't happen. Nobody came. John not only returned our booth fees, but he offered us free space at his next show. He lost a lot of money that day, but he still wanted to take care of us vendors." Spider, a supplier of riding gear and helmets who has been both a vendor and an organizer of swap meets, says, "John never failed to give a man a leg-up in this business. If you showed up and could not pay for your booth space, he would let you go ahead and sell and pay him at the end of the show. He was always honest and helpful, and he treated everyone else the way he would like to be treated."

John's philosophy toward running motorcycles shows was the same as at swap meets. Customer satisfaction was always the goal, because sending the participants home happy was the best way to make the promotions grow and become more profitable. At the shows, John developed an awards program that distributed as many trophies as possible by creating many different classes of competition. John laughs and explains, "A fellow will go home just as pleased as he can be after winning second place in his class, and he doesn't have to tell his buddies that there were only two bikes in his class. He is going to put that trophy on his mantle with pride, and his good experience and positive word-of-mouth are going to make your next show bigger and better."

Because many of the events were held indoors over the winter months, travel was sometimes treacherous. On one occasion, John, Jill, and two other employees were on their way to Kalamazoo, Michigan, driving a maxi-van on Interstate 80 through a snow storm that was approaching white-out conditions. John recalls, "Snow was building up on the highway and it was getting slick. A

J&P Super Series Shows made bike builders happy and brought back satisfied customers with cash prizes and a vast array of awards and trophies. Above is the Custom Chrome Inc. presentation stage at Chicago, 1996.

Below: John's good friend Lonnie Isam receives his award at a J&P Promotions Bike Show in Houston, TX. 1994.

Nostalgic Antique Flat Track Races at the Davenport, IA AMCA meet.

Below is the Board Walk Bike Show organized by J&P Promotions at Daytona Beach, 1997.

tandem UPS truck just ahead of us began to lose it. He started fish-tailing one way and then the other. Because it was a tandem, there was no way of telling which way he was going to go. I tried to get by, and in two or three more seconds I would have made it, but his trailer swung around and clipped the back of the van." The big rig slid off the highway into the median, and the J&P van was knocked to the right, off the highway and down an embankment. John continues, "The snow was so deep that as we plowed down the embankment, it piled up clear over the windshield. The impact from the truck broke the gas tank filler spout, and there we were, off the road, half buried in the snow, smelling the van fill up with gas fumes." The crew got out and up the embankment. It was bitterly cold, and when a highway patrol car finally arrived, Jill was allowed to sit in the back seat to try to stay warm. John says, "The wreck shut down I-80 for three hours, and it seemed like it took forever for a wrecker to arrive that could handle the UPS truck. When he got the truck out of the median, he was just going to drive off and leave us there. He said he was not equipped or allowed to handle small vehicles and was afraid he would roll our van over, trying to get it up the embankment." John finally persuaded the wrecker driver to help. He said he would take full responsibility for his van and attach the cable himself if the wrecker would just winch it back onto the road. Back on the road, the crew limped on to Kalamazoo, smelling fuel fumes all the way. It was too cold to sleep in the van, so they found a discount motel to grab about two hours of sleep before it was time to set up the show. Jill adds, "Yeah, and it was really a dump. The kind of place where you want to sleep with your clothes on."

J&P Promotions developed a colorful crew. Doug Hessing was a mainstay, but there were also Bill McGill, called Swill McGill for his consumption of great quantities of beer, and Hosehead, so named for the long, braided ponytail of red hair that hung down his back. Doug recalls, "Sometimes, to get a crew, we would just empty the bars on our way out of Anamosa. We would go in a bar and ask who wanted to go to Chicago, or Milwaukee, or wherever, and earn some money. There were always a bunch of guys who would grab their beer, climb off the stool, and get into the van." Doug laughs, "We would make a stop somewhere along the way, and when people opened the doors, beer cans would come rolling out on the pavement around the van."

The shows also always brought unexpected adventures. John relates a story when the crew was just blocks away from the Amphitheater in Chicago when they hit a bad pot hole and destroyed a tire.

He says, "It was November and really cold, in a very bad neighborhood, and we discovered we had no lug wrench. The crew got out and was standing around with the street people around burning oil drums trying to stay warm while I got to a phone to call Triple-A." John laughs, "It was really a scary place. The guys were standing around waiting, and Doug had just finished drinking a carton of milk. Out of boredom, he set the cardboard carton down on the ground and stomped it. It made a loud explosion, and Hosehead instantly hit the deck. He thought it was a gun shot and dropped and spread out flat on his face on the pavement."

John relates, "The Triple-A guy took about 45 minutes to show up, then he saw our company name on the side of the truck and said, 'I don't do commercial!'" He continues, "I asked if he would just let me borrow his tire iron. He refused, said he didn't have time, and had to get to another customer." "By this time," John says, "Locals were hanging around watching, and some old guy said he could help us out. He took us down this dark street to an area that looked like some kind of permanent flea market. There was even some guy living in an old bread truck that was up on blocks. The guy was really trying to help us because he wanted to earn a few bucks, but we weren't finding anyone with a tire iron." John and Swill McGill began to feel uncomfortable as they went deeper into the rough neighborhood. They began to wonder if they were being taken on a wild goose chase, and finally turned around and headed back for the van. John says, "We had been stranded there for about an hour and a half by then, and we had no idea what we were going to do. Then I saw the Triple-A guy coming back down the street." John ran into the middle of the street and flagged down the truck. He told the man he would rent his tire iron for fifty dollars, which did the trick. John says, "He took my fifty bucks and just stood there and watched while we changed the wheel."

Sometimes, John and Jill would take Zach to the shows where he would stay in the ticket booth to help his mother, shadow Doug during setup before the crowds arrived, or stay in the J&P Cycles booth during the show. Jill says, "We tried to keep a close eye on him and always keep him under reliable adult supervision." Once at the Chicago Amphitheater, however, when Zach was only five, Jill was selling admission tickets and suddenly realized Zach was nowhere to be seen. She says, "I was freaking out. We had the crew looking everywhere for Zach, and we kept paging him over the public address system." John says, "We were about to get the police involved, then we look up and here comes Swill McGill, wandering down the aisle with Zach following him.

Young Zachary got an early start in the motorcycle show and swap meet business, helping distribute J&P catalogs by the thousands at the various events.

Below: J&P's shows attracted large crowds across the country as seen here at the St. Paul, MN Super Series show in March, 1995.

John with friends Tom Hinderholtz and Dick Betchkal on a motorcycle riding trip in August 2008. Pictured here in front of the Gay Bar in Gay, MI.

He had gone out to the van to do something, and Zach went along. He had not heard the P.A. announcements, but I think he was so unconscious, he didn't even realize he had Zach in tow."

By 1993, several of the shows in major cities had become well established and successful. John had the idea of grouping these into a "Super Series." That year, the J&P Promotions Super Series was launched with shows in Milwaukee, St. Paul, Chicago, Harrisburg, and Belleville. The following year, venues at Boston and Secaucus, New Jersey, were added, and the Super Series grew to seven. By now, some venues, such as McCormick Place in Chicago, were drawing 10,000 people, and the creation of a Super Series achieved a critical mass that made the J&P schedule attractive for sponsorship. Custom Chrome signed on as the presenting sponsor for the series. By 1996, the Custom Chrome Super Series grew to nine venues. J&P Promotions had become the biggest promoter of motorcycle events in America, and its flagship show, at McCormick Place, was the largest motorcycle swap meet in the world. With over 200,000 square feet of exhibit space, J&P's McCormick Place show drew as many as 800 vendors and 200 custom motorcycles. In both size and scope, John Parham raised motorcycle shows and swap meets to a new level. Dick Betchkal, who would later acquire several of the leading shows, says today, "John wrote the book on this business. He sorted out the problems and created the rules and procedures that are still used today. I still use the forms and paper work and policies that he created back in the 1980s."

Below: Custom bikes on display at a J&P Promotions show. St. Paul, MN Super Series 1995.

John and Ray Kittel at J&P Cycles Open House 2008. Ray began judging bike shows for John in the early 90's and still does so today.

Chapter Five:
J&P Promotions, The Turning Point

While the shows were a successful business in their own right, they had also become a powerful marketing engine for J&P Cycles. Ever increasing numbers meant that many more J&P product catalogs could be distributed at the shows. Also, using drawings for door prizes as an incentive, the shows began to generate huge mailing lists, which John used to distribute catalogs and promotional flyers. John and the J&P Cycles staff were learning how to effectively use direct-mail, and good mailing lists became a highly-valued commodity. Doug Hessing laughs when he says, "Sometimes I think John was more excited about the door prize ticket box than he was about the money box."

The shows and swap meets were a cash business, and, once established, they could be very lucrative. When Jill went to the shows, she supervised the sale of tickets and was responsible for all of the cash. When the schedule became very crowded with events as far away as the West Coast, some of the crew would fly. Ed Ahlf recalls, "At a big event where a lot of money was being transported back to Anamosa, John and Jill

Large crowds at the shows began to generate ever-larger mailing lists, driving sales to J&P Cycles. At right is one of J&P's biggest and most successful shows: Chicago, 1995.

Some shows, such as Peotone, included biker rodeos. Above, the barrel roll. Below, John judging a slow race.

would sometimes split up the cash between key members of the crew. More than once I went through airport security and got on an airplane with a carry-on bag containing ten or twelve-thousand in cash. You sure as heck couldn't do that today," he laughs. Thinking about cash receipts from big events, Jill smiles and adds, "I had to hide a lot of the money from John so he wouldn't buy things. He was apt to see some Indian or Harley he liked, and buy it on the spot." John adds, "She's right. I always had a problem with cash. If I had it and saw something I liked, I would probably just buy it."

Although the shows hosted by J&P Promotions were providing strong and consistent income in the late 1990s, J&P Cycles was doing even better. A significant change was taking place in America's attitude toward motorcycles that had resulted in improved sales, not just for new motorcycles, but in the aftermarket business as well. It was a positive trend that would eventually cause John Parham to re-evaluate his allocation of resources and make some tough decisions in regard to the future of his various corporations.

ℛ

After the Second World War, motorcycling took a step down the social ladder. The powerful new medium of television portrayed an idyllic suburban life where conformity was necessary for upward mobility and realization of the American dream. This image of America glossed over the countless GIs who returned home physically and emotionally damaged. While the government tried to reintegrate veterans into society with the opportunities provided in the GI Bill, too many of them were not capable of boot-strapping themselves back into the expanding and competitive peacetime economy, or they simply chose not to do so. Still young and restless, and cursed with deeds and memories that polite society did not want to know about, they became a forgotten underclass. Some rode the rails and wandered America, panhandling or looking for menial jobs that would get them to their next meal. Others found their release in motorcycles, which gave them freedom and conspicuously set them apart from the norm. They gathered in groups and blew off steam, sometimes deliberately mocking and intimidating the "straight society" that had declared them outsiders. Casual groups became clubs with names like Booze Fighters, Galloping Gooses, and PoBobs, the Pissed-off Bastards of Bloomington. It was just such people who kicked up dust at Hollister, California, over the Fourth of July weekend in 1947, and while police records show that little damage was done, the national media, including *Life* magazine and later *Time*, turned the incident into a fearsome riot that they warned was apt to be visited on any American community at any minute. The story, which had already become larger than life, was told on the silver screen in "The Wild One" in 1954, and in this movie the motorcycle thugs caused the death of an innocent citizen (which never happened at Hollister), and somberly declared to its viewers in the opening credits, "This really happened!"

Suddenly, America had a new threat to worry about, and a vigilant press shifted its imaginative reporting into overdrive. Any boisterousness at a motorcycle race or rally became another "riot," though similar behavior at sporting events was generally accepted and ignored. America's highways were depicted as being overrun by vast hoards of violent, drunken or drug-crazed bikers, intent on rape and ruin. If you had never seen such a thing, don't worry, it had probably already happened in the next town over, and this myth was reinforced by an endless series of B-movies where lawless bikers brought decent American society to its knees. Call it life following art, but to a certain extent the myth did become reality when the Hell's Angels (in fact named after a movie) realized that their tough and lawless image appealed to enough angry young men that they could franchise chapters in cities throughout America, and eventually Europe, Australia, and New Zealand. Unwittingly, the American Motorcyclist Association greatly enhanced their prestige when one of its officials declared that the bad guys were only one percent of the people who own and ride motorcycles. The Angels and other outlaw clubs made up little patches that said "1%er," and sewed them to their vests and jackets with defiant pride.

By the 1970s, there were Hell's Angels chapters in many major cities, from Oakland to New York City. Other outlaw clubs formed as rivals to the Angels, generally claiming a region of the country as their territory. In the Midwest were the Outlaws, a club that rivaled the Angels for membership, with chapters in many industrialized cities throughout Wisconsin, Illinois, Michigan, Ohio, and Florida. In New Jersey, Eastern Pennsylvania, and down the Eastern Seaboard, the Pagans claimed their turf. In the Southwest it were the Banditos. Across the lower Midwest, from Denver to Indianapolis, were the Sons of Silence. Others with less territorial reach included Warlocks, Devil's Disciples, and Huns. Oddly, it was not usually straight society from which the groups had become outcasts that they waged war against. More often, they fought each other. Tribal in nature, they maneuvered for turf and battled their rivals on sight. Unfortunately, it was often legitimate motorcycle shows, rallies, swap meets, and races that they chose for their battlefields.

At many of their venues in major cities, John and Jill Parham had to deal with an outlaw presence which, at best, was an annoyance, and at worst laid waste to their efforts. John reports that sometimes individuals would rent a booth, pretending they had parts to sell. Rather, they would show up with fifty cases of beer, lay one or two motorcycle parts out on the table, put on their club colors (their vests bearing the club insignia), and sit and scowl and drink all weekend, watching for people wearing the colors of other outlaw clubs. He recalls that one pair made such a mockery of being vendors that they set a box of rubber bands out on the table with a sign that read "Rubber Bands $1 each", and would give out a free beer with the purchase of a rubber band. The dominant club in

The Chicago show at McCormick Place became the largest show and indoor swap meet in the world, justifying its own logo, designed by M.K. John. Here we see a Special 10th Anniversary logo by M. K. from 1994.

Below: The shows always provided an opportunity for J&P Cycles to sell some parts. Pictured here is Peotone, 1992.

J&P promoted modern dirt track races and a ride-in bike show at Elkhart Lake, Wisconsin, in conjunction with the annual AMA national championship road races at Road America. Above, a 1995 bike show prize winner.

Below: J&P Promotions provided a great opportunity for J&P Cycles to pass out thousands of catalogs to gain new customers. Employee seen here stocking the catalog table at the Harrisburg, PA Super Series show in March 1997.

a city would come to Parham and demand special benefits and tell him that it was his responsibility to keep other patch-holders (outlaw club members) out of the show or meet.

John found the behavior of the Chicago Outlaws hard to understand until he and Doug Hessing were summoned to a meeting at their clubhouse. Doug recalls, “Everyone thought we were crazy for driving to Chicago for a meeting at the Outlaws clubhouse. The clubhouse was really a frightening place. It was surrounded by a tall fence with barbed wire, and there were actually gun ports in the cement block walls of the building.” He continues, “Inside it was a different matter. It was clean and well furnished and had a bar, pool tables, and a dance floor.” The meeting began with the Outlaws demanding 200 tickets, and John refused. He asked why they were putting so much heat on him, then the underlying issue emerged. They wanted him to admit he was a member of the Sons of Silence, which meant his show was a serious encroachment on their turf. John was astonished, and wanted to know how this idea had even occurred to them. Well, they explained, John was from Iowa, and there was a Sons of Silence chapter in Waterloo, so he must be a member of the Sons of Silence. This was the point of view of the outlaw biker. If you were not from their side, you had to be from the other. John and Doug spent two hours trying to convince them they were not Sons of Silence, and in the end John negotiated his ticket tribute from 200 down to 25, plus a free vendor booth where they could sell their t-shirts. The Outlaws turned down the heat, but they remained a hovering presence at his Chicago shows, though there was never any major conflict. Jeff Carstensen, who worked some of the J&P Promotions shows and now manages the National Motorcycle Museum, says, “We never had any open conflict at McCormick Place, but John had to hire 43 Chicago police officers at $22.50 an hour. They were even stationed in the overhead maintenance walkways, and everyone who came to the show, including the public, got patted down. Luckily, the Chicago Police, especially Pat Shannon, were always great to work with. ”

John ran into an equally serious and ultimately less successful confrontation with the Outlaws in Milwaukee. John heard that his upcoming show there was going to be a battleground for the Outlaws and the Hell’s Angels, and he called the Milwaukee police to notify them that there might be trouble. When he arrived for the show, the president of the local Outlaws chapter approached him, leaned into his face, and said, “Look, you ever think you have a problem with us, you bring it to me.” John realized that the Outlaws had friends on the inside of the Milwaukee police force. The police had immediately passed his remarks on to the club, which left John with the sobering realization that he could expect no support from local law enforcement.

John Parham was doing three shows in Milwaukee, including one of his Super Series shows. He had an agreement with the Mecca Arena management that they would not book a bike show and swap meet

60 days on either side of his events, so effectively he had a monopoly on the arena for motorcycle shows. But facility management changes, especially in cities where it is tied to local politics, and in 1996 John learned that a local promoter who was friendly with the local bike clubs had booked the arena for a swap meet. John spoke to the woman who was managing the arena and said, “What are you doing? You've put another show right in front of mine?” She said, “Don't worry, he says this is something different. You are doing a show and a swap meet, and he's only doing a swap meet.” John protested, “Look, you've been had. It's the same thing, and you have broken our agreement. I'm done here. This will finish me.” The manager said a deal was a deal and she could not change it. When John's show opened the next day, the other promoter stood right at the front door and handed out flyers for his upcoming event. John went to him and said, “You have a booth here, why don't you hand out those flyers at your booth.” The man replied, “No, I think I'll keep handing them out right here.” As John and the man conversed, a group of about 25 Outlaws, all wearing colors, closed in around them and stood silently, listening to the conversation. Ed Ahlf recalls, “I saw John in the middle of this big group of Outlaws, and every one of them was at least a head taller than him. I knew we would never do another show in Milwaukee.” They didn't.

Doug Hessing says, “There were bike clubs at most of our shows. If you saw them coming in with a girlfriend, or even their wives and kids, you knew there was not going to be any trouble. If they came in groups with no friends or family members, you knew that anything could happen.”

In Secaucus, New Jersey, in 1995, some members of the New York City chapter of the Hell's Angels set up a booth, entered two bikes in the show, and wore their colors. John recalls, “About forty Pagans arrived wearing colors, and it was like they knew the Angels were going to be there. They all walked right down the aisle to a booth near the back of the hall. The guy in the booth bent down and pulled a big box of axe handles, fender struts, and fork tubes out from under his table. The Pagans each grabbed a weapon and started slowly circling the hall, occasionally banging the butt of an axe handle on the floor.” He continues, “It was very intimidating. A lot of people didn't know what was going on, but I did, and so did the Hell's Angels.” John's rented security, who were not about to deal with a gang of Pagans, called the Secaucus Police. John says, “It was getting more tense inside the hall, and the Pagans were circling closer to the Angels' booth. The Hell's Angels got up and posted themselves at the corners of their booth, all facing outward. They stood there with their right hands inside their vests, like they had guns.”

John continues, “The police arrived and about a dozen of them were in the lobby. I went out and said, ‘You better get in there. We need some help,’ and they told me they had to wait for their sergeant.” When their sergeant arrived, he refused to order his men into the hall, but called for his lieutenant. In the meantime, however, he

George Barnard hands out cash to a lucky door prize winner.

Below: Awards galore, in this case for the Road America bike show in 1996.

J&P Promotions organized shows both indoors and outdoors. Here we see the July 1994 Peotone, IL event.

Above and below, the Boston Super Series Show boasted over 100 motorcycle entries in the bike show and had several thousand attendees, 1997.

put out an alert call to all local law enforcement agencies, and police cars started arriving from neighboring communities, including a SWAT team. John recalls, "By now there were police all over the place and the street out in front of the hall was filled with cop cars with their lights flashing. We had sold about 4,000 tickets, and people were still arriving, just walking around the police and the cop cars to get into the building. By the time a lieutenant arrived, there were about 60 police out in the lobby, many in full riot gear. But still, they would not come into the hall. The lieutenant said he was going to wait for the Chief of Police to arrive."

John went back into the hall and told the Pagans that the cops were there in force and would be coming in. The president of the Pagans said, "Are you telling us to leave?" John replied, "I'm not telling you anything except that the cops are going to be coming in here." John offered to let them out a back loading dock door so they would not have to leave through the lobby, but they would not budge. John went back out to urge the police to do their job, but they said they were going to wait for their Chief. At the show was a motorcycle club of off-duty policemen called the Wild Pigs, and John got them to go out to the front lobby to explain that the situation was urgent, but still local law enforcement would not come into the hall. John reported to the Pagans that more cops were arriving, and finally the Pagan president sent a member out to the front lobby to confirm the report. John again offered to let them out through the back of the building. In defiance, the Pagans made one additional slow circle around the hall and around the Hell's Angels booth, then left. Once they were gone, John went back out to the lobby, where the Chief had arrived. He explained that everything was cool now and that there would be no trouble. The Pagans had gone. The Chief said, "What do you mean they are gone?" John explained what he had done to solve the problem. The Chief was obviously upset and demanded to know why the Pagans had been allowed to leave. By now Parham was quite irritated and said, "I had to do something because your people were too chickenshit to do their job." The Chief responded, "Okay, I'm shutting this show down!"

By now, it was only 12:30, there were 4,000 people who had paid to see the show, and normally the awards program did not begin until 3 p.m. John insisted that there was no longer a problem, there was no reason to close the show, and explained his obligation to his paying customers. The Chief told John to start his awards ceremony as soon as possible, ordered that no more tickets be sold, and insisted that the show was going to be terminated. John could see that the police wanted to take action against someone, and he got one of his staff aside and told him to go into the hall to alert the Hell's Angels to the situation. "They had done nothing wrong, but we told them the cops were pissed and would be looking for someone to blame," John explains. "The Angels understood, and began to load up to leave." John says, "It took them a good half hour to dismantle their booth and load everything into two vans, including the two show bikes they had brought, and still the police had not yet come into the hall." He continues, "We got the awards ceremony underway about 1:30, and I tried to stretch it out as much as I could for the sake of all the people who had paid to see the show."

Finally, as the program was coming to a conclusion, about 60 police in full riot gear came storming into the hall. John relates, "They came running down either side of the hall and did a crossing maneuver right in front of the stage. Those who came down the left side of the hall marched right through the crowd and lined up in formation on the opposite side of the hall. Those who came down the right side crossed over to the left, and they all stood there in defensive posture with their batons, helmets, plastic shields, the whole works. It was really a stupid show of force, and I announced, 'Let's hear it for the New Jersey Police. Better late than never!'" He adds, "I was really disgusted. They refused to do their job, then they just destroyed a good show for no reason. I ridiculed them from the microphone because I already knew I wouldn't be coming back there." John concludes, "These guys frightened our customers far more than the Pagans did," then he adds, "I never, ever, had any negotiations with any outlaw gangs that were as bad as the mismanagement of the New Jersey police on duty the day of the Secaucus, N.J event."

When the motorcycle gangs were not threatening John's shows, their pervasive image would haunt him in every aspect of his business, as it did all Americans who rode motorcycles during the 1960s through the mid-1980s. John recalls, "We always tried to stop on the way home from a good show and treat the crew to a really good meal." Jill adds, "We never had any money going into the shows, and I made a big cooler of sandwiches for the crew. After everyone had been eating cold sandwiches all weekend, we wanted to give them a nice meal when we could." John continues, "We were still wearing our biker gear, and there were many times when nice restaurants told us they had no seating, even when the place was half-empty." He continues, "I remember one night when we stopped at a restaurant. At first we were told the kitchen had just closed, but we insisted we really needed to get a meal. The lady who owned the place looked us up and down, then took us through the restaurant, past all the other diners, and back to a corner at the far end of the back room." He concludes, "That really frosted me. We had had a great show, and I probably had enough cash on me to just buy the whole place, and it was all I could do to keep from telling her so."

On another occasion, John and Jill were traveling home from a show, and stopped at Paul's, a discount department store in Clinton, Iowa.

John, Jill, and R.T. Shaw (with back to camera) at the All-Harley Drags East/West Shootout at Sturgis in 1992.

Below: J&P Cycles sponsored the Drag Races at the Sturgis Rally for several years. (1997)

Trophies at the Daytona Boardwalk Bike Show.

Below: J&P Promotions brought fun, excitement, glitz, and glamour to the motorcycle show circuit. But with J&P Cycles profitable and growing rapidly, by the late 1990s John began to wind down his promotions business. In 2002, the J&P Promotions corporation was dissolved.

John says, "We got a shopping cart and went on a spree, mostly buying office supplies for J&P Cycles. We had the cart filled to the top, and I noticed this guy was shadowing us." Jill adds, "This is when the distressed leather biker jackets were popular. John was wearing an expensive jacket, but it looked scruffy, and this guy kept eyeing that jacket." John continues, "This guy wasn't subtle at all. He was staying right with us all over the store, and I finally got annoyed and turned to him and said, 'May I help you?' He said, 'What do you mean?' and I replied, 'You keep following us around. Is there a problem?' He said, 'I'm not following you,' but he didn't leave." John and Jill continued to shop, but soon a second man joined the first and continued to follow them. John says, "It finally pissed me off so much that I just rolled the cart up to the checkout station, shoved it against the counter, and said 'Here!' and we left it sitting there and walked out. We left better than $300 worth of stuff sitting in that cart." He adds, "What did they think? Our gang was going to show up any minute, overpower everyone, and help us steal a cart full of merchandise?"

By the end of the 1990s, the attitude toward motorcyclists in America had changed significantly. Motorcycles had grown in popularity, and sales had begun to soar. In 1998, when the Guggenheim Museum in New York opened its "The Art of the Motorcycle Exhibition," it was clear that motorcycles were not just popular, they were fashionable. At the same time, the era of J&P Promotions was coming to an end. In part due to motorcycling's new popularity among middle-class Americans, sales at J&P Cycles had really taken off. Since 1994, sales had been growing at a rate of 40 to 50 percent per year. John had developed a huge product selection, a powerful mail-order machine, and a mechanized fulfillment system while Jill and a more professional senior staff had turned accounting and information processing into an efficient and fluid operation. In terms of operational control, predictable income, and return on investment, J&P Cycles had become far more important than J&P Promotions, and maintaining a high standard of customer service in the face of rapid growth demanded much more of John's attention. It was not the biker gangs who brought an end to the shows and swap meets, but they certainly provided a good incentive for John to revisit his priorities.

J&P Promotions began to sell off its shows and its racing program to other promoters, and in 2002 the corporation was dissolved. In retrospect, the timing seemed to be right. With escalating fuel prices and the advent of internet sales, the life of a vendor has become much harder. And because the public has many more choices for entertainment, including their computer screens, it has become harder for promoters to earn a living. Dick Betchkal, who acquired the Madison, St. Paul, and Chicago shows and remains a good friend of John's today, says, "John built it up, got it going, and got out at the right time. The big ones, like Chicago, are still big, but it is a much tougher business today. It's harder to get the vendors and it's harder to get the people through the door." It would appear that John's storied vision and uncanny sense of timing were still intact.

Chapter Six: Building a Business at J&P Cycles

The qualities of the classic American entrepreneur are vision, genius, hard work, and willingness to defy conventional wisdom, as John Parham did in the mid-1970s when he decided to pursue the Harley-Davidson aftermarket when others in the industry had little faith in the future of the brand. But there comes a time in most entrepreneurial ventures when the dedication and hard work of the visionary alone will no longer suffice. At this point, a business structure must be created and individuals with skills in management must be brought aboard to move the venture forward. They must not only be able to grasp the vision of the entrepreneurial leader, but sometimes they must have the ability to slow him down, help him focus, and establish priorities. If this transition to a structured organization does not take place, the entrepreneurial venture often stalls or fails entirely. This moment of critical transition is exactly where John Parham found himself when J&P Cycles experienced record growth in 1989 and 1990, but failed to turn a profit. That an entrepreneurial genius needs help to succeed is not to his discredit. For example, had he not met Takeo Fujisawa, Soichiro Honda might have lived out his days building excellent engines hidden behind the brand names of other companies. Instead, Honda and Fujisawa together

In 1991, Jill quit her job and went to work for J&P Cycles at a loss of $5,000 a year, but it proved to be the right move as John and Jill formed a partnership that slowly built J&P Cycles into the world's largest motorcycle aftermarket retailer. They are seen here celebrating their 20th Anniversary in 1999.

As mail order brought greater geographical outreach, J&P Cycles began to exhibit at shows outside the Midwest. Pictured above are Tom Hinderholtz and George Barnard at a rally booth, and below driving J&P's Buck Truck, so called because it cost more than any vehicle J&P had ever purchased.

made Honda one of the world's greatest companies and strongest brands.

When John Parham found himself in unexpected and serious financial trouble at the end of 1990, he traveled to Janesville, Wisconsin, to meet with Fred Fox, CEO of Parts Unlimited, one of J&P's suppliers and one of the largest, most successful distributors in the motorcycle industry. Fox is highly respected as a man who knows how to maintain an efficient organization and a profitable business under the pressure of rapid growth. John's purpose for meeting with Fox was to ask for a loan, but he got advice instead. Fox listened to John's problems, then told him that he was at the stage of his business where he needed to stop trying to grow. Growth in the absence of control, he explained, would only result in failure, and J&P needed for the moment to quit worrying about sales and start worrying about the cost of doing business. J&P needed to know more about where it was spending money and why. It needed to organize its data and improve its accounting so it could identify and eliminate waste and inefficiency. John was trying to run a $1 million business with inadequate attention to what he had, what functions brought a better return on investment, and where the company was bleeding money. With growth, he had begun to achieve his vision, but that vision had begun to outrun reality. J&P needed not just more people, but better-qualified people. Fox told John, "Stop trying to get bigger. Start getting better by getting what you have under control."

Who would have better understood John's vision or been better qualified to install information management at J&P than Jill? She had been married to him for 15 years and had struggled beside him for a decade to build their independent motorcycle business, spending weekends on the road to work at swap meets. Jill wanted to devote more time to support John's ventures and be with Zach, who had just started school, and she proposed to Roger Kelley, her boss at Keltech Information Services, that she work only part-time. When he refused, she quit, and, taking a $5,000 cut in annual earnings, went to work full-time for J&P Cycles. Years later, Kelley would say, "Jill was a rock star. She was a hard worker, paid attention to detail, and our customers really loved her. She worked like a tornado, but always knew where she was going and what she needed to do next. I wish I had owned a copier that could have produced ten of her." But Keltech's loss was J&P's gain, for Jill would bring to the company the energy and focus that Kelley described, and the very business management qualities that J&P needed. With the title of Vice President, Jill assumed broad responsibilities, including information processing and human resources. Business organization at J&P was primitive, and personnel matters needed a lot of attention. Virginia Dearborn, who started part-time in 1986 and had been handling the bookkeeping on a full-time basis since 1988, says, "We had a computer, but the only thing on it was mailing lists." In short, the business had not been mechanized and human resources policy was non-existent. Ron Payne describes a situation when an employee was caught stealing parts from inventory. Payne relates, "John sat down with him and said, 'Why are you stealing from me?' and the guy replied, 'Doesn't everyone steal from you?'"

Undoubtedly, this was not the case, and the idea that J&P was there to be exploited by all of its employees was surely just one man's distorted perception. But still, there were not adequate controls in place to prove otherwise, and the fact that an employee would make such a remark to John revealed that screening and hiring practices were woefully inadequate. John admits, "I was an easy touch. I would hire just about anyone who said he liked motorcycles." Employment at J&P had doubled since 1985, from 12 to 23, in an effort to keep up with the ever-increasing work load, but in too many cases this had been a matter of indiscriminate hiring, with little regard for qualifications and job descriptions. Jill took these matters in hand, and within a month of her arrival, six people—more than a quarter of the staff—resigned. Jill is a good-natured person who fits in well with any group, and she laughs easily, but within her outgoing personality is a no-nonsense attitude toward business, and she is more than willing to make the hard decisions. This included requiring employees to adjust to better management and more discipline. Over the years at J&P, Jill has earned the nickname "Queen Bee," at which she laughs with genuine mirth and says, "Yeah, and I don't think the 'B' is for 'Bee!'" She is also affectionately known as "The Warden," a facetious reference to the fact that the only other large institution in Anamosa is a high-security state prison. It is Jill who brought discipline and order to the company, and even John's father has said, "Things didn't really start humming at J&P until Jill came onboard." And John's brother, Mark, concurs, stating, "The smartest thing John ever did was to marry Jill, then bring her into the business."

Due to its strategy to limit growth, regroup, and put stronger business systems in place, J&P Cycles experienced a decline in gross sales in 1991, down three percent from 1990, which had seen growth of 80 percent over the previous year. Yet, the company became profitable, while taking steps to return to growth in future years. For example, its catalog was increased to 96 pages and a storefront for Bike Week sales was opened in Daytona Beach. The application of better business controls worked so quickly that revenue rebounded to $2 million on a 34 percent increase in sales in 1992, and this time there was a nice profit. That year, for the first time, the local newspaper, *The Anamosa Journal-Eureka*, took notice of what was happening in the gray and white building on Highway 151 just outside of town. A front-page story in the April 16 edition stated, "J&P Cycles is one of the largest mail-order dealers of parts and accessories for Harley-Davidson motorcycles in the United States." In that story, John described the fertility of the Harley-Davidson market and the fact that J&P could have sold even more, but he stressed the importance of not letting growth

In 1991, J&P Cycles opened a temporary store on Main Street in Daytona Beach, Florida, pictured here during Bike Week, 1996.

Below: Jill working inside the Daytona Beach store in 1997.

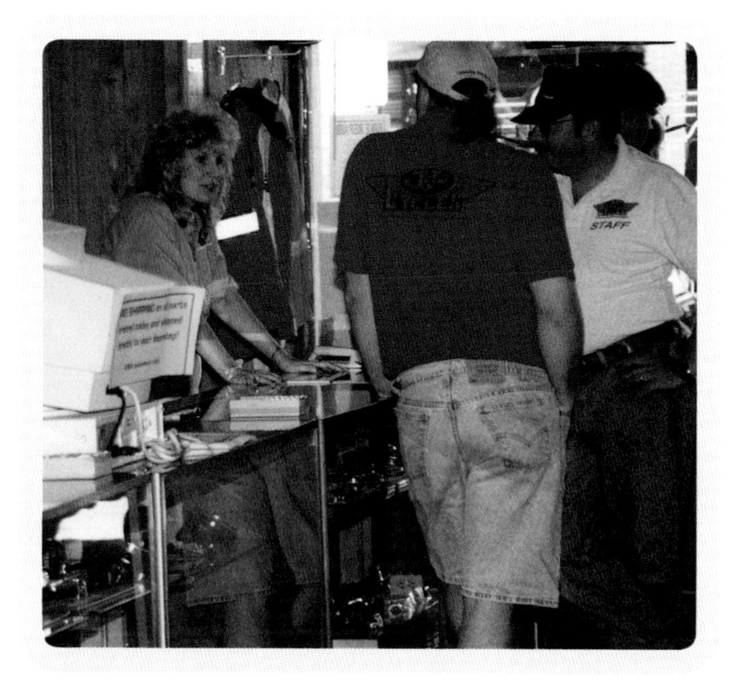

J&P Cycles began to promote its business in Europe in 1993. At the European Super Rally in Italy that year, John ran into his friend Arlen Ness, America's most famous custom bike builder.

Below: John and George Barnard, seen here in St. Mark's Square, Venice, soaked up the culture when they weren't chasing sales.

outstrip the ability of his business systems to handle it. It was a lesson well-learned that would put the company on a path of steady growth into the foreseeable future.

1992 was also the year that John met Ron Helle, of Honkamp, Krueger and Company, an accounting and business consulting firm in Dubuque. Helle recalls, "John was working with an accounting firm in Cedar Rapids. For them, J&P was small fry, so he wasn't getting much help." He continues, "When we got involved, J&P's systems were pretty basic. People would take an order over the phone, write it out on a piece of paper, then stick it on a spindle, almost like a waitress would do for the cook in a diner. Someone would come from the warehouse and take the paper, then go out and fill the order." Helle's company wrote a distribution software package for J&P that included packaging and distribution systems. Helle adds, "John is a quick learner; a real self-study guy. When he started seeing the possibilities of software-driven, mechanized fulfillment and distribution, he got very involved. He could see bottlenecks that others couldn't, and come up with really good ideas to increase the speed and reduce the cost of order fulfillment." Helle claims that over a couple of years, J&P found ways to eliminate a quarter-million dollars in expense in the warehouse alone. He adds that he could see the partner relationship between John and Jill bearing fruit immediately. He says, "John is the idea guy and Jill is the execution gal. John is such a forward thinker, he does not bother to backfill his idea. That's where Jill comes in. She fills in the detail and makes the ideas work. She helps build the systems around them." Helle adds, "Jill was also good at setting priorities. John is a guy who wants to do it all and do it now, and Jill can help him decide what is next and what can wait." With efficiency improving, the company profitable, and stronger business controls in place, John found it easier to focus on forward thinking rather than the problems of business survival. One of the ideas John decided to explore was the potential of the European market.

☙

With Harley-Davidson beginning its resurgence in the mid-1980s, by 1990 the popularity of the Milwaukee machine had become a global phenomenon. The Motor Company was exporting as much as 20 percent of its production, and overseas there was a voracious demand for the big V-twins to the extent that brokers were rounding up containers of used Harleys and shipping them to Europe. Along with the Harley culture went the American craze for customizing and a demand for aftermarket parts. In 1993, John traveled to the Super Rally in Italy to study the market. Coincidentally, his friend Arlen Ness—known in America as the King of the Customizers—was there as well. The Super Rally was an event oriented toward custom and high-performance motorcycles that moved to different venues throughout Europe each year. John was not thinking of promoting shows in Europe, but was exploring the opportunities he might find there for J&P Cycles, and he shipped over a pallet of J&P catalogs to distribute at the rally. George Barnard became one of John's main men in Europe. Barnard started at J&P in 1991, working in the back room, changing tires and keeping stock in order. He proved to be hard-working, resilient, and good on the road, and still today works on contract for the company, driving its trucks and working at meets and rallies. After John had made business contacts in Europe, he later sent Barnard over on his own to manage the J&P Cycles presence at the Super Rally and several trade shows throughout Europe.

In addition to the Super Rally in Italy in 1993, J&P attended the rallies in Denmark, Belgium, Finland, the Netherlands, Germany, and Austria in successive years. Barnard did not speak any European language, but he had no trouble getting by. He says, "I would stand out in front of the booth waiving a J&P catalog in my hand, shouting 'Gratis! Gratis!' Wherever we were, that worked. Everyone knew what 'gratis' meant." It was not cost-effective to ship a lot of parts to Europe for sale at the rallies, so in addition to its free catalogs, J&P pushed the sale of its Gold Card membership. The J&P Gold Card is a special customer membership that costs $49.99 a year, and it gives its owner discounts and other special benefits, such as advanced notification and access to special sales. Barnard says, "We pushed group use of the Gold Card in Europe. In other words, we would sell a card to a member of a club with the offer that everyone in his club would receive the discount by ordering through his Gold Card membership." The Gold Card worked especially well with American military personnel. Barnard explains, "A lot of GIs came to the Super Rallies. We would sell one a Gold Card with the commitment that everyone in his unit could benefit from it." Parham was still not sure that sales in Europe would prove cost effective, but he knew that selling to military personnel would work because J&P could use the APO mailing system where mailing motorcycle parts to a GI in Europe cost no more than shipping to New York.

Attendance at European rallies and shows proved a worthwhile learning experience for John, but was discontinued after five years. Success in Europe was subject to many factors beyond J&P's control, not the least of which was fluctuation in the value of the dollar. John explains, "We made some real progress in establishing J&P as an international brand, and we were getting enough sales penetration that in order to continue I was going to have to put a warehouse and distribution center in Europe. Custom Chrome had already done this, and I realized I would have to do it too." Barnard and business associates in Europe scouted property for John, but in the end he decided not to make the move. He says, "J&P Cycles was really taking off, and we were overwhelmed just trying to serve our customers in America. With this, and the promotions business, it was just too much. A European operation would be the least cost-effective way we could use our resources, so we decided not to jump in." Still, through establishment of the J&P brand, the Parhams were able to elevate and expand the image of their company. Artist Kenny John recalls, "One day John Parham called me and said, 'You need to modify our logo. We need to change 'Keeping America on 2 Wheels' to 'Keeping the World on 2 Wheels.'" This slogan is supported by the fact that even without a physical presence in

In 1995, J&P Cycles undertook its first expansion in Anamosa, adding 15,000 square feet. The aerial view (below) shows how the floor space was more than doubled.

In the mid-90s, artist Kenny John created a distinctive new logo for J&P Cycles and the company slogan was changed from "Keeping America on 2 Wheels" to "Keeping the World on 2 Wheels."

Below: The logo for John's Nostalgic Toys business.

Below: Nostalgic Toy Creations sold collectible toy banks produced by John as well as Harley-Davidson, M.B. & Strings and other manufacturers.

Europe, today J&P Cycles does over $4 million in international sales per year. As for George Barnard, who no longer has to shout "gratis" to distribute catalogs on the road throughout the United States, the European foray returns some fond memories. He says, "I can remember sitting at a sidewalk café with John on a canal in Amsterdam, drinking Crown Royal and smoking Cuban cigars. I said, 'Boss, I can't believe you have to pay me to do this!'"

❧

By 1994, J&P Cycles was definitely on track, growing to $2.6 million in sales. In 1995 that figure jumped to $4.1 million. Employee head count grew to 50, and ground was broken for a 15,000-square-foot warehouse expansion in Anamosa. By now, John Parham Enterprises consisted of four companies: J&P Cycles, J&P Promotions, Zacharia Advertising and Publications, and Nostalgic Toy Creations, a company formed to manufacture and distribute high-quality, die-cast toys and banks. These had become popular among motorcyclists who purchased and collected examples decorated with various motorcycle-related logos. Those produced by Nostalgic Toy Creations functioned as promotional vehicles for J&P Cycles, but there were also commemorative designs for other companies in the motorcycle industry, such as Biker's Choice, Dave Perewitz, and the National Motorcycle Museum, as well as special events, such as the Laconia Rally and Races. When producing these toys under license from J&P's business partners, Nostalgic Toy Creations paid royalties to the licensing organization. They also sold toys produced for other motorcycle events, like Sturgis and Daytona, that were produced by M. B. & Strings.

In the midst of this growth and expansion at the headquarters in Anamosa, J&P Promotions continued to increase its show and race schedule while the page count of Zacharia publications continued upward. It was at this time that John commissioned Kenny John to create a crisp, modern, new J&P logo, featuring the company name in stylized yellow letters inside a red oval, backed by a pair of blue wings. With its catalog distribution going to every corner of North America and its reach going global, J&P began to create a corporate identity more powerful than that of any other aftermarket motorcycle retailer in America. In this respect, J&P was blessed with not having a franchisee relationship with a motorcycle manufacturer. Other retailers are obliged to promote the brands they sell, but J&P was in a position to promote strictly its own name and identity. Ron Helle observes, "John Parham was doing branding before a lot of small businesses even grasped the idea, and I know of no other retailer in the motorcycle industry that has even come close to achieving the identity and recognition of J&P Cycles." To increase sales and further enhance its identity, J&P put a big rig mobile showroom on the road in 1996, carrying its logo on a brightly-painted truck to motorcycle rallies and special events all over America, and *The Motorcycle Dispatch,* now reaching 20,000 in circulation, publicized a schedule of events where J&P Cycles would have a presence.

Sales continued upward, but the company began to notice something else that is quite unusual at the retail level of the motorcycle industry. Based on its reputation for good customer service, people were developing brand loyalty toward J&P. They loved the big J&P catalog and they were beginning to take pride in buying their parts, clothing, and accessories from J&P Cycles. Sales in 1996 increased again by more than 50 percent, to $6.48 million.

☙

J&P Cycles has built its business on two key principles: easy access to a huge selection of products and superlative customer service. Access has been achieved by developing a large catalog that is distributed free of charge at events and through direct mail. When sales began to come in from the early 24 and 36-page catalogs that John distributed at swap meets during the 1980s, it was not long before the mail-order business began to surpass on-site sales at the Anamosa store. John grasped early the potential for direct mail, and took himself to school. He began to subscribe to trade magazines in the direct mail industry, and joined the National Catalog and Operations Forum, attending its seminars and workshops every chance he could get. In addition, J&P Cycles became a member of the Direct Marketing Association. John says, "These organizations were a great source of information and guidance. They taught us a lot about effective direct marketing." While lists of names and addresses were collected at all the swap meets for promotional use by J&P Promotions, they also became a golden asset at J&P Cycles. With growth in J&P's product line, reflected in a steadily-growing catalog, the catalog became a significant gift in its own right, sent out annually by the thousands to J&P customers and potential customers all over the nation.

As for customer service, while it proves to be a good business practice, it probably arose from the way John was raised and some of the things he learned working at Pamida. His parents always instilled in him honesty and courtesy toward others, and Pamida taught the importance of making customers happy. These practices were consistent with the storied Iowa work ethic, and something you did just because it was the right thing to do. Brad Mrstik, J&P's comptroller, who has been with the company since 1994, says, "John never stops stressing the importance of customer service. Even in the early years, he would say, 'We may not be the biggest, and we may not even be able to give the best price, but we can treat our customers better than they will be treated anywhere else.'" It is a concept that is drummed into the psyche of every employee, and built into every system within the organization. J&P's call center is a case in point. The men and women on the phones understand motorcyclists and are rigorously trained in the company's product line. They are taught that they are not there just to make sales, but that if they focus on

In 1996, J&P Cycles made its entire catalog available through its web site, and put a mobile showroom on the road to chase an exhaustive schedule of events and rallies throughout the nation.

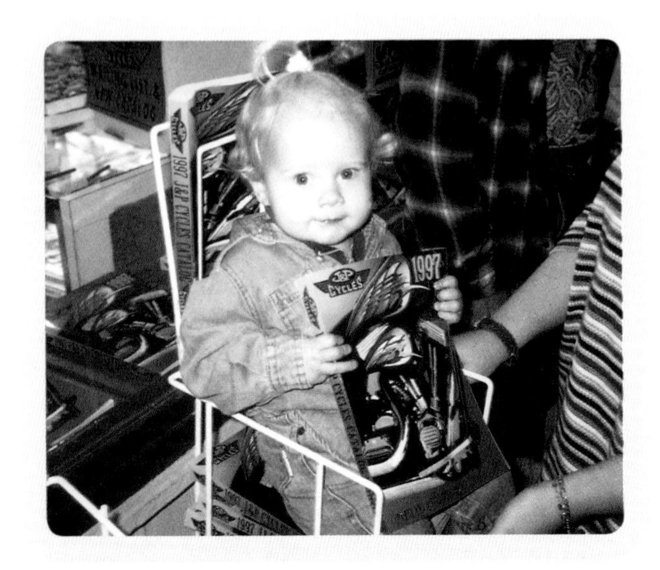

Exceptional customer service turns J&P customers into outright fans. Below, Alastair Burt, for example, who built his chopper mostly from parts acquired from J&P Cycles, rode all the way to Anamosa from British Columbia, Canada, just to meet John and Jill and shake the hands of the people who had treated him so well. (Ed Youngblood photo)

helping customers, the sales will follow. When a customer's questions go beyond the scope of a call center worker, the call is turned over to a "Tech." Techs are first and foremost trained motorcycle technicians who have been taught how to work on the phones. They are certified mechanics that J&P has turned into consultants, and they will converse with customers in great detail to solve their technical problems, to make sure they are ordering the right part, and to make sure a certain part will fit the motorcycle they are buying it for. Currently, J&P's crew of 40 techs represent 750 years of experience in building and repairing motorcycles.

This attention to detail not only creates good feelings among customers, but it is good for J&P Cycles as well, because it benefits no one—least of all J&P—if a wrong part has to be returned and restocked. George Barnard recalls a time when a Tech stayed on the phone for 45 minutes with a customer in Germany, taking him through each step of a carburetor installation. And Bernard adds, "We know there are times when we are helping out a guy who bought his problem from one of our competitors, but that's okay too, because when it is done, he is going to have good feelings about J&P Cycles and not the company that maybe sold him the wrong thing." Bernard adds, "We know who he is going to buy from next time." Because J&P's technical support of customers is so important, the company eventually set up a separate call center in Daytona Beach, Florida, where it could attract personnel with the right qualifications, because there are motorcycle technician training schools in that city. As the staff grew at Anamosa and it became difficult to attract enough qualified technicians to Iowa, with its sometimes harsh winters, John simply moved a portion of his operation to a location where the right people were readily available.

Customer service carries into the fulfillment operation as well. While the system has been continuously updated and improved to reduce waste, speed of fulfillment is also a cardinal objective, since next-day service and quick delivery goes a long way to enhance J&P's reputation and achieve a high level of customer satisfaction. Buying the right products and maintaining inventory are also important to good customer service. Some companies will list products in their catalogs and their web site that they do not have in stock, making customers wait days and weeks while they back-order the part. J&P's product fulfillment rate consistently runs from 92 to 95 percent, and extraordinary effort goes into making sure that the company can immediately deliver what it has advertised for sale. Call center workers have access to current inventory information while they are talking with a customer, to make sure the company can deliver. If there is a back-order situation, the customer will be advised and alternative solutions will be explored. The company also maintains detailed records on the performance of suppliers, and any supplier who is not able to meet J&P's inventory demand will have its products removed from the next year's catalog. Good customer service drives every aspect of the J&P operation, and its employees will readily claim that it is the company's greatest asset in a very competitive industry.

Motorcycling is a fraternity, and what its members talk about when they get together are the ride, their motorcycles, and the companies they deal with. Nothing is more powerful than word-of-mouth. No amount of advertising or public relations will overcome a bad rap, but good word-of-mouth is solid gold. This was born out at the 2007 J&P Customer Appreciation Open House when Alastair Burt, age 68, rode his beautiful orange custom-built chopper all the way to Anamosa from his home in British Columbia, on the west coast of Canada. About 60 percent of the motorcycle were components that Burt had ordered from J&P Cycles. He had spent three years building the machine, and during that time set a personal goal of riding it to Anamosa. During the construction process, he ran into the inevitable problems, and says, "J&P's tech team was very helpful. They got me out of more than a few binds." Burt claims he knows another 10 or 12 bikers who have started buying from J&P because he talked about his good experience. About his trip of more than 2,000 miles from his home to the Midwest, he says, "I just wanted to come here and meet the people who have been so nice to me. I wanted to shake the hands of people who behave like this toward their customers."

In his latest book, "The One Minute Entrepreneur: The Secret of Creating and Sustaining a Successful Business," business consultant Ken Blanchard says, "To keep customers today, you can't be content to merely satisfy them; you have to give them legendary service and create 'raving fans,' customers who are so excited about the way you treat them that they tell stories about you." Customers like Alastair Burt would indicate that J&P Cycles has risen to, and adheres to this "legendary" level of performance.

In 1996, J&P Cycles put its whole catalog on the Internet, accessible through the J&P website, **WWW.JPCYCLES.COM**. With sales still growing at a consistent rate of 40 to 50 percent per year, the company laid plans to develop a second seasonal location, breaking ground on Lazelle Street in Sturgis, South Dakota, for a 12,000-square-foot retail store, which had its grand opening at the 1997 Sturgis Rally. In 1999, another 50,000 square feet were added to the facility in Anamosa, and *Dealernews*, the leading motorcycle trade magazine in America, named J&P Cycles a Top 100 Dealer. Business consultant Ron Helle recalls an incident that illustrates how much clout the company had developed in the motorcycle industry during its decade of growth. He was traveling to Sturgis and checking in to board a flight to Rapid City. He relates, "The lady at the desk looked at my ticket, but did not give me a boarding pass. She asked me to take a seat and said she would call me. I started worrying that the flight was overbooked and I was going to get bumped. Finally, just as the airplane was ready to board, she called me and handed me a first class boarding pass. She said, 'Here, sir, I kind of thought I could find you a first class seat.'" Helle continues, "I was very surprised and asked her why. She said, 'I recognized the J&P logo on your shirt. You're a good company and do an awful lot of business with us.'" Helle concludes, "That's when I realized how important J&P had become."

Clearly, after 20 years in business, J&P Cycles had finally arrived, mainly as a result of its intensive effort to improve business systems and master the techniques of direct-mail marketing during the 1990s. There were now more than 130 employees, and its catalog had grown to over 800 pages. John says, "Suddenly, people around the motorcycle industry were talking about J&P Cycles, the 'overnight success.' I never knew how to respond to that. I know people intended it as a compliment, but it couldn't be further from the truth. 'Overnight' was more like twenty years of struggle and hard work. We may have looked like an overnight success to the people in the industry who finally noticed us, but we had been around for a long, long time." Still, the coming years would show that J&P Cycles had only just begun.

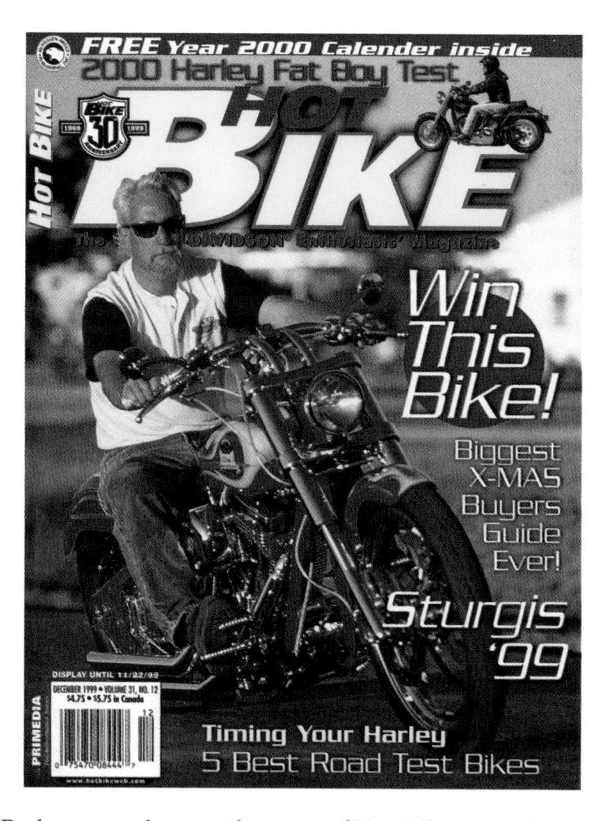

John Parham, seen here on the cover of Hot Bike *magazine, made J&P Cycles one of the biggest advertisers in the motorcycle industry. By J&P's 20th anniversary, it was being heralded as American motorcycling's "overnight success," but everyone at Anamosa knew it had been a long, hard road to earn such recognition.*

J&P Cycles Anamosa, IA showroom. (December 1994)

As you can see, long before the National Motorcycle Museum came to Anamosa, John housed a fantastic Antique motorcycle display in the J&P Cycles showroom . (December 1994)

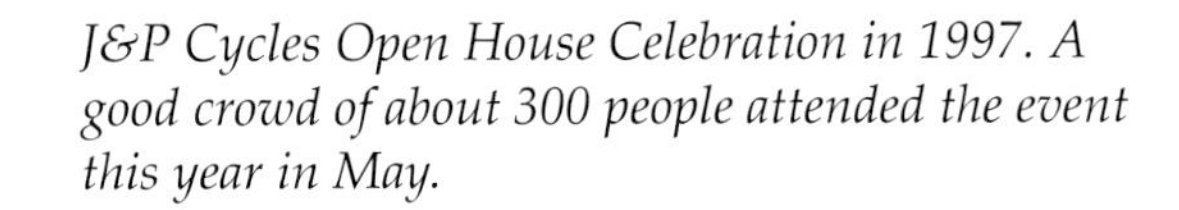

J&P Cycles Open House Celebration in 1997. A good crowd of about 300 people attended the event this year in May.

In 1998, the showroom was expanded. Where the Stamper jewelry case is, the wall right behind was previously the parts counter (see top left photo on this page).

With the 1998 expansion, John had more room to display his growing antique collection of motorcycles and memorabilia.

Chapter Seven: Sturgis

In the heat of August they come, thundering across the yellow grasslands of South Dakota, past the strangely eroded pinnacles and spires of the Badlands, heading toward the dark silhouette rising on the horizon, toward the Black Hills, what the Lakota Sioux call the Paha Sapa, their sacred place. They travel alone, or in groups of twos and threes, or sometimes in long columns of scores of men and women astride powerful, rumbling motorcycles. On Interstate 90 they speed down through Montana and Wyoming, or northward through Nebraska, or south from Canada, through North Dakota. They fly into Rapid City from the four corners of America, and from Europe, Australia, Japan, anywhere that bikers love the sound and mystique of an American V-twin. By the tens of thousands they converge, and before they are done, the small town of Sturgis will have grown from 6,000 to as many as a half-million souls. They are on a kind of pilgrimage, descending on their motorcyclist's mecca, where they will experience the uniquely American phenomenon of the Black Hills Classic, what many just call "Sturgis," an annual gathering that has captured the imagination of motorcycle enthusiasts the world over.

Sturgis Rally, the mecca for motorcyclists the world over.

John and his brother-in-law Doug Hessing first attended the Sturgis Rally in 1985, sleeping in their booth in Mr. Al's Alley, and paying two dollars for a shower at the Lantern Motel.

Below: living rough in Mr. Al's Alley, Sturgis 1987.

The Black Hills are a geological phenomenon, so-called because their forest cover of pine and spruce make them appear black from a distance, rising up in dark contrast to the tan table of the surrounding grasslands. Dating back millions of years, this 20 by 50 mile area was driven upward to a height of over 7,000 feet by volcanic pressure under what was once a vast inland sea. Cracking and shifting the geological layers above it, the magma's pressure forced caches of minerals upward, turning the region into coveted ground for gold hunters and the mining industry during the mid-19th century. But a century before that, the Black Hills region was populated by the Lakota Sioux, an aggressive nation who drove out the Cheyenne, Crow, and Pawnee, who themselves were the successors of indigenous people dating back thousands of years. Despite arriving relatively late on the scene, the Lakota declared this beautiful place their axis mundi, the spiritual center of their world.

Spirituality was the last thing that white men had on their minds when, in 1874, a party headed by General George Custer discovered gold in the region. This event, post-dating the discovery of gold in California by a quarter-century, turned southwestern South Dakota into the first American region not settled by westward movement. Rather, the adventuresome, rough-cut, wild-catting people who had already moved west for the gold rush of '49, returned eastward, responding to the promise of riches from the land. They were a resourceful and hard-scrabble people, more than willing to put up with the hard winters of the Dakotas for the prospect of wealth and a better life. And, as it turned out, gold was only a part of the mineralogical bounty of the Black Hills. From Spearfish on the west to Rapid City on the east, the region became a center of mining for coal, lead, and other valuable minerals. The growth of mining towns created a local lumber industry, and along with the miners and speculators came a wild-west lifestyle, spawning drinking and gambling centers like Lead and Deadwood, famous for Calamity Jane and the site of Wild Bill Hickok's last card game. The clashes between frontier and native cultures led to the last of the great Indian Wars, ended by a treaty that is under dispute by the Lakota Nation still today. Sturgis–named after Major Samuel D. Sturgis—emerged as a "scoop town" for the nearby Fort Meade Cavalry Post, so called because it was a place where hapless soldiers on leave went to get their pockets "scooped" by local gamblers, merchants, prostitutes, and other opportunists. On balance, however, Sturgis was a fairly sedate community, certainly not as notorious as nearby Deadwood.

With the arrival of the Great Depression of the 1930s, the Black Hills Region fell on hard times. Mining had begun to play out, and America's great interstate highway system that would eventually turn the area into a center for tourism, had not yet arrived. In this climate of limited prospects, a young man born and raised in Sturgis named Clarence "Pappy" Hoel, decided to try his hand at selling motorcycles. Prior to the Second World War, the American motorcycle industry was nothing like it is today. There was not a plethora of brands or a vast range of styles and models. Thanks to protective tariffs enacted by the federal government after the First World War, motorcycle sales were almost totally controlled by the two surviving domestic manufacturers, Harley-Davidson and Indian. There was already a Harley-Davidson dealer in Rapid City, and Hoel applied to become a sub-agency for Sturgis. The deal did not come through, so in 1936 Hoel applied to the Indian Motocycle Company and was granted a franchise for the whole of the Black Hills Region. That year he set up Hoel's Motorcycle Shop in his garage, and within a decade he would become Indian's top dealer in the nation, selling a grand total of 44 motorcycles in 1947.

Motorcycling is and has always been a social activity, and smart dealers have always created clubs to stimulate camaraderie and promote sales through word-of-mouth. With this kind of grass roots marketing technique, towns throughout America often became "Harley towns" or "Indian towns," depending on who was the most aggressive and successful dealer. Within a market divided between only two brands, intense rivalry between brand-partisan owners also became a characteristic of the American motorcycle scene. The Harley-Davidson dealer in Rapid City had long since turned it into a "Harley town," and its motorcycling social scene was run by the Rapid City Pioneer Motorcycle Club, known for short as the RPMs. With Sturgis quickly becoming an "Indian town" at the hands of a promotionally-savvy Pappy Hoel, a local club of mostly Indian riders began to take shape, and would soon call itself the Jackpine Gypsies, seeking an American Motorcycle Association charter under that name in 1936. In 1937, the Jackpine Gypsies decided to invite their rival, the RPMs, to a day of competitive activities that would include field contests and a race at the local fairgrounds. It was a surprisingly successful event, drawing participants and spectators from throughout the region. This success did not escape the attention of the local merchants.

In the throes of the Great Depression, beleaguered communities throughout the nation looked for any reason they could find to create a summer festival in order to stimulate the local economy. Noting the success of the 1937 races, the Sturgis business community created a new organization they called the Black Hills Motor Classic for the purpose of developing an annual event. The BHMC remained distinct from the Jackpine Gypsies, and a certain social tension existed between the two (Gypsies scoffed at the businessmen because they "blonded" their coffee rather than drink it black, like real men), but a cooperative business relationship emerged, thanks largely to the vision and skills of Pappy Hoel. Hoel was foremost a Gypsy and a biker, but as the owner of an important business in the community, he also had one foot squarely in the camp of the BHMC. In addition, his wife, Pearl, proved an invaluable asset in the development of the Sturgis Rally

Though J&P did not promote the drag races at Sturgis, they proved to be an advertising opportunity for J&P Cycles, which became a lead sponsor for the event.

Below: John, with fatigue showing on his face, helps a customer find the part he needs. J&P's early days at Sturgis brought 18-hour days and nights in a sleeping bag on an air mattress.

Above and below: In addition to Mr. Al's Alley, J&P Cycles soon erected a large tent during Sturgis with which to increase its sales and expand its inventory.

and Races. She was not only an indefatigable supporter of Pappy's causes, but as the elected county auditor, she had access to the political leaders of the region.

A joint effort between club and town first known as the Sturgis Rally and Races, and later as the Black Hills Classic, took place in 1938, and, again, it was Pappy Hoel's promotional expertise that undoubtedly contributed to its lasting and legendary success. Hoel invited a nationally-recognized Indian racer named Johnny Spiegelhoff to come show the local talent how it was done. Spiegelhoff had begun his career as a Harley-Davidson factory rider, but had fallen out with the Motor Company. Switching to Indian, he looked for every opportunity to advance the Massachusetts brand over its legendary Milwaukee rival. Later, he would become one of only three men to win the prestigious Daytona 200 for Indian. As an American Motorcycle Association top-ranked rider, Spiegelhoff informed Hoel that if he were to compete, the races would have to be sanctioned by the AMA. So, the Jackpine Gypsies applied for and received an AMA sanction, which, over time, attracted other nationally-ranked riders, which greatly enhanced the reputation and quality of the races. It was not long before this little South Dakota backwater became one of the favorite venues on the AMA professional racing circuit. The national riders loved Sturgis. They were treated well by the fans and promoter, and a trip into the scenic Black Hills was a welcome respite from the mind-numbing grind of crisscrossing the American flatlands, traveling from one dusty fairground to the next.

Over time, as touring riders began to travel to Sturgis from all over the nation and the rally crowd grew larger and larger, racing became less critical to the success of the event, which eventually became a kind of happening where hard rock and country-and-western concerts would attract more people than the races. Except for a hiatus during the Second World War, the phenomenon known as "Sturgis" has steadily grown into an international event. Some have called it a "Biker's Woodstock," but this is not an apt comparison. Rather than an inexplicable, one-off success like Woodstock, Sturgis happens every year as mind-boggling numbers of the committed make their annual trek across the nation to experience the world's largest and greatest motorcycle rally. They come for the camaraderie and the fun. They come to see and be seen. They come for exquisite scenery that includes not only the natural beauty of the Paha Sapa, but also mankind's most grandiose works of art, at Mount Rushmore and the Crazy Horse Monument. They come because Sturgis is the axis mundi of motorcycling. Reflecting on the unique quality of Sturgis, John Parham says, "It's a rider's rally. Other rallies are a destination. People go there, then they hang out, kick tires, and drink beer. All the same things happen at Sturgis, except here everyone also rides. Every day they saddle up and head out to see the exquisite scenery. They come in such numbers because of the beauty of the place, and once they come and see it, they want to come back." Jill adds, "It is also a place where people make lifelong friendships. They meet at the campgrounds, and they return every year, looking forward to old friends and happy reunions."

ଓ

Jill Parham reminisces about the humble beginnings of J&P Cycles as a swap meet vendor, describing a memorable event in the early days. It was late August, and she and John were working a swap meet in Davenport, Iowa. Because it was little more than an hour from home, they had brought Zachary, who was still in diapers. It was sweltering hot; a perfectly miserable day. J&P's table was positioned by a building that had a water faucet on the side, and people would come by to get water or wash their hands, leaving a big, wet, mud puddle. Zach had found the cool spot and was sitting in the mud, gleefully splashing. He was covered with mud, and apparently the only comfortable, happy person anywhere on the grounds. Jill explains, "It wasn't a problem. He was having such a good time, I wasn't about to stop him then have to fight with him about wanting to get back into the puddle. We were camping, and they had a nice shower facility for the campers. Later I was going to take a shower, and I planned to just take Zach into the shower with me, remove his diaper, and wash him off." But passersby didn't know this, and Jill recalls, "You should have seen the looks we were getting. You would think we were practicing child abuse. People looked down their noses at us like we were some kind of gypsies." Then she pauses, thinks for a moment, and burst into laughter: "We were gypsies! That's exactly what we were."

This was the humble context in which John Parham came to Sturgis to vend his wares in 1985. John embarked on the 800-mile trip with his brother-in-law, Doug Hessing, in a van full of parts pulling a badly overloaded homemade trailer. Hessing recalls, "We had it so loaded down that the tires were rubbing the fenders. We were going down the road with smoke pouring off the tires, and we had to stop and get a tire iron and bend the fenders back away from the wheels." In Sturgis there was a local merchant named Al Colton who had a 100 by 150-foot building with a 26-foot-wide alley at 1219 Main Street, which at that time was the main drag for visiting bikers. During rally week, Mr. Al, as his clients called him, turned this property into a swap meet. John rented enough space in Mr. Al's alley for two tables, which he used to display his products during the day, and under which he and Doug slept at night. Doug says, "I had never been to Sturgis and I didn't know what to expect, but I had heard it could get pretty wild. I took along a shotgun for protection, and I slept with it in my sleeping bag."

Mr. Al with John at Sturgis, 2008. John and Al became fast friends when they met back in 1985. Throughout the years Al has been a staunch supporter of John, especially when dealing with city politics.

Below: As J&P's business grew, John leased a storefront from the National Motorcycle Museum on Junction Avenue. It was a step toward a permanent presence in the city during the rally. (Photo taken in 1991)

The J&P staff slept in a loft at the Junction Avenue store, often for only a few hours a night before it was time to start the next sales day. Sturgis 1993.

John was a new father, a struggling motorcycle dealer, and deep in debt. Jill did not come along because it was so far away, and the rally was going to last a full week. Besides, they needed to hold down expenses and it was still the income from Jill's day job that fed the family. But John knew that Sturgis was where he needed to be, not only because it was where his customers would gather, but because it was where he could immerse himself most deeply in the activity and culture he loved. Sturgis was the place to sell, and learn, and to learn what to sell. Not only did he immerse himself in the biker lifestyle that was emerging as the resurgent Harley-Davidson brand began to come into its own, but he met others who shared his love for traditional American motorcycles. Still, this first trip to the Black Hills was a pretty trying experience. Hessing explains, "It rained like crazy, almost every day. We didn't have a decent tent, just blue plastic tarps strung over our tables, and they were useless." He continues, "Mr. Al's building had this arched roof, but no gutters. The water just roared off that building and turned the alley into a river. I actually saw Harley gas tanks floating around like boats. It was so bad, John wondered if we should just pull out and go home, but we decided we had come this far and were going to stick it out." John adds, "And it wasn't just rain. It hails in Sturgis like no place else I've seen. I've seen storms in Sturgis that filled the streets with hail so deep that you couldn't see the curbing." About living rough in Mr. Al's alley, John adds, "We went each day to the Lantern Motel and paid two dollars to take a shower." While J&P's first year at Sturgis did not turn a profit, at least it provided some useful cash flow for the company.

Ever on the outlook for opportunities, and still in the period when his event promotions were yielding more revenue than motorcycle accessory sales, in 1989 John decided to step into the entertainment side of Sturgis by promoting a swap meet and bike show. Doug says, "John told me to go rent the biggest tent I could find, and we put up a 150 by 300-foot circus tent at the Sturgis drag strip." Unfortunately, the promotion was a bust, completely incompatible with the free-ride culture that prevailed at the time. John explains: "Sturgis had not become as commercialized as it is today, with its concerts and staged entertainment. It was a wide-open place where people rode into town, parked on Main Street, and walked around. If they wanted to buy something they would, but looking was free. The idea of paying admission to get into a bike show just didn't compute with these people, and they weren't about to do it." To make matters worse, John's show went up against a show promoted by a friend of his named Spider. John laughs and says, "Spider and I had the same idea at the same time, and neither one of us knew the other was doing it. We both had a flop that we could laugh about later. We both lost our shirts! I lost $30,000 and Spider had to lose tens of thousands also." With a more sober tone, he adds, "For all intents and purposes, Sturgis marks the end of the big selling season for motorcycle accessories. If you don't go home with a pocketful of money, it is going to be a hard winter. If you go home worse than broke like I did in '89, you're really in trouble."

John learned something else from the experience. He learned that Sturgis and its surrounding jurisdictions can change the rules. John explains, "One reason we set up our show and swap meet at the drag strip was because it was outside the city limits. The City of Sturgis had a vending license fee, but the county did not. However, as soon as we started promoting our event, the County changed its laws and created a vending license fee." On another occasion, John almost ended up in jail due to Sturgis' moveable rules after he had rented a lot on Lazelle Street to set up a tire-changing tent. John says, "We had extra space, so I invited CCI to park their big truck there, and I went to the city and got permission." He continues, "The CCI guys had the rig almost set up, which is a pretty big effort, when the cops showed up and said we were too close to the street. They wanted us to tear everything down and move the truck back about five feet. We did. Then, when we were set up again, another cop car comes by and said we can't park trucks there. I explain that we have permission from the City, so then they say it should not be within line of sight from the stop sign at a nearby intersection, and we needed to tear it down and move it again. I had had it, and I said, 'This is bullshit! We're not moving it again.'" The police had John handcuffed in the back seat of the cruiser when the city official who had given permission showed up and persuaded them to stand down. Similarly, John discovered that the Sturgis open container rule is subject to interpretation, having once almost been jailed for having a can of beer in the back of his booth at Mr. Al's alley. John says, "This is where we lived, all week! It was more like having a beer in your own living room, and these cops come along and bust us for being in the street. At least, that's how they saw it." Again, John and his crew almost got a free ride to the city jail. But John promised the police it would not happen again and police let them go.

J&P Cycles Sturgis Rally Store in the National Motorcycle Museum on Junction Avenue. J&P sold new and used parts at the rally. (1994)

Through their shared failures at the 1989 Rally, John and Spider became even better friends. Spider, who was a manufacturer of the small "beanie" helmets that had started to become popular, was a vendor in many of the J&P Promotions shows and swap meets, and he became a kind of a confidante and business adviser for John. Spider recalls, "John had started handing out a little flyer for mail-order sales in 1985. He was the only guy in our business who had even thought of mail-order. We were talking one day about how hard it was to travel and sell the way we were doing it, and I said, 'You know, someday we're both going to get old and its going to get too hard to keep chasing customers like this. We gotta figure out how to get the customers to come to us.'" Spider continues, "John told me about how his little flyer was working, and I told him I thought he had something. I thought he should expand it, and he did. I like to think it was out of that conversation that John began to realize that a catalog could become the very heart of his business."

Custom Chrome's president Nace Panzica bringing stock into the J&P store during the Sturgis 50th Anniversary in 1990. This was great customer service from CCI.

Below: The 50th Anniversary Sturgis bike as it is now, on display at the National Motorcycle Museum. It was originally donated to the National Motorcycle Museum by CCI president Nace Panzica for a raffle bike fundraiser.

John had an understanding with Mr. Al. Year-by-year, as vendors turned over and their space became available, John asked to be given first right of refusal. But he never refused. As J&P Cycles continued to grow, each year John would secure more vendor space in Sturgis until eventually his operation was under a 20 by 60-foot tent. Over time, Sturgis became his company's biggest pay day, and in addition to on-site sales, it was the most fertile ground available for distribution of the J&P catalog. Today, Jill says, "People who were not there cannot understand what it was like. Everything has changed so much at Sturgis, and at J&P. Now, a trip to Mr. Al's alley is part of our orientation for all new employees, just so they can see where it all began."

By 1988, John had established many friendships at Sturgis, and he had met kindred spirits who loved old motorcycles as much as he did. With some of the members of the Jackpine Gypsies, John got involved in the creation of a non-profit organization for the purpose of starting a motorcycle museum. John had some collectible motorcycles he could lend for display, but not enough to make a suitable exhibit, so he solicited the support of his friend, Lonnie Isam, and E.J. Cole, a major collector from Houston, Texas. John flew to Houston at his own expense to talk to Cole and Lonnie on behalf of the proposed museum. By 1990, which was the 50th anniversary of Sturgis, the project had taken shape, and space was rented at a former supermarket storefront at 2348 Junction Avenue to locate their ambitiously-named National Motorcycle Museum. Local motorcycle collectors, Jackpine Gypsy members, John, Lonnie, and E. J. Cole provided most of the motorcycles that went on display. John also brought in CCI as a sponsor for the Museum. Nace Panzica, CCI President, commissioned leading custom bike builder John Reed to create a pearl white Harley-Davidson with gold-plated trim for a fund-raising raffle. The bike raised $25,000 for the museum, then Panzica bought it back from the raffle winner and later donated it to the Museum for a second time in 1999.

The new museum enjoyed an excellent location, near Exit 32 on Interstate 90, and because it did not need—nor could it afford—all of the space that was available, John opened an outlet for J&P Cycles at the storefront adjoining the museum. In addition, he kept his space in Mr. Al's alley where he had begun. The pundits were predicting as many as a million people for Sturgis's 50th, so it was both an opportune time to open the museum and for John to expand his sales operation to a bigger and better-looking location. Not only could the museum bring additional traffic to the J&P store, but arrangements were made to continue to distribute catalogs at the Sturgis Community

Center on Lazelle Street, Rally Headquarters at the National Guard Armory on Main, and at Mr. Al's swap meet as well. To provide rally-goers a high level of customer service, J&P guaranteed that items not purchased on site, but from the catalog, would be shipped from its Anamosa warehouse by second-day service, either to the rally or to the customer's home.

J&P had become one of the biggest single retail operations in Sturgis, and a crew of eight was brought from Anamosa to man its various retail and promotional locations. A loft with a shower and a small kitchenette was built at the Junction Street storefront to provide low-cost housing for the crew, who slept there on air mattresses. John and Jill slept on air mattresses in a spare bedroom at the home of R.T. Shaw, a local realtor whom they had met at Sturgis Dragway, which he managed. It was certainly a step up from Mr. Al's alley. About the loft, Doug Hessing recalls, "The roof leaked, and during rains we hung black plastic garbage bags from the ceiling to act as funnels to catch the water. We would cut the corner out of a bag so the water could drip into barrels set all around the store." Rob DeSotel, who has been on the Sturgis crew since 1992, says, "At the Junction Avenue store we were so busy we had to eat lunch on the job, and there were only two places we could get food. These were Mother's Restaurant and Taco John's, and by the end of the week we were pretty tired of everything on their menus." One long-serving J&P employee says, "Sometimes it is crazy. Everyone looks forward to it, but Sturgis is really a killer. We were doing 13-hour days, then sometimes another three or four hours during the night, filling out paperwork, cleaning up, doing the accounting, and transmitting mail orders back to Anamosa. You would grab five or six hours of sleep and do it again." He adds, "I have seen times when John was lying flat on his back on the floor, talking on the phone to Anamosa or to suppliers, just too exhausted to remain on his feet or even sit in a chair." Jill adds, "It was about this time that we started the tradition of having an employee cookout at the end of the week. Everyone worked so hard and ate nothing but carnival food all week, so we started doing a big feed at Shaw's place when it was over."

The Sturgis 50th Anniversary proved a bonanza for J&P and other vendors. John recalls, "I have never seen anything like it. Even with the big growth in motorcycle popularity in recent years, I've never seen gridlock in Sturgis like we had at the 50th. I don't think anyone has any idea how many people were actually there." Even with its new larger retail facility, J&P Cycles was overwhelmed. John continues, "We had all this additional floor space, and we went out very well stocked. We knew it would be a big year, and we planned for it. But we were nearly wiped out by the fourth day, and we were selling stuff faster than we could bring it in overnight." He adds, "We were so overwhelmed, even Nace Panzica, the president of Custom Chrome, was helping us sell and stock products." There was so much cash flow, Jill couriered cash back to Anamosa at mid-week. She recalls, "I got on a little

John, Ed Ahlf and R. T. Shaw enjoy a friendly game of "Butt Darts" at R.T.'s house in Sturgis 1994.

Below: In December, 1997, construction was begun for J&P's permanent home on Lazelle Street in Sturgis.

12-passenger airplane coming out of Rapid City, carrying a bag containing $50,000. I was the last one aboard, and I walked on and there was one empty seat, one other woman, and ten Hell's Angels, fully decked out in their colors. The whole flight I had this paranoid feeling that somehow they knew what I had in the bag and they were going to knock me over."

Proud moments for John Parham: In 1997 when J&P Cycles shared space with two of the world's leading brands as a major sponsor of the Rally.

Below: The new store was opened for business at the 1998 Rally. It provided over 7,000 square feet for the National Motorcycle Museum. An Evel Knievel's sky cycle went on display when J&P opened its doors.

Late summer, 1990, on the occasion of Sturgis's 50th anniversary, it seemed like a high time for John Parham. J&P's sales were booming, John had begun to collect vintage motorcycles, he was in on the ground-floor development of a motorcycle museum at the American mecca of motorcycling, and he had turned J&P Cycles into the Rally's biggest and most visible aftermarketer. But by early 1991, it all proved an illusion when J&P's year-end bookkeeping was completed. With record income, the company had unknowingly spent more than it earned, finding itself near bankruptcy. It was during the hard struggle to survive—at Sturgis in 1991—when John confessed to his friend Spider that he was so discouraged that he might sell J&P Cycles to anyone who would just take the inventory off his hands. However, as business systems were improved at Anamosa, and the company returned to profitability in 1992, John continued to rely heavily on Sturgis for both sales and exposure to advance the company brand. In 1992, J&P Cycles became a sponsor of the All-Harley drag races at Sturgis Dragway, and in 1993 it became an official sponsor of the overall event, the Sturgis Rally and Races. John says, "Our arrival at Sturgis that year was one of the proudest moments of my life. There was a big billboard on the highway welcoming the bikers, and on the billboard were three logos: Harley-Davidson, Coca Cola, and J&P Cycles. We were up there in some pretty serious company."

By mid-decade, J&P Cycles' sales had grown dramatically, the J&P staff had grown to more than 50 people, and with consistently good profits, John and Jill made a major commitment to their accessory sales business by purchasing property on Lazelle Street in Sturgis, just west of the Sturgis Community Center. John says, "It was three-and-a-half blocks away from the center of town, and everyone thought we were crazy. At that time, no one even went down there. For the first year we only used it to park cars for five dollars a pop." He adds, "But things changed quickly in that part of town. I paid about $200,000 each for nine lots. Three years later, when I wanted to buy another three, the price of land had almost doubled."

On December 4, 1997, ground was broken for a new two-story building that would, eventually, become the new home of J&P Cycles and the National Motorcycle Museum. Construction had to await a decision about space for the Museum because it's board of directors had to also evaluate offers from two other Sturgis property owners, but eventually construction began, based on a plan to provide J&P a 6,000-square-foot showroom, and 7,300 square feet for the National Motorcycle Museum, which was nearly a 50-percent increase over its first home on Junction Avenue. John recalls, "By offering space to the Museum, it added about $100,000 to our construction costs. It required a change in zoning, we had to hire a state-licensed architect to review our plans, and we had to provide bathrooms and other features for handicapped visitors." Still, John offered the Museum rent on a sliding scale, so it did not have to pay as much during the off-season when tourism was down. In keeping with the history and ambiance of the town, John commissioned an old-west style for the façade of the building. The new facility opened and was dedicated during the Rally in 1998.

Over time, as adjoining property on Lazelle became available, John purchased it, and by 2005 his Sturgis store was at the center of a full city block that provided paved parking for 300 motorcycles, plus ample space for J&P's clients and business partners to put up their own displays. These included Küryakyn, Drag Specialties, Progressive Suspension, Custom Chrome, Biker's Choice, Redneck Engineering, Tower Machine, Memphis Shades, and others. Jeff Carstensen, who has worked on the Sturgis crew since 1994, explains, "John kept buying old residential homes near the Lazelle store. Our crew from Anamosa got bigger every year, and each year we would use one of the old houses for our living quarters. Then John would acquire another house that we would move to the next year, and he would tear down the old one and improve the property. Eventually, the entire block was converted to commercial use except for the sandstone Annie Tallant House, which is listed on the historical registry. Named after a famous frontier school teacher who became the first white woman to arrive in the Black Hills as a member of the Gordon-Russell expedition in 1874, the Tallant House was in a state of disrepair when John bought it. Carstensen relates, "It was disgusting. Some old guy had been living there, and both the yard and the inside of the house were about a foot-deep in garbage. We even found a deer carcass under the trash in the backyard!" Carstensen continues, "We cleaned it up, John restored the place, and today it serves as our permanent crew headquarters."

Tire sales and installation are a major activity for J&P Cycles at Sturgis.

Below: J&P Cycles full city block on Lazelle Street has grown to become a huge sales and customer service complex. It now includes two J&P Cycles showrooms, vendors and several of the industry's leading manufacturers.

Above: J&P Cycles' Sturgis store promotes the different companies, brands and products it sells at the rally. (2006)

Below: John Parham making his acceptance speech at his 2006 Sturgis Hall of Fame induction breakfast.

In 2004, John built an additional 3,500-square-foot building at the Lazelle property to serve as a separate store for the sale of metric bike accessories, and as a tire service center. Zach Parham, who now runs J&P's Sturgis retail operation, explains, "In dollar volume, tires are our biggest seller. It is amazing how many people arrive in Sturgis on worn-out tires, and our sales are limited only by our ability to install tires. We have six lifts going all day every day, with people lined up and waiting, and we could sell even more tires if we had more technicians to install them." By last count, more than 150,000 customers visited the J&P Cycles stores during rally week. In addition to more than 500 tires, the company sold more than 150 custom exhaust systems and more than 400 windshields, for which it offers free installation. Doug Hessing laughs, "A lot of people make their first ride to Sturgis with no windshield. By the time they get there they are so sun- and wind-burned they look like a lobster. They've learned their lesson and are not about to return home that way, so they buy a windshield."

John says, "You wouldn't believe some of the things we see with customers who come to get tires. There must be some kind of big honor in making it all the way to Sturgis on your old tire, because we see tires that should have been replaced a few thousand miles ago." For example, John recalls an experience with the Banditos, who ride from Texas and make a traditional grand entrance into the town late in the week. He says, "They arrive on Friday, and some of them are on tires that never should have left home." He smiles and relates, "This one big Bandito rolls in on a ratty old Panhead that looked like it would not make it across town, but he has ridden from Texas. He had a bald rear tire and knew he had to replace it, so he's there pulling money out of all of his pockets and counting it. He bought the cheapest tire that would fit his rim, then he left the bike with us and walked off to look around town." John continues, "When our technician pulled the axle, about 20 washers and nuts fell out all over the floor. This guy had used all kinds of junk as spacers for the rear wheel. I said, 'I hope you can figure out where all that stuff goes, because if he has a wreck and comes back here, I'm going to let him kill you, not me!" When the Bandito returned to get his motorcycle, the technician had thoroughly cleaned the rear wheel, which had been caked with grease and grime. With his mood lightened by several beers, the Bandito was overwhelmed with gratitude, and gave John a big bear hug. John says, "I really didn't need that, but then he starts telling me how great we J&P guys are, and he asks me if I would like some grass. I say, 'No, I better not,' and he ups his offer to some crystal meth. I turn that down too, and he says, 'How about some PCP?' I said, 'Isn't that stuff bad for you?' and he says,

'Naw, that's just a bunch of propaganda.'" John laughs and adds, "Another satisfied J&P customer!"

To meet customer demand, today the J&P Sturgis crew is 45 people, plus a dozen local kids who are hired to help direct traffic, police the parking lot, and keep the place tidy. Four semi-truck loads of parts and supplies are shipped in from Anamosa, and an advance crew spends more than a week just setting up the sales and service operation. George Barnard, who came to Sturgis with the J&P crew in 1991 and now drives one of the company show trucks, says, "It has changed a lot over the years. It is still long, hard days, but it is better organized and a little easier than it used to be. We still take lunch on the job, but we no longer have to run out to Taco John's. The company has catered meals brought in for lunch, and while we are cleaning up late in the day, a nice dinner is being grilled on site." When not being used by J&P for the Rally, John Parham's Sturgis property is rented to a local automobile dealer. Recently, Parham has bought an additional full block in Sturgis for commercial development, not strictly related to the Rally.

ଊ

Along with the explosion of Harley-Davidson's sales, and the entrance of the Japanese companies into the American cruiser-style motorcycle market, Sturgis—both the Rally and the town—changed significantly during the 1990s. J&P Marketing Supervisor Nicole Ridge, who first joined the Sturgis crew in 1997, says, "Rally attendees are a broader demographic than they used to be. Whereas it used to be mostly hard-core bikers, today you also see lots of half-million-dollar motor homes and $60,000 pickups, pulling enclosed trailers full of $50,000 show bikes." With standard motorcycles selling for more than $20,000, and customers buying another $10,000 or more in accessories, or paying $30,000 or more for a custom motorcycle, the amount of money that flowed into the American motorcycle market has been phenomenal. Likewise, the money that flowed through Sturgis during the Rally grew exponentially during the decade. Well-funded outside investors began to buy Sturgis property because they could make a return on their investment in only the two weeks each year that the bikers were in town. This kind of outside investment sometimes caused resentment among the locals, especially if an outsider cared only about Rally income and made no effort to maintain his buildings year-round. These people were seen as carpetbaggers with no real interest in the welfare of the community or their neighbors.

Pepper Massey, who is now director of the Sturgis Motorcycle Rally, was there to see it all, initially as an outsider, then as a resident. Massey came to Sturgis in the mid-1980s as a representative for the National Coalition of Motorcyclists, a California-based advocacy and lobbying group for motorcycle owners. Coming out of the cement sprawl of Los Angeles, she flew into Rapid City, was enamored with the beautiful scenery of the Black Hills, and fell in love with Sturgis. In 1997, she left California behind and came to Sturgis to work for the National Motorcycle Museum, then later as publisher for the Meade County Times Tribune before becoming

John with friend Bob Illingworth at Sturgis, 2008. Bob has fought for motorcycle rights all his life. He is the main fundraiser and promoter of the Sturgis Motorcycle Museum & Hall of Fame and has helped shape it into the fine museum it is today.

Below: John with his longtime friend Mike Corbin. Mike has been a true leader and innovator in the motorcycle industry Mike nominated John for the Sturgis Hall of Fame in 2006.

Rally Director in 2007. Massey says, "John Parham has a good reputation in town. He puts up first-class buildings on his land, and always keeps his property maintained and active when the Rally is not on. His interests in Sturgis clearly go beyond his motorcycle interests, because he has just bought another block and is putting in a commercial mall, which is going to be beneficial to the community. His investment in the community gives it a return. He is not one of the people who just take the money out of town."

Al Colton, who met John when he rented him a small vendor space on Main Street in 1985, says, "John is a wonderful person. He was one of the favorite vendors I had, and I would like to have more just like him. He has become one of our main assets in Sturgis. He has done a lot of wonderful things for the town." John's old swap meet friend Spider would concur, stating, "You could make the case that John's investment on Lazelle Street was what triggered a whole wave of renewal and property improvement in Sturgis." R.T. Shaw, who managed Sturgis Dragway when J&P Cycles became one of its sponsors, and is now owner of Hog Heaven Campground, says, "John and Jill are seen here as hardworking and honest business people. They are an asset to the community and maintain their property very well. I don't know anyone who does not respect John and Jill Parham." Parham's acceptance as an "insider" with the Sturgis community was made clear on August 9, 2006, when he was inducted into the Sturgis Hall of Fame, nominated to that honor by his longtime friend and business associate Mike Corbin, of Hollister, California. Outlining Parham's 30 years of achievement in the motorcycle industry as well as his contributions to Sturgis, Corbin says, "I was honored to nominate John for this recognition. He is well-deserving for his years of service and dedication to motorcycling."

ଓ

The Sturgis Rally has come a long way from its roots as a friendly challenge between two local motorcycle clubs in 1937, and in fact its greatest growth and change has taken place since J&P Cycles arrived as a vendor a little more than two decades ago. Once confined to the town of Sturgis, today's Rally week has become a collection of concerts, motorcycle races, bike shows, campgrounds, and manufacturer's displays that sprawl for 100 miles along the I-90 corridor, from Rapid City, South Dakota, to the Devil's Tower region of Wyoming. The growth and influence of J&P Cycles has been equally impressive. Beginning as a struggling and near-bankrupt company with two rented swap-meet tables in Mr. Al's alley, today it is a major Sturgis property owner with more than 15,000 square feet of sales and service facilities under roof on Lazelle Street, setting J&P Cycles apart as the largest retailer at the Sturgis rally.

John with the legendary Malcom Smith. John proudly displays one of Malcom's motorcycles at the National Motorcycle Museum.

Below: John and Jill have an opportunity to meet old friends in Sturgis. Slider and Charlie Gilmore are two hog farmers from Iowa known as the ZZ Top brothers.

Below: John and Jill with Brian Klock (left) of Klock Werks and long time friend Charlie St. Clair of the Laconia Rally and Races (Sturgis 2008). J&P Cycles is a proud sponsor of Laconia each year and Charlie has been a great supporter of J&P over the past two decades.

Chapter Eight: Protecting Motorcycling's Heritage

As was the case throughout the industrialized world, motorcycles began to appear in America upon the arrival of the 20th century. One or two brands were launched during the last decade of the 19th century, but the nation's first successful and enduring brand—the Indian—appeared in prototype in 1901 and went into mass production in 1902. Its ultimate great rival, Harley-Davidson, appeared in 1903 or 1904, depending on whether you follow documented research or the Milwaukee marque's "official" history. An inexpensive automobile had not yet arrived in large quantities, so for the next decade the motorcycle became the motor vehicle of choice to replace the horse as the leading means of personal transportation. New brands proliferated from industrial centers all over the eastern United States to the extent that historians have identified as many as 200 American-made brands in existence prior to 1920. Indian especially prospered, with sales growing steadily until 1913, when the Massachusetts-based firm sold 32,000 motorcycles. Harley-Davidson grew more slowly during the period, but still achieved an undisputed second place in market share, followed by the Chicago-based Excelsior, manufactured by bicycle maker Schwinn.

With a love for rare and classic motorcycles, John Parham has become one of the nation's leading collectors and museum patrons. He is seen here with Jill in a 1917 Harley-Davidson with sidecar.

The first home of the National Motorcycle Museum was on Junction Avenue in Sturgis. It opened in 1990 for the 50th Anniversary of Sturgis. It also housed J&P Cycles first retail store at the Sturgis rally.

By 1913, the American motorcycle industry was feeling its strength. Approximately 100,000 motorcycles were sold that year among a national population of 92 million. Indian held a clear third of the market with Harley-Davidson and Excelsior combined earning another third of the sales. The remaining third was divided among a great many brands, most of which had less than five percent market share. These included Thor, Yale, Flying Merkel, Cleveland, Henderson, Reading-Standard, and others. For the leaders especially, the future looked bright. Indian had become the largest motorcycle manufacturer in the world, with significant international sales and a network of 3,000 dealers worldwide. With a huge manufacturing facility, Indian even published a plan to nearly double its sales to 60,000 in 1914. But it was not to be. Instead, as a result of greater production and lower pricing achieved by Henry Ford's famous Model T, in 1914 the American motorcycle industry began to crash, unable to match the Tin Lizzy for its combination of price and convenience. Indian would never again come close to 30,000 motorcycles a year, and by 1920 most of the minor brands had become extinct. Thanks to conservative product development and prudent management, Harley-Davidson would continue to inch upward until it had surpassed Indian in the decade following the First World War. But with only 10,000 units per year, its first-place position was due more to Indian's decline than the Motor Company's own growth. Excelsior would hang on until 1931 when, during the Great Depression, Schwinn would make the strategic decision to cease motorcycle production in favor of bicycles only. By the mid-1930s, total motorcycle sales in America had fallen to only 6,000 units a year, with Harley-Davidson outselling Indian by two to one, and both companies barely earning enough to keep their doors open.

The Second World War kept Harley and Indian in business with military production, but Indian was already a broken company going into the war, and afterward it continued downward until it declared bankruptcy in 1953. Changes in U.S. tariff rules, plus the devaluation of the British Pound after the Second World War, caused motorcycle sales to rebound, but mostly among imported British and European brands. Still, by the mid-1950s no more than 50,000 motorcycles a year were being sold in America, and it would not be until the arrival of the Japanese brands at the end of the decade that the market would move into its modern era of robust growth and expansion. This era, beginning in 1959, saw near-dominance by the Japanese for two decades, followed by Harley-Davidson's remarkable resurgence as a leader in sales and a dictator of design and style in the late-1980s.

Today, the market is at the end of a steady 19-year period of growth that can be compared only to the 13 years of uninterrupted growth that took place at the beginning of the 20th century. Interestingly, to a large extent this latter-day growth has been driven by a strong interest in nostalgia and a demand for modern-technology motorcycles that imitate the styles of a yesteryear.

The two great motorcycle sales booms of the modern era—from 1960 through 1975, then 1985 to the present—were driven largely by the phenomenon of the post-war Baby Boom. It was young and affluent Boomers who became teenagers just as the Japanese manufacturers arrived to market their products to the American middle class in the 1960s, and it was these same Boomers, three decades later, after having raised families and managed careers, who returned to motorcycles, driven by nostalgia and fond memories of their youth. It was mostly Harley-Davidson that figured out how to grab the Boomers their second time around, becoming the industry benchmark for marketing nostalgia and the mythos of the rugged American motorcycle outlaw, or as some would rather say, the "motorcycling individualist." Ironically, most of these "individualists" go to great lengths to dress and act in strict conformity with their motorcycling friends, a behavior that has turned the traditional grease-stained motorcycle shop into a modern, upscale fashion boutique, and earned fortunes for Harley-Davidson as well as competing aftermarket companies, including J&P Cycles.

ଓଃ

Fifty years after the formation of the Harley-Davidson Motor Company, four men who revered motorcycle history founded the Antique Motorcycle Club of America. These were Ted Hodgdon, Emmett Moore, Henry Wing, and his son, Henry Wing, Jr. Both Hodgdon and Moore had experienced the full metamorphosis of the American motorcycle industry. They had begun their careers in the pre-war era of American exclusivity, working for Indian, both had moved to the British firm BSA after Indian failed, and Moore even continued into the modern era of Japanese dominance, working for Kawasaki. These men understood the richness of America's motorcycle history, and they formed the AMCA in 1954—the year that both John and Jill Parham were born—to encourage the restoration and preservation of antique motorcycles.

As late as 1980, America had only one motorcycle museum, which was the Indian Motocycle Museum in Springfield, Massachusetts, a private venture owned by Charles and Esta Manthos. A few major automotive museums or museums of science and industry owned modest motorcycle collections, but these were usually shunted aside and inconspicuously displayed. But with the arrival of the 1980s, and the Boomers' self-conscious obsession with their youthful past, a greater interest in motorcycle history and motorcycling traditions took hold. In part because of a presentation that Emmett Moore made to the American Motorcyclist Association Board of Trustees in 1980, two years later the AMA created a separate non-profit foundation for the purpose of protecting the nation's motorcycle heritage and one day creating

John on a 1912 Indian (left) and his friend Dave Ohrt aboard a 1914 Harley-Davidson board track racer, helping create a History Channel special television show about early motorcycle racing.

Below: John's ride aboard the Indian inspired an original oil painting by David Uhl. (Michael Lichter photo)

Through J&P Promotions, John Parham developed a successful program of nostalgic dirt track racing, including classes for the pre-1920 board track racers, pictured above.

Below: Jim Long brings riders to the line at the nostalgic races at Davenport.

a museum. Also, the AMCA—now more than 11,000 members strong—began a period of steady growth, and the idea of motorcycle museums became a national movement. From 1995 through the present, scores have been opened throughout the United States, often built around the private collections of AMCA members. In addition, following the model of the Guggenheim Museum's The Art of the Motorcycle Exhibition, launched in 1998, many established museums and art galleries have clamored to create motorcycle exhibits, often treating motorcycles as objects of art. Today, America has many of the world's leading motorcycle museums, including the Barber Vintage Motorsports Museum in Birmingham, Alabama, the Wheels Through Time Museum in Maggie Valley, North Carolina, the Motorcycle Hall of Fame Museum in Pickerington, Ohio, The Sturgis Motorcycle Museum, and the National Motorcycle Museum in Anamosa, Iowa.

Individually and collectively, these represent huge investments in the preservation of the nation's motorcycle heritage.

ૹ

Typically, nostalgia is a state of mind that grips a person 25 to 30 years after his teens. In other words, those who look fondly upon the culture and artifacts of their past, usually begin to do so in their 40s and 50s. In this respect, John Parham is not typical. By the age of 25, when he was founding J&P Cycles and prowling the motorcycle swap meets of the American Midwest, Parham had already become gripped with a passion for the motorcycles of old. He says, "I cannot remember a time when I was not in love with old motorcycles. The 1980s, when I first got involved, were the heyday of swap meets. The old and original stuff had just begun to come out of barns and basements. I remember swap meets where there were old Harley Springer front ends lined up by the dozen, laid out in rows on the ground, and I was just crazy about them. I wanted them all!" Parham's passion for the old machines sometimes got in the way of good business sense, as evidenced by the purchase of his first great collectible, his yellow 1955 Harley Panhead, which he could ill afford and once had to part with because he could not make ends meet.

In 1988, still not 35 years old, John Parham got involved in two significant contributions to the preservation of America's motorcycle heritage. He had been promoting races for modern motorcycles at the half-mile track at the Mississippi Valley Fairgrounds in Davenport, Iowa, when Paul George, a long-time Indian collector, approached Parham with the idea of promoting some vintage races at the same facility over Labor Day weekend, on the occasion of the big AMCA national meet at Davenport. Paul was an active member of the Blackhawk Chapter of the AMCA, the organizer of the meet, and he helped facilitate an arrangement to schedule the races on Friday night the following year. There were only 26 motorcycles at the

1989 race, but one of them was a pre-1920s flat-tank Flying Merkel, one of the rarest and most exciting of the factory board-track racers, which John let make some exhibition laps. The crowd of about 1,000 responded enthusiastically to the program, and especially to the ancient board-track motorcycle. This gave Parham the idea to offer a racing class for these rare machines, and in 1990 he had two of them show up, plus a pre-1920s racing sidecar rig. Because they were obviously big crowd-pleasers, in 1991 John offered to waive the entry fees for board track machines in order to create a larger field. The few of these fragile, powerful, smoking, thundering machines that still exist were rarely started by their owners, much less run at speed on a racetrack. But John was part of the brotherhood, he was known and trusted by the owners, and for 1991 he mustered 10 machines, which were enough to put on a spectacular race. By now, 70 or 80 motorcycles in the various vintage classes were turning out, the annual crowd had grown to 3,000, and the races had become one of the favorite features of the Davenport AMCA swap meet.

Steve Boggs, who was at the initial meeting with Parham and Paul George in 1988, and who has raced the Davenport vintage races every single year—winning his class in 1998 and 2007—attributes the success of the event to Parham's organizational skills and attention to detail. Boggs says, "John is a good promoter. He is very thorough and very well organized. He knows how to put on a professional show." Jeff Decker, a fine artist, motorcycle collector, and friend of John's, says, "Before John got involved, there were about 10 guys out there who knew or cared much about the early board trackers. John putting them on the track at Davenport has opened a whole new dimension to the motorcycle community. Not only are they the most popular class at Davenport, and you have more guys collecting and restoring them, but now you have all these custom bike builders creating a whole new genre of customs that look like and take their inspiration from the board trackers. If it were not for John Parham, I don't think any of this would be happening."

The Parhams have become leading patrons of motorcycle artists. They are seen here with Jeff Decker (right) and his life-size bronze of 1937 speed record setter Joe Petrali.

Below: John with additional examples of his Jeff Decker bronze motorcycle sculptures. (Ed Youngblood photo)

Among the other regular participants every year at the Davenport races were Paul George's five sons, all of whom raced both vintage and modern motorcycles. Matt George started promoting dirt track races in Iowa in 1997, and in 1999 he signed on to do John's track preparation at Davenport. Life at the Parham's had changed significantly since John started promoting the event in 1989. J&P Cycles had nearly failed, weathered the crisis, and become a growing concern, and John and Jill's priorities were changing. J&P Cycles was growing and required more of their attention, and their son Zachary was entering high school. John had spent a lot of time working and

When the National Motorcycle Museum in Sturgis became insolvent, John Parham paid its bills and relocated it to Anamosa, Iowa, reopening in 2001.

Below: some of the first visitors were the Blackhawk Chapter of the Antique Motorcycle Club of America, for whom John had promoted the Nostalgic Races at their annual meet in Davenport.

away when Zach was young, and he wanted to have more time to spend with Zach and support his activities, including high school football. In 2000, the last year that Parham promoted the race at Davenport, he departed the fairgrounds at 4 p.m., entrusting the running of the event to subordinates. Zach had his first high school football game that evening, and John told Jill, "This is it! I'm going to sell the race." Parham approached Matt George and suggested he take over the

Davenport promotion, offering to mentor him in the business aspects of the event. George agreed to take over in 2001, and has continued the races as one of the most popular aspects of the big Davenport weekend. George says, "John built this race into a success because he treats the racers just like they treat their customers at J&P. When you treat people good, it all comes back to you in good ways." George adds, "And John has stayed involved as a strong supporter. His staff designs and he produces a new collectible poster for the race every year, and we use J&P's mailing operation to distribute over 20,000 flyers a year. He is a good guy to work with, and always is ready to help when it involves vintage motorcycles."

Also in 1988, John Parham joined like-minded enthusiasts in Sturgis to explore the idea of creating a motorcycle museum. By 1989, by-laws were set down and a not-for-profit corporation was created, just in time to put a museum together for the 50th anniversary of the Sturgis Rally, which took place in 1990. It was called the National Motorcycle Museum and Hall of Fame, and was located in a storefront on Junction Avenue, close to Exit 32 on Interstate 90. J&P Cycles took adjoining space to open its first indoor store in Sturgis. Parham also flew to Houston at his own expense to meet with motorcycle collectors Lonnie Isam and his uncle, E.J. Cole, whom he persuaded to loan motorcycles for the inaugural exhibit. Local collectors and members of the Jack Pine Gypsies Motorcycle Club also provided strong support. However, over the next decade the project struggled. The Museum did not draw the kind of attendance that its founders had hoped for, even during the crush of motorcyclists who came in August for the Rally. Jeff Carstensen, a longtime J&P employee who now runs the National Motorcycle Museum in Anamosa, says, "They never had the budget to market it properly. There was probably an assumption by its founders that it would succeed on its own merits, without much promotion." Pepper Massey, who is now Sturgis Rally Director and was at one time the executive director of the National Motorcycle Museum, concurs. She says, "The board members were enthusiasts and had great belief in the project, but they probably should have looked at it more from a business point of view." During her tenure,

JASON LEFFLER

2003 NASCAR CRAFTSMAN TRUCK SERIES

JASON LEFFLER AND THE ULTRA MOTORSPORTS TEAM ASE/CARQUEST #2 DODGE RAM

One of the hot, young drivers on the NASCAR Craftsman Truck Series circuit, Jason Leffler burst onto the scene in 2002 by posting 11 top-five finishes. His performance earned him fourth place in the overall drivers' standings and gained him a lot of respect from his NCTS peers.

Once again this year, Leffler sports the red, white and blue colors of the #2 Team ASE/CARQUEST Dodge fielded by Ultra Motorsports. Veteran crew chief, Tim Kohuth, moves into the General Manager role for 2003 and Winston Cup veteran Buddy Barnes takes over as crew chief, flanked by the "Ultra Bad Boys."

The 27-year-old Leffler brings a wealth of racing experience to the table at Ultra Motorsports. In 1999 he became the first driver in 37 years to win three straight USAC National Midget titles.

The following year, Leffler made the move to stock cars, running for Rookie of the Year honors in the NASCAR Busch Series. In 2001 Leffler joined the NASCAR Winston Cup fraternity wheeling Chip Ganassi's #1 Dodge Intrepid.

In his rookie season in NASCAR's top division, Leffler collected one top-10 and seven top-20 finishes, including his first career Winston cup Bud Pole in the inaugural Protection One 400 at the all-new Kansas Speedway.

Leffler believes his varied experience will serve him well racing the Team ASE Dodge Ram. He said, "I've raced just about anything on four wheels, from Winston Cup and Busch to the IRL. With all the experience I have in different divisions, I don't envision any big hurdles that we should have to overcome."

He concluded, "Our racing program at Ultra Motorsports has been very strong over the years. With the exception of a few bumps in the road, we've been contenders for the win on almost every track or superspeedway where we've raced. I don't expect that to change."

Of course, Leffler knows to drive with power even when he's not on the track. During his everyday life, he drives the truck with the most powerful line of engines in its class: the Dodge Ram.

When anyone wants to talk about dominating performances, they have to include the Dodge Rams in the NASCAR Craftsman Truck Series. Dodge has stayed at the top of the NASCAR Craftsman Truck Series by combining superior engineering and drivers who never want to take a backseat to anyone. Look for more of the same this season from the talented Dodge Ram truck series teams.

CLIMB INTO JASON LEFFLER'S #2 DODGE RAM

Want to know what it's like to drive a NASCAR Craftsman Truck Series Dodge Ram? Check out all the racing action on the Dodge Web site, **www.dodge.com**.

Here you'll find the inside scoop on Jason Leffler's #2 Dodge Ram, along with detailed information on Ultra Motorsports and all the latest results from the NASCAR Craftsman Truck Series. In addition, you'll get a good look at the cool Dodge race team merchandise, including hats, shirts and other collectibles.

WHAT'S NEW FROM DODGE?

Go to **www.dodge.com** for a complete look at all Dodge cars and trucks. Get the inside line on the latest product information and specifications. Visit your local Dodge dealer in your area to see Dodge cars and trucks up close or to take a test drive!

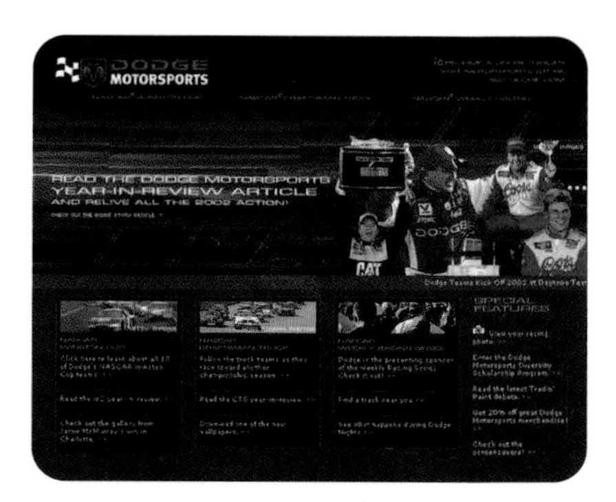

2003 DODGE RAM NASCAR CRAFTSMAN TRUCK TECHNICAL SPECIFICATIONS

Length:	202 inches
Width:	80 inches
Wheelbase:	112.0 inches
Weight:	3400 pounds
Engine Type:	5.9L Magnum V8, Mopar Cast Iron R-3 Block and Mopar W-8 Aluminum Heads
Horsepower:	700+
Redline:	8500+ rpm
Gearbox:	4-Speed Manual
Brakes:	4-Wheel Disc Brakes

BRENDAN GAUGHAN

2003 NASCAR CRAFTSMAN TRUCK SERIES

BRENDAN GAUGHAN AND THE ORLEANS RACING #62 DODGE RAM

One of the rising stars in racing, Brendan Gaughan has made an impressive transition from the world of high-powered, off-road truck racing into the arena of high-speed truck competition. With his performance in the Orleans Racing #62 Dodge Ram, Gaughan has firmly established himself as one of America's hottest racing talents.

Earning the 2000 and 2001 NASCAR Winston West Series Championships, Gaughan and Orleans Racing added selected NASCAR Craftsman events to their schedule. "Our plan was to take home a second Winston West crown and we did just that," explained the popular Las Vegas resident. "The second part of our plan was to gain as much experience in the truck series as possible. And, again, we were able to accomplish our goal."

Leaving no doubt as to his skill on the track, Gaughan definitely showed his prowess in the Craftsman Truck Series. Of the 22 races he entered, he won two, had five top-five finishes and nine top 10s. This effort earned Gaughan the Raybestos Rookie of the Year award. Quite an impressive beginning for the youthful Gaughan.

"I started racing in trucks," smiles Gaughan. "I really feel at home behind the wheel and, better yet, they are really fun to drive. The Craftsman Truck Series offers incredible competition and I couldn't be happier than to be in the series full time. There are some great drivers and the racing is aggressive. In short, it is a terrific series for both drivers and fans."

From desert buggies to full-sized trucks, Gaughan's off-road career boasts five championship titles and a wealth of knowledge. A lengthy union with Walker Evans Racing (1992–1999) groomed him to make the full-time transition to high-speed NCTS competition. Of course, Gaughan knows to drive with power even when he's not on the track. During his everyday life, he drives the truck with the most powerful line of engines in its class: the Dodge Ram.

When anyone wants to talk about dominating performances, they have to include the Dodge Rams in the NASCAR Craftsman Truck Series. Dodge has stayed at the top of the NASCAR Craftsman Truck Series by combining superior engineering and drivers who never want to take a backseat to anyone. Look for more of the same this season from the talented Dodge Ram truck series teams.

CLIMB INTO BRENDAN GAUGHAN'S #62 DODGE RAM

Want to know what it's like to drive a NASCAR Craftsman Truck Dodge Ram? Check out all the racing action on the Dodge Web site, **www.dodge.com**.

Here you'll find the inside scoop on Brendan Gaughan's #62 Dodge Ram, along with detailed information on Orleans Racing and all the latest results from the NASCAR Craftsman Truck Series. In addition, you'll get a good look at the cool Dodge race team merchandise, including hats, shirts and other collectibles.

WHAT'S NEW FROM DODGE?

Go to **www.dodge.com** for a complete look at all Dodge cars and trucks. Get the inside line on the latest product information and specifications. Visit your local Dodge dealer in your area to see Dodge cars and trucks up close or to take a test drive!

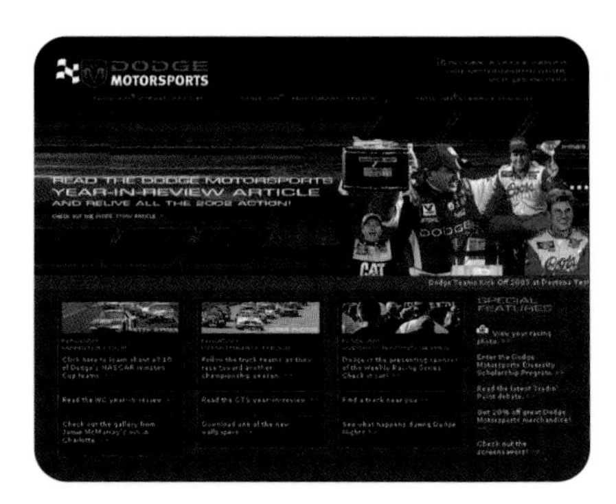

2003 DODGE RAM NASCAR CRAFTSMAN TRUCK TECHNICAL SPECIFICATIONS

Length:	202 inches
Width:	80 inches
Wheelbase:	112.0 inches
Weight:	3400 pounds
Engine Type:	5.9L Magnum V8, Mopar Cast Iron R-3 Block and Mopar W-8 Aluminum Heads
Horsepower:	700+
Redline:	8500+ rpm
Gearbox:	4-Speed Manual
Brakes:	4-Wheel Disc Brakes

Massey did everything she could to cut expenses to the bone, but the Museum was still not able to pay its way.

By 1997, the Museum was on the verge of losing its lease at the Junction Street facility, and John Parham was planning to break ground for a purpose-built store for J&P Cycles on Lazelle Street in Sturgis. Parham proposed to revise his plans to create a new home for the Museum. Because he understood the problems faced by the operation, he negotiated a deal that provided for rent on a sliding scale so the Museum would pay less in the off-season. After the Museum board explored two other opportunities for housing, it confirmed an agreement with Parham, and John revised his building plans to provide more than 7,000 square feet of space for exhibits. It seemed like a very good idea. There would be ample parking at the new Lazelle Street property, and the traffic generated by J&P Cycles would feed Museum attendance, and vice versa. In retrospect, Massey believes that the advantages offered at J&P's new building were probably offset by the fact that the National Motorcycle Museum lost its proximity to the I-90 off-ramp. She recalls, "Attendance still did not come up to expectations. The Museum still could not earn enough to meet its obligations."

Jeff Carstensen reports that within a year of moving into the Lazelle Street property, a bank to which the Museum owed money was requesting additional collateral, and at its meeting after the Rally in 1999, the board began to discuss the idea of closing the Museum. Carstensen says, "John and some of the other board members were opposed to this idea. They did not want to see the Museum disappear." In addition, E.J. Cole signed a note at the bank so additional collateral would not be required. With these developments, the Museum board decided to give the project another year, hoping its fortunes would improve in 2000. Unfortunately, this did not happen, and as the 2000 Rally and Museum board meeting approached, there was a lot of informal discussion about the fate of the project. Parham recalls, "Within the board there was a lot of discouragement, and there did not seem to be sufficient will to continue. A consensus seemed to be forming that the Museum should be closed." Carstensen explains, "John was still not willing to give up, and he agreed to take full responsibility for the project. As a result, at the 2000 meeting he was elected president, and then the entire board resigned so he could form a new board of individuals who wanted to keep the Museum open." In fact, so few showed up for the 2000 meeting, there was barely a quorum, and it was clear that a new board had to be selected if there would be any hope of moving the project forward.

As the new president of the corporation, Parham was in a position to get a

The actual Captain America bike from the movie "Easy Rider" holds a special place in the museum and the exhibit is complete with artwork, memorabilia and the certificate of authenticity signed by Peter Fonda.

Below: Maria Tuttle, John, and Jeff Carstensen receive the Iowa Tourism's "Attraction of the Year" Award for the National Motorcycle Museum in 2001.

A display of Harley-Davidsons, historical advertisements, and pedal toys at the National Motorcycle Museum. In the center is John's 1955 Panhead.

Below: A display of drag bikes, featuring the late Elmer Trett's top fuel machine, the fastest drag racing motorcycle on Earth.

full and accurate picture of the financial situation. He says, "It was worse than I realized. I knew the Museum was in debt $50,000 to the bank, but then I discovered it was in debt another $20,000 to suppliers. The Museum had goods on consignment it had sold, but still owed the consigners because that money had been spent on operations." He continues, "We could not even find consignment receipts, and we actually had to call consigners to ask what we owed them." Today John laughs, "I still think I have some refrigerator magnets and stuff that were left over from the Museum when it was still in Sturgis." He continues, "It was not my intention at that time to move the Museum, but it became clear we would lose another $10,000 over the winter." Parham and the new board watched the attendance figures go from 100 in September to 60 in October, then in November a grand total of 15 people walked through the door for an income amounting to one-half visitor per day! "Finally," he says, "I had to make a decision with my business head, not my motorcycle heart. I knew there was nothing I could do to improve the situation from 800 miles away while the place continued to hemorrhage money, so if there were any hope of keeping the National Motorcycle Museum alive, it would not be so in Sturgis." Parham paid off all the Museum's debts and made plans to move it over the winter to Anamosa.

Despite the fact that Parham bailed out the organization by paying off the Museum's debts, there were people in town and some members of the board who felt he had an obligation to keep it going in Sturgis. Neil Hultman, a Jackpine Gypsy, former Rally Director, and a strong supporter of the Museum project from its inception, says, "I understood it was going to stay in Sturgis, but within six months he was making plans to move it to Iowa. I told him, 'You can take Mount Rushmore as far as I'm concerned, but please don't take the Museum!'" Others in the community had feelings even stronger than Hultman's, and they leveled harsh criticism toward John. Regardless of what members of the Museum board and community might have understood, Parham was convinced he could not make the operation survive in Sturgis, especially since he would not be there to manage it most of the year, and having discovered that its balance sheet was much worse than he had been told. Parham was deeply hurt by the public criticism he received for closing the Museum. Buzz Kanter, the publisher of *American Iron* and a longtime friend of John and Jill, says, "John felt like he had done everything he could to rescue the project, and he spent a lot of money to bail out the organization.

There were some unhappy locals, but I suspect they had no idea how deep he had reached into his own pockets."

Carstensen, who had worked at J&P Cycles since 1992, had departed recently to pursue an opportunity in the agriculture supply industry, and John urged him to return to manage the Museum and help turn it into a going concern. Carstensen says, "We went out to close and mothball the Sturgis facility in November 2000, and we spent the winter renovating a former hardware store that John had purchased on Main Street in Anamosa, then in March 2001 we began to bring back about 40 bikes that belonged to John, or to lenders who wanted them to stay on display with the museum in Anamosa. Other lenders were asked to come collect their bikes in Sturgis. We opened the new National Motorcycle Museum in May 2001 with about 60 motorcycles and John's toy collection on display." Some in Sturgis remained critical of Parham for moving the Museum, but for most it is a closed chapter. They realize that John Parham chose to protect the motorcycle history and traditions that he loves rather than see the National Motorcycle Museum disappear. Those who criticize the moving of the Museum fail to remember that its own board of Sturgis-based supporters had no plan for making it solvent, and was ready to let it go under until John paid off its debts. And for some of the most unhappy critics, time and unfolding events have softened their feelings. For example, Neil Hultman, who was very angry about the relocation of the Museum, now thinks it might have been a blessing in disguise. He says, "I think people in Sturgis took it for granted. They thought it would always be there, and they did not appreciate it until it was gone. I think this caused some community people to get serious about creating and supporting another new museum in Sturgis who never offered any support to the first one."

George Barnard, a J&P contractor who witnessed the drama surrounding the survival of the Museum, says, "I think it turned out for the best. It woke the board up and made the City adopt a more involved and positive attitude toward having a museum. As a result, they have done very well." Indeed, Hultman's and Barnard's opinions seem to be supported by the facts. When it became clear that the National Motorcycle Museum was moving to Anamosa, the people of Sturgis—including school children—began volunteering time to renovate an old church. Gene and Nancy Flagler, the owners of the church, offered it as a new museum site for a rent of one dollar per month. Bob Illingworth, a motorcycle dealer who had recently retired and moved to Sturgis from Minneapolis in 2000 for the beauty of its scenery, became a leader in the development of the new museum. Illingworth says, "People were upset,

A collection of Harley-Davidsons at the National Motorcycle Museum in front of an original billboard from the 1920s.

Below: The engine collection at the National Motorcycle Museum includes over 50 different motors.

Vincents and Broughs, the two most valuable brands among classic British motorcycles.

Bottom: A display of Von Dutch artifacts, including a Triumph motorcycle painted by Von Dutch and customized by Bud Ekins.

and I told them, 'Look, it doesn't matter if the National Motorcycle Museum moved out of town. We still have something that no other motorcycle museum can have, and that is the name 'Sturgis.'" Perhaps the name "Sturgis" did bring a pride and power to the project that a "National" museum had never enjoyed, because before Illingworth was through, he had acquired $150,000 in grants from the State. In addition, most of the lenders who did not want motorcycles to go to Anamosa were more than willing to be part of the new plan. Illingworth says, "Among the lenders who wanted their bikes to stay in Sturgis, we had more than enough to start a new museum." The Sturgis Motorcycle Museum and Hall of Fame opened its doors at its new and temporary home on June 1, 2001. Soon, Sturgis Mayor Mark Ziegler offered the city's former post office building as a permanent home for $100 a month. But Illingworth brought his negotiating skills to bear once again, and came away with the post office as an outright gift, with the provision that it would be returned to the City if the Museum were ever to be dissolved. This put the new Sturgis Motorcycle Museum and Hall of Fame at the corner of Main Street and Junction Avenue, which is the epicenter of activity during the Rally. The new Museum opened in July 2002, and has since expanded from one to two floors, and continues to benefit from strong community support. More than 80 motorcycles are on display. John Parham says, "If it had not been for the arrival of Bob Illingworth in Sturgis, I doubt that the new Museum would have ever gotten off the ground. In fact, I wish he had arrived a couple of years sooner, before the National Motorcycle Museum failed in Sturgis and had to be moved to Anamosa to survive. With Bob's energetic support and good marketing ideas, perhaps things would have been different."

Illingworth, however, was not yet finished in healing the wounds that were caused when the National Motorcycle Museum left town. Except among a few people who would not let go of their anger over the issue, John Parham had become an important and beneficial investor in the community, and when Illingworth learned that Mike Corbin had nominated John to the Sturgis Motorcycle Hall of Fame in 2006, he saw it as an opportunity to complete a healing process. Illingworth became one of the strongest supporters for John's induction into the Hall of Fame, which brought closure to the issue for the great majority of the people of Sturgis. Mike Corbin recalls, "Actually, I think it was Bob's idea. He thought it was necessary for healing old wounds and recognizing John for all the good things he has done for Sturgis, and I was more than happy to be the one to put forward the nomination." Corbin adds, "I guess it does not matter who had the idea, and maybe we both did. The point is that nobody loves motorcycles more than John. He is doing something good for motorcycling 25 hours a day, and no one is more deserving of the Hall of Fame recognition." About the recognition, John Parham says, "That was a great honor for me. Sturgis has become a very important part of my life, and especially after some of the controversy around the National Motorcycle Museum, it was very important to me to receive this honor and gesture of acceptance." Jill adds, "John's acceptance speech had people in tears. I think they all know how important being part of the Sturgis community is to both of us."

☙

The new National Motorcycle Museum and Hall of Fame opened in Anamosa in May, 2001. Ironically, this too brought a bit of controversy, which in retrospect, seems quite amusing. When word began to circulate that the museum was being moved to Anamosa from Sturgis, a misunderstanding traveled through the rumor mill that John had somehow arranged for the entire Sturgis Rally to move to Anamosa. This was a prospect that some locals were not too excited about, and, incredibly, there were still those who believed in the 50-year-old idea, advanced by the movie "The Wild One," that hoards of bikers were prowling the nation and capable of swooping down to take over small rural communities in the heartland. In fact, great numbers of motorcyclists had been descending on Anamosa for J&P Cycles' annual open house for years, but most of them came in and out on Route 151, and had no reason to detour through the heart of town. In 2001 it was different, and Main Street filled up with motorcyclists who came into town to visit the new National Motorcycle Museum. Anamosa Mayor John Hatcher grins as he recalls, "This farmer with his eyes bugging out came to me and demanded, 'Have you called the National Guard yet?' I didn't know what he was talking about, and I started laughing, and he shouted, 'No, I'm serious, the street is full of bikers and there's going to be trouble!'"

Today, Anamosa has gotten used to the great number of motorcyclists who are attracted annually by the now nationally-famous J&P Cycles and the National Motorcycle Museum. Speaking for the community, Mayor Hatcher says, "The Museum is a positive contribution to Main Street. The visitors spend money, buy food, and stay overnight. Except for the coldest months of the winter, you can always see motorcycles in the hotel and local business parking lots, bearing license plates from all over North America." He adds, "I find the bikers enjoyable. You can learn more from a total stranger than you can from the people you know. We get as many as 12,000 motorcyclists in town for the Open House, and it is clearly a benefit to the local economy." With the amount of traffic the Museum has brought to Anamosa, Parham has broadened his collection in deference to his visitors. He says, "If I displayed only what I like best, most of the motorcycles would be pre-1920. I really love the old stuff. But I

John and Jill with good friend and fellow Hall of Fame inductee John Reed at the 2006 Sturgis Rally.

Below: John and Jill on the set of the Tonight Show with fellow motorcycle collectors Jay Leno and Somer and Loyce Hooker.

"American Thunder" hostess Michele Smith and Arlen Ness with John, Jill, and Zach at Daytona Bike Week 2008.

Below: John with Willie G. and Nancy Davidson at Davenport. Willie G. subsequently purchased this Harley WR racer from John for his personal collection.

know our visitors like to see a wide variety of brands, styles, and periods, so we have tried to develop our collection accordingly."

Today, with 14,000 square feet of exhibit space, the National Motorcycle Museum has more than 225 motorcycles on display that range from 1904 through 2000. They represent brands from every part of world, plus there are custom motorcycles and oddities, such as a homemade steam-powered machine, one-off "art bikes," and V-eight powered monsters. The collection includes an excellent group of early Harley-Davidsons, beginning with a 1905. Among them are some of the oldest, complete original-paint Harleys in the nation, including examples from 1908 and 1909. There is also an array of Indians, starting with a 1903 and including eight-valve and six-valve racers, and an extremely rare 1905 Indian Tri-car. For those who like the great British classics, there are four Broughs and eight Vincents, including an example of the rare and beautiful China Red Touring Rapide, plus Ariel Square Fours and Sunbeams. For the Baby Boomers looking for nostalgia bikes, you'll find a Mustang, Cushmans, a Vespa, and many of the early Japanese brands from the late 1950s and early 1960s. The artifacts include nice collections of Von Dutch and Evel Knievel memorabilia, and a vast array of photographs, posters, product literature, accessories, apparel, engines, plus one of the largest motorcycle toy collections in the world.

Arguably, one of the most valuable motorcycles in the collection is the Captain America chopper ridden by Peter Fonda as Wyatt in the movie "Easy Rider," which was released in 1969. Its strange chain of custody adds even more to its value. For filming, four surplus police bikes were acquired from the LAPD. All four were chopped and customized, resulting in two Billy Bikes, the yellow and red chopper ridden by Wyatt's sidekick Billy, and two Captain America choppers with their sparkling chrome and stars-and-stripes fuel tanks. In the final scene of the movie, one of the Captain America choppers was destroyed, literally, which was accomplished by pushing the bike out of the back of a speeding pickup. The three other bikes—the two Billy Bikes and the Captain America chopper—were retained by Fonda and subsequently stolen from a storage facility. No one has ever seen or heard of them again, and since the movie at that time had not yet achieved its iconic status, there is little doubt that the thieves quickly dismantled and cut them up for parts. The wrecked Captain America bike was given by Fonda to Dan Haggerty, who played a bit part in "Easy Rider" and later earned fame on television as Grizzly Adams. Haggerty restored the machine, thus finding himself many years later with a collectible that had gained enormous status as the most recognizable motorcycle in the world, due to the popularity of "Easy Rider," which had become a cult classic. Parham acquired the bike, and while there are many Captain America replicas in museums all over the United States, this one is the only to have a certificate of authenticity signed by Fonda and Haggerty. The museum also has pedigreed machines once ridden by Steve McQueen, Malcolm Smith, and the artist Von Dutch. During its inaugural year in Anamosa, the National Motorcycle Museum was named by the Iowa Department of Tourism as "Attraction of the Year," and since that time, Parham has continued to add motorcycles and artifacts, building it into one of the leading motorcycle museums in North America. As a result, it has attracted some famous visitors as well. On July 19, 2003, for example, while campaigning for his bid to become President of the United States, Democratic nominee John Kerry selected the museum as a backdrop for a speech, then took a spin through Anamosa on a new Harley-Davidson V-Rod.

☙

John Parham's interest in the preservation of the nation's motorcycle heritage has not been limited to the promotion of events and the development of his own museum. In fact, he has generously collaborated with other museums and supported high-profile exhibits. One leading museum with which he has collaborated is the Motorcycle Hall of Fame Museum, affiliated with the American Motorcyclist Association, in Pickerington, Ohio. The fact that both museums were maintaining halls of fame led to a discussion in 2004 that resulted a year later in Parham resigning the hall of fame function to the AMA-affiliated museum to focus on the collection and presentation aspect of his own facility. While the National Motorcycle Museum in Anamosa still honors the Hall of Fame inductees, the job of managing the program has been turned over to the organization in Ohio. As part of the arrangement, Parham was offered a seat on the board of the Motorcycle Hall of Fame Museum. Its Executive Director, Mark Mederski, says, "We value John's role on our board. He is connected and knows the world of collectible motorcycles. He brings valuable knowledge to our organization, and his presence on our board undoubtedly enhances our credibility." Mederski adds, "He is a good businessman, and he is interested in the advancement of all motorcycle museums, not just his own."

Over the years, Parham has generously shared motorcycles from his collection with temporary exhibits in major museums and galleries throughout the nation. These include the Wonders Museum in Memphis and the Orlando Museum of Art, both of which hosted the Guggenheim's legendary The Art of the Motorcycle Exhibition. He has also lent his bikes for display at the Columbus College of Art and Design in Columbus, Ohio, the Saratoga Automobile Museum in Saratoga Springs, New York, the Petersen Automotive Museum in Los Angeles, and the Legend of the Motorcycle Concours d'Elegance, staged annually at the Ritz Carlton Hotel in Half Moon Bay, California. In fact, in 2007, his Steve McQueen Indian chopper provided the backdrop for the prize-giving ceremony at the event, presided over by Chad McQueen and Steve's widow, Barbara. Parham has readily supported other exhibits and institutions because it is consistent with his desire to promote motorcycling, which dates back to his teenage years.

In addition, Parham has advanced motorcycling as a patron of fine art. Two decades ago, no one would have thought of the motorcycle as a subject suitable for art, but as motorcycling became more popular, artists began to treat them seriously in painting and

John, Jill and Indian Larry on Jill's 50th Birthday in Sturgis 2004 right before his passing.

Below: John and Branscombe Richmond at the 2003 National Motorcycle Museum Hall of Fame Induction breakfast.

sculpture. These include David Uhl, Jeff Decker, Tom Fritz, Scott Jacobs, Steve Posson, Ric Stewart, and Stanley Wanless. Decker relates, "When I started doing bronze based on motorcycle history, the fine art world did not take us seriously, and it was hard to find ways to get exposure. I had been going to Davenport as a motorcycle collector and trader, and one year I set out some of my bronzes in my booth. John Parham was the first guy to leave his card with a note, 'I want one of these. How much?'" Decker met Parham and over the years has become a family friend, and John has purchased every motorcycle sculpture Decker has ever produced. Decker says, "He is more than a friend and a customer. He is a patron. He gave me confidence because I always knew I could pay for my molds, because I would sell at least one of my works to John's collection, and I knew it would be displayed at his museum."

Scott Jacobs also speaks of the evolution of motorcycle art to fine art status. Today he has clients in 82 countries around the world, and half of his paintings are privately commissioned, but it was not always that way. He says, "I started painting for Harley-Davidson in 1993, but I was not happy with how the work was being received. It was quite popular among Harley-Davidson owners, but they were buying prints and hanging them in their garage. They did not yet understand that this art could be shown in their dens and living rooms. It was not enough to paint the motorcycles, we had to start painting them in historical and classy settings that told a captivating story about the role of the motorcycle. Then people began to see that this wasn't garage or barroom art." Jacobs believes John Parham had a material role in this process. He explains, "When John bought a painting, I knew it was going to end up in the National Motorcycle Museum. It was going to be hung in a serious setting and be seen by thousands of people. This undoubtedly helped popularize motorcycle art and helped people understand it could be the subject of fine art, just as much as landscapes, portraits, and still life."

David Uhl, a painter who works in oils and uses light and shadow reminiscent of Rembrandt, has sold a number of his original paintings and numbered prints to Parham, and has been commissioned by John to create an original portrait. Uhl says, "In creating a portrait of John, I felt it was my task to not just picture him in an Indian jersey with his board-track motorcycle, but to capture his love of the vintage era. John, I believe, was born in the wrong time, and I wanted to paint him in a style that looked like it was done in 1917. I did not want to do photo-realism; I wanted it to look like it came from the period where John and his Indian both belonged." Listening to Uhl describe his creative task, it becomes clear that John Parham is not just a collector of fine art and patron of artists, but that he provides inspiration as well.

Surely, when he was struggling to establish J&P Cycles in the late 1980s and early '90s, John Parham could not have imagined that one day he would have the resources to develop one of the top personal collections of motorcycles, memorabilia, and motorcycle fine art in America, and become both an art patron and sponsor of one of America's leading motorcycle museums.

John with Willie G. Davidson in 2006 when John was inducted into the Sturgis Motorcycle Hall of Fame.

John, Jill and Michael Lichter with John's 1911 Flying Merkel Board Track Racer at Michael's 2005 Journey Museum exhibition during the Sturgis rally.

Chapter Nine: The John Parham Collection

John Parham's first collectible motorcycle was his beloved 1955 Harley-Davidson FLH Panhead, which he acquired in 1978. Although he realized it was of collectible value, it also became his and Jill's main rider. Today it is a focal point of the National Motorcycle Museum among the more than 225 motorcycles that are on display. The great majority of these are from Parham's private collection, which today numbers more than 170 motorcycles, plus thousands of pieces of memorabilia, including apparel, engines, photographs, posters, art, literature, and motorcycle toys.

About his collecting, John acknowledges that his tastes and objectives have changed over the years. He explains, "First it was Indians and Harleys. That's about all I was interested in. Then, as I began to take an interest in other American brands, I got into the shiny stuff, acquiring a number of fine motorcycles that by today's standards would be considered over-restored. My personal taste tends toward the very old motorcycles, mostly pre-1920, but with the opening of the National Motorcycle Museum in Anamosa, I began to pay attention to the interests of our visitors. I began to acquire later model motorcycles and European brands to provide a broader and more eclectic exhibit. Lately, my attention has turned toward the very rare original paint machines. These have a purity that appeals to my sense of history and antiquity. A motorcycle can be restored any number of times, but you can never recreate original paint. These original, complete, and un-restored machines, in my opinion, are a great treasure that should be preserved at any cost."

We hope you enjoy the following pages depicting examples from the John Parham collection. You can learn more about John's collection by taking his personal tour on the free DVD included with this book.

John Parham and his rare 1938 Crocker.
(Ed Youngblood photo)

1903 Indian Single
During 1902, its first year of production, Indian built only 143 motorcycles. In 1903, 376 were built. With barely more than 500 produced in the first two model years, and only a couple of authentic '02s known to exist, a 1903 Indian is a very rare and desirable collectible motorcycle. With a reliable engine designed by Oscar Hedstrom, and chain drive when most motorcycles used a troublesome leather belt, Indian won national endurance competitions in 1902, 1903, and 1904, establishing the reputation that would quickly take it to the top of the industry. During its first decade of production, Indian became the largest motorcycle manufacturer in the world. As with early Harley-Davidsons, early Indians have been totally replicated, making the real McCoys even more valuable.

1906 Curtiss Twin
Glenn Curtiss was a brilliant early motorcycle designer who would later become a leading aeronautical engineer. He built his first motorcycle in 1901 and his first V-twin, as pictured here, in 1905, two years ahead of Indian and four years ahead of Harley-Davidson. His finest hour as a motorcyclist came in 1907 when he piloted a special V-8 machine to a world speed record of 136.36 mph at Ormond Beach, Florida. Subsequently, Curtiss ceased motorcycle manufacturing, shifting his attention entirely to aviation. Because of their rarity, Curtiss motorcycles are extremely desirable among collectors.

1908 Harley-Davidson, Original Paint
There is a debate among historians as to whether Harley-Davidson produced its first motorcycle in 1903 or 1904. Today, the Motor Company insists that it dates back to 1903, but, curiously, for fifty years it acknowledged that its first motorcycle was built in 1904. At any rate, early Harley-Davidsons are so rare that complete and accurate examples have been reproduced in replica form, and a collector must be very careful as to the pedigree and originality of such machines. Certain proof of the correctness of a rare collectible is original paint, as is the case with this 1908 model. As a very early original paint machine, it is one of the most valuable Harley-Davidsons on Earth.

1908 Indian Twin Racer
Indian, which began production in 1902, developed an early reputation for good performance and reliability through racing. The Springfield, Massachusetts company built its first V-twin motorcycle in 1907, and in 1908 it offered a production racing model, featuring low handlebars, open exhaust pipes, and a rear-positioned seat so the rider could lie down over the gas tank to reduce wind resistance. The racing twin had seven horsepower – nearly twice that of the standard twin – weighed five pounds less, and, at $350, cost nearly 50 percent more.

1908 Reading Standard
Reading-Standard, based in Reading, Pennsylvania, began in 1903 with a single-cylinder model that fairly copied the Indian, including the same engine, manufactured under the Thor brand. In 1906, Reading-Standard started building its own engines, designed by Charles Gustafson, who would later take his knowledge and skills to Indian. In 1908, Gustafson produced a new F-head, V-twin design that proved to be a superior engine for street machines that was even moderately successful in racing. It embodies Gustafson's ideas that would later go into the spectacularly successful Indian Powerplus engine. As a rare and early v-twin, this motorcycle is very valuable. R-S continued production until 1922, when it was acquired by the Cleveland Motorcycle Manufacturing Company.

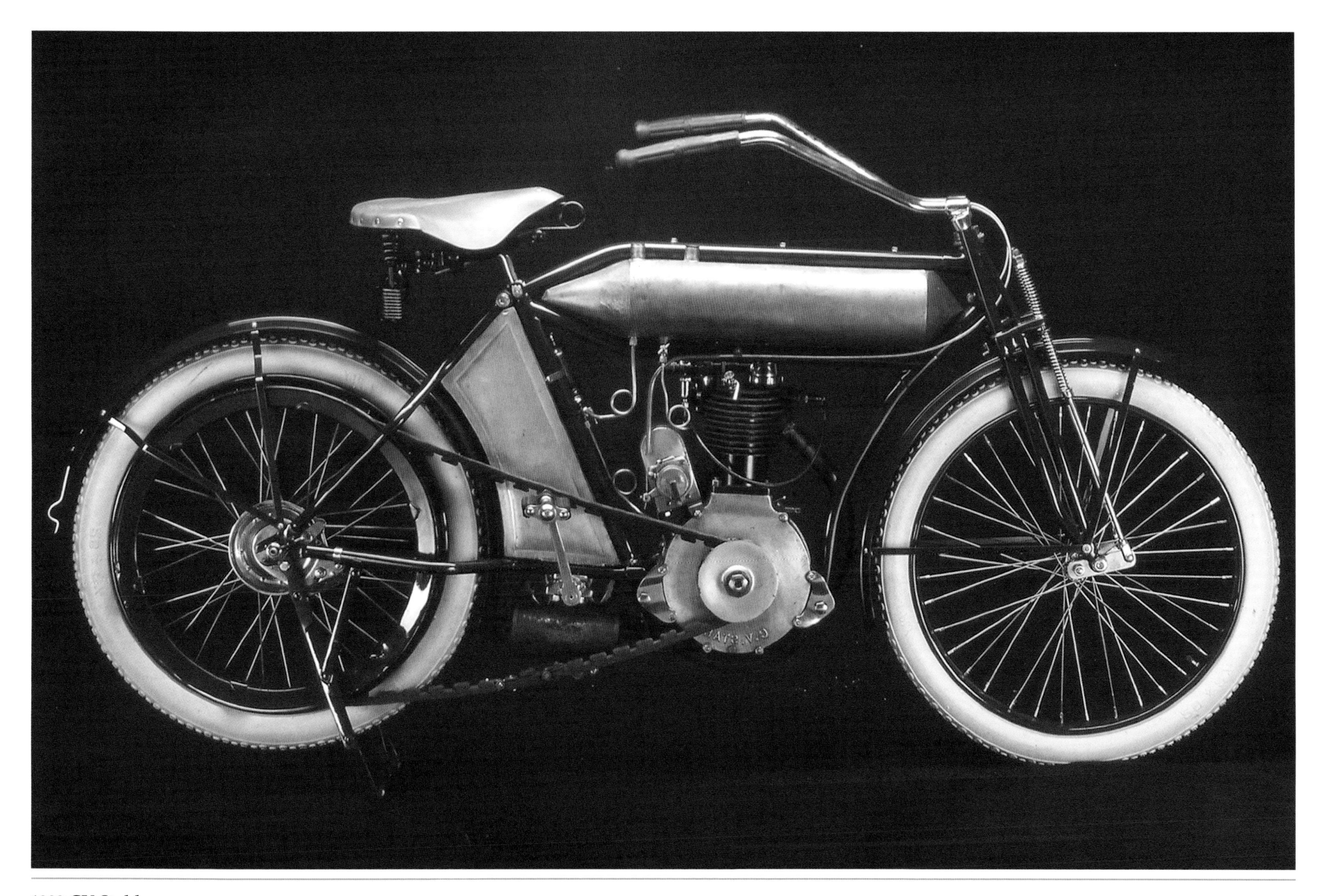

1909 CV Stahl

The Home Motor Manufacturing Company, later called CV Stahl, was based in Philadelphia and began in 1901 to offer small engines designed to be mounted on a bicycle. Later, it began to offer complete motorcycles with 500cc single and 1,000cc twin-cylinder engines. Like most of the early minor American brands, CV Stahl did not survive the teens, ending motorcycle production in 1917. Today, examples of the CV Stahl are extremely rare.

1910 Harley-Davidson Single Cylinder Belt Drive
In 1912, Harley-Davidson updated its product significantly by moving from belt to chain drive with multi-plate clutch, and by improving comfort with a "spring post" seat. Until the Motor Company offered an olive green color in 1919, gray was its trademark livery, giving rise to the nick name "Silent Gray Fellows." Unlike other leading American brands, in this period Harley-Davidson refused to get involved in racing. Rather, it built its reputation on robust construction and reliability, aiming its product at tradesmen and people who wanted trouble-free commuters. This example has original paint except for the gas tank and battery box which were repainted over 50 years ago.

1911 Flying Merkel
Merkel, founded in Milwaukee in 1902, built its reputation on early racing success, much of which can be attributed to the innovative engineer/rider Maldwyn Jones. Thanks to the brand's success as a speedster, in 1910 its name was changed to "Flying Merkel." Although a small and under-funded company, Merkel gave both Indian and Harley-Davidson fits on the race track. As one of the first motorcycles to use both front and rear suspension, the company boasted, "All roads are smooth to the Flying Merkel." Flying Merkel production came to an end in 1915. This example is the rare flat-tank board track racing model.

1912 Henderson

In addition to Indian and Harley-Davidson, the third great early American brand was the Henderson. Designed by William Henderson, this luxurious motorcycle first appeared in 1912. Its unusually long frame was intended to provide a smooth ride over the rough roads of the era, and a passenger seat could be mounted in front of the rider so a female passenger might be better protected from the elements by the car-like floor board of the machine. Though expensive, the Henderson was valued for police work because its engine could lug along at a walking pace, then accelerate to high speed without being taken out of top gear. Later, William Henderson went on to design the four-cylinder Ace. After Henderson's death, the company was acquired by Indian, and his design evolved into the famous Indian Four. Examples of the 1912 Henderson that still exist can be counted on one hand, and this one is especially valuable because it is the only original paint 1912 model known to exist. Even the leather and tool box are original.

1912 Indian Six-Valve Racer

As the level of competition among the brands escalated during the first decade of the 20th century, Indian engineer Oscar Hedstrom was determined to keep his brand at the head of the pack, and in 1911 he created an eight-valve, v-twin, 1,000cc racer, utilizing the latest aero engine technology. Indian's eight-valve machines dominated racing into the teens, until they were finally displaced by the company's new Powerplus engine, which was more reliable and cheaper to build. Still, the multi-valve racers held sway until 1920. While eight-valve models are quite rare, this six-valve (three valves per cylinder) is even more unusual because the Indian racing department never built such a machine. The three-valve heads—featuring two exhaust and one intake valve—were an aftermarket product installed by a private owner. This recreation began as an engine only, owned for many years by Bob McClean, the President of the Antique Motorcycle Club of America. After acquiring the engine, which is built from a 1912 lower end, John Parham had his friend Dave Ohrt create a racing-style chassis by using a 1912 Indian frame. This type of construction is historically accurate because many privateer racers who could not acquire an Indian factory machine did exactly the same thing, building racing machines with high-performance engines in modified street chassis. Because of its short wheelbase, the 1912 frame was excellent for home-built racers.

1913 Indian Twin
In its early days, Indian outpaced its competition with constant innovation and design improvements. In 1909 it introduced a stronger frame, in 1910 it offered an improved leaf-spring front suspension, and in 1913 it became one of the first to offer rear suspension, also utilizing automotive-type leaf springs. It was this year—1913—when Indian achieved its all-time highest production, with sales of 32,000 motorcycles. Although there were over 100 brands available by the middle teens, one of every three motorcycles in use was an Indian. Well-suited for the road, an Indian such as this could also be outfitted with gas lighting.

1913 Sears
Sears, Roebuck, and Company began offering motorcycles in 1910, built by Aurora Automatic Machine, the same company that once supplied Hedstrom engines to Indian. In 1912, Sears switched to the Excelsior Cycle Company, a Chicago firm that produced for several early brands. These models, which continued until 1916, used single and twin-cylinder DeLuxe engines built by Spacke. Like many American manufacturers, Sears abandoned the market in the mid-teens. The Sears DeLuxe Twin is an extremely rare model. This example was restored by Steve Huntzinger for Otis Chandler, then acquired from the Otis Chandler collection.

1914 Yale Twin

Yale, based in Toledo, Ohio, entered the motorcycle market in 1903 when it acquired the California brand, which had just distinguished itself by becoming the first motorcycle to be ridden from coast to coast by George Wyman. In 1913, Yale introduced a V-twin, a beautiful engine that featured unique horizontal cooling fins. Although the company offered sporting models, such as this example, Yale was better known for endurance than for speed racing. Consolidated Manufacturing Company, which built the Yale, ceased motorcycle production to focus on war materials in 1915. Noted for their quality and attention to detail, Yale is considered by many collectors to be the most beautiful and stylish motorcycle of its era. When noted custom bike designer Arlen Ness visited the National Motorcycle Museum in 2005, he declared that this motorcycle was his favorite of all because of its styling and beautiful lines.

1916 Iver Johnson

Iver Johnson was long known for the manufacture of guns, and had been building bicycles for over 20 years when it decided to get into the motorcycle business in 1907. Reflecting its tradition as a precision weapons manufacturer, the company produced a high-quality motorcycle with excellent fit and finish. Unlike other designs of the era, its V-twin engine had its crank pins spaced to give it a regular firing order that made it sound more like a vertical twin. Owners had a choice of a rigid frame or a swinging arm rear suspension. With the outbreak of World War I, Iver Johnson ceased the manufacture of motorcycles and turned its attention to munitions. While any Iver Johnson is a valued collectible, this one is unique and has an incredible history. It was assembled entirely from new-old-stock parts left over after Iver Johnson ceased motorcycle production. The footboards and a few other parts have been fabricated, but 90 percent of the motorcycle is brand new. The beautiful paint you see here is not the result of restoration. It is original, as applied at the factory. The engine is brand new and has never been run, other than its initial starting at the factory.

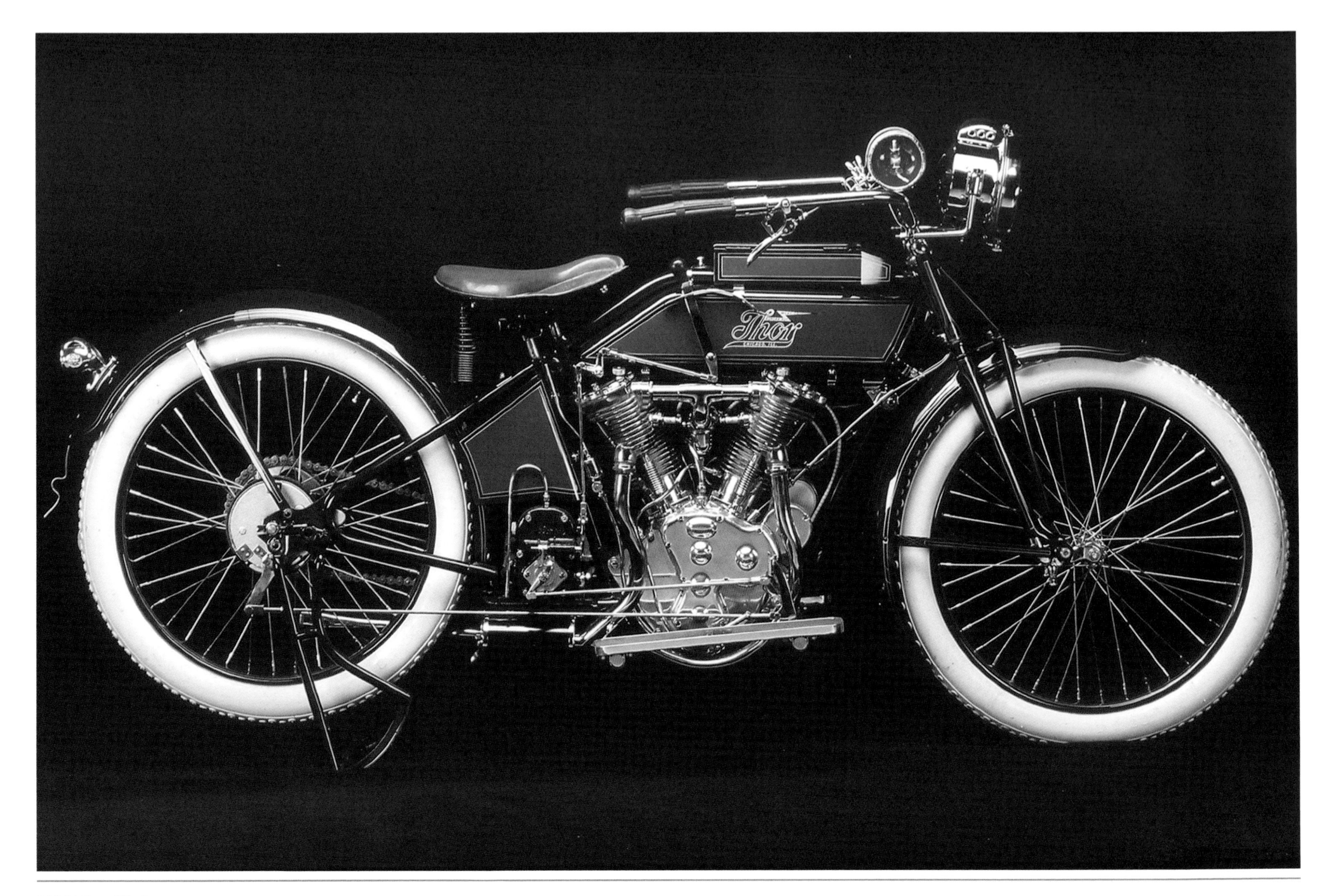

1916 Thor Twin
The Aurora Automatic Machine Company, which built engines for Indian from 1902 through 1907, decided to launch its own Thor brand in 1902, with rights to use Indian's Oscar Hedstrom-designed engine. Thor introduced its own V-twin engine in 1910 which set several speed records. However, unable to keep up with Indian and Excelsior, Thor withdrew from racing in 1915. A model with full road equipment, such as this example, sold for under $300. After 1916, Aurora sold its motorcycle inventory to concentrate on the manufacture of power tools.

1921 Harley-Davidson Model J Racer
Harley-Davidson stayed out of racing until 1914, at which time it introduced a production racing model and hired Thor engineer William Ottaway to set up a factory racing department, aiming to overtake Indian's long experience in racing. By 1921, Harley-Davidson had become dominant on the race track, and in that year proudly awarded a plaque to its team rider Otto Walker for becoming the first person to be clocked on a board track at a speed of 100 miles per hour. This 1921 Harley-Davidson racer from the John Parham collection is not like the eight-valve factory machine that Walker rode; rather it is a beautiful example of the Motor Company's Model J, modified for racing. It is typical of the kind of motorcycle a privateer would have built and raced at the time. The 1,000cc Model J was very popular among sporting riders, even when maintained in street trim and not modified for racing.

1927 Brough Superior SS100
Known as "the Rolls Royce of motorcycles," the British-built Brough Superior is considered by many the best motorcycle ever made, and today it is arguably the most desirable of all collectible classics. Some of its mystique may be attributed to the fact that T.E. Lawrence (of Arabia) was a devoted fan who owned seven, wrote romantically about them, and was finally killed aboard a Brough. Their desirability is clearly enhanced by their rarity, since in 21 years of production only 3,048 were built, and about 1,000 are known to still exist today. The SS100, manufactured from 1921 through 1940, is the most desirable model of the Brough. Brough enjoys a stunning reputation for a motorcycle brand that never mass produced its own engines, but bought in engines from Matchless and JAP.

1929 Harley-Davidson JDH
In 1929, the Model JDH was the top of the Harley-Davidson line. With its 1,200cc twin cam engine, it was considered a high-performance motorcycle, and, at $370, the most expensive motorcycle the Motor Company had offered to date. This was also the only year that Harley-Davidson offered the stylish twin headlights. In many ways it represented the end of an era. When the stock market crashed in October that year and the Great Depression arrived, Harley-Davidson began to focus for the next six years on a line of motorcycles with simpler and less-costly side-valve engines.

1930 Moto Guzzi Falcone Sport
Established in 1921 by two Italian WWI aircraft pilots and their mechanic, Moto Guzzi is now Europe's oldest manufacturer of motorcycles in continuous production. Its history shines with technical innovation and racing success. The company's first engine design was a 500cc horizontal single—as seen in this Falcone Sport—which remained a trademark of the brand for 45 years. The Falcone Sport is a sport touring machine that traces its roots back to Guzzis' earliest racing motorcycles. In addition to its large, distinctive, deeply-finned horizontal cylinder, it is characterized by its large external flywheel, which some call a "bologna slicer."

1936 Norton International
Founded in 1902, Norton established its sporting reputation very early by winning the inaugural Tourist Trophy races at the Isle of Man 1907. Norton won the TT again in 1924, '25, and '27, the latter of which was with a new overhead-cam engine that would become the brand's signature design. During the next decade, its 350cc and 500cc overhead cam engines won no less than 14 TTs. The Norton International, introduced in 1933, made the 500cc overhead-cam engine available both in a fully-equipped road machine, or a highly competitive production racer. Norton's big singles were eventually displaced on the race track by a new generation of Italian multi-cylinder machines, but the Norton Manx—a racing machine similar to the International—continued to make its mark into the 1950s, earning victories in both the Senior and Junior TTs in 1961.

1938 Crocker
Taking his styling cues from the high-performance "bobbers" that appeared on California streets in the 1930s, in 1936 Albert Crocker introduced a hand-crafted, limited-production motorcycle that has become one of the most valuable collectibles in the world. It is to American collectible motorcycles what the Brough is to British, because of its reputation for speed and because less than 100 were built. Making liberal use of light alloys, it had more horsepower, but weighed more than 80 pounds less than a Harley-Davidson Knucklehead. It was considered an expensive motorcycle in its day; at $550, it cost 25 percent more than a Knucklehead. The last Crockers were built in 1940. This piece came from the Bill Harrah collection and was owned by Otis Chandler before being acquired for the National Motorcycle Museum.

1939 Harley-Davidson Knucklehead Bobber

Motorcycle sales were so bad during the Great Depression that Harley-Davidson was down to a two-day work week. Under these dire circumstances, the Motor Company took one of the biggest risks in its history, allocating resources to design a totally new motorcycle. Nearly five years in development, it appeared in 1936 as the Model EL, a revolutionary machine with overhead valves, a re-circulating lubrication system, and totally new frame and styling. It made its name immediately by setting speed and endurance records in 1937. This is the motorcycle that became known to its fans as the "Knucklehead," supposedly because the large chrome nuts on the right side of the cylinder heads look like the four knuckles of a fist. The Knucklehead became a great favorite for its performance, and was ridden hard by its owners. This example was built by Dave Ohrt to look like the kind of motorcycle a working-class biker might have ridden during the 1940s, modifying it somewhat with the ornamental reflectors on the rear fender and the name of his motorcycle club on the gas tank, in this case the Piston Splitters MC from Elm Grove, Illinois. Other than these slight changes, it is a no-nonsense machine, clearly intended to be serviceable rather than pretty. The white paint is original, and the skull-and-crossed pistons insignia on the gas tank was created by George Sedlak, the artist who painted Evel Knievel's motorcycles.

1940 Vincent HRD, Series A
The Vincent is one of the most famous and romantic brands in the world, the subject of legend and song. Philip Vincent bought the previously-existing HRD brand in 1928 to launch his own motorcycle, which featured a sophisticated rear suspension that was well ahead of its time. Vincent introduced its own 499cc single-cylinder engine in 1934, then added a second cylinder in 1937 to create the 998cc Series A V-twin.

Complex-looking and cluttered with external oil lines, it became known as the "plumber's nightmare," but it was a very robust engine that, when later redesigned, established Vincent's reputation as the world's fastest motorcycle.

Vincent reduced motorcycle production for war materials manufacturing in 1939, then launched its all-new Series B line in 1946. Consequently, only 79 of the Series A Vincent twins were built, making it the most desirable model among Vincent collectors. This one is a special collectible because it was the last one made. It was acquired by John Parham from a collector in Japan.

1946 Harley-Davidson Knucklehead Dragster
When it was introduced in 1936, the Harley-Davidson Knucklehead immediately captured national speed and endurance records. Its engine was robust enough to take a lot of high-performance development, and as drag racing became a popular national sport after the Second World War, the "Knuckle" proved highly competitive. This dragster, raced by Bill Pearson, of Kansas City, is a good example of the drag bikes of the period. Because lightweight performance parts were not yet readily available, builders often extensively drilled holes in their motorcycles to reduce weight. This motorcycle has over 70 holes drilled in its front forks alone. In 1955, Pearson set a quarter-mile record of 125.76 mph on this motorcycle. Knucklehead production ended after 1947.

Steve McQueen's 1947 Indian Chief Chopper

Steve McQueen, an active motor racing enthusiast and motorcycle collector, could afford to ride or drive anything he chose. What he chose, however, was this ratty-looking 1947 Indian Chief chopper. This motorcycle was part of McQueen's emotional protection from the pressures of celebrity. As his movie career progressed, he became more uncomfortable with his fame and lack of privacy. Part of his solution was to buy this motorcycle in 1977, about the same time he gained 30 pounds and grew long hair and a bushy beard. When McQueen rode around on the Indian, no one but his motorcycling buddies knew who he was. He even attached the old sleeping bag so he would look like an itinerant out-of-towner. Consistent with its unimpressive appearance, McQueen named the motorcycle "The Blob." After McQueen's death in 1980, this motorcycle sold at auction for $6,000 in 1984 to a collector from Texas. Later, celebrity chopper builder Jesse James bought the motorcycle, and John Parham acquired it from James. It was displayed at the Petersen Automotive Museum in Los Angeles in 2006, then taken to the Legend of the Motorcycle International Concours in Half Moon Bay, California, where Barbara McQueen was the guest of honor. Parham recalls that she wept when she saw the motorcycle and thought of the memories associated with it.

1947 Marman Motor Bicycle
After the Second World War, several companies offered small "clip-on" engines to attach to bicycles. These included Whizzer, Johnson, Dayton Motor Wheel, Monark, Marman, and others. The Marman Products Company was founded in 1941 by Herbert "Zeppo" Marx, of Marx Brothers fame. Having helped with the production of small drone aircraft engines, Marx developed a two-stroke opposed twin for use on bicycles. The Marman was a good-quality machine that was faster than a Whizzer, but is much rarer today because it was more expensive.

1948 Harley-Davidson Bobber
The 1948 Harley-Davidson is a valuable collectible in its own right because it was the first year for the Panhead engine and the last year for the Springer front forks. With its more reliable engine and stylish forks, hearkening back to the Knucklehead, it also became a favorite for customizers in the 1950s and '60s. With its flamed paint job, up-swept pipes, bobbed rear fender with tombstone tail light, ample use of chrome, and no front fender, this is a classic example of the customizing trends of the period.

1952 Vincent Series C Touring Rapide
The Vincent Series C models were introduced in 1948. These were the machines that would cement the brand's legendary reputation for speed and power, especially after American Rollie Free piloted one, un-streamlined, to 150.313 mph at Bonneville in September, 1948. HRD had been a well-known and respected name in Great Britain, and these initials remained prominent in the design of the Vincent's logo through the 1940s. But, as Vincents gained popularity in the United States after the Second World War, Philip Vincent learned that many riders thought HRD stood for Harley R. Davidson. This simply would not do, and he redesigned the logo to give more prominence to "Vincent," then eventually dropped the HRD letters altogether. Due to a poor dealer network, Vincents never achieved their sales potential in America, and in the early 1950s, Phil Vincent sought to improve this situation by arranging to have them sold through Indian dealers. Typically, Vincents were black, but the Indian Sales Company ordered some in China Red for better appeal in the North American market. Only 117 red Vincents were built from 1950 through 1952, so they are especially valuable today as rare collectibles. Vincent ceased motorcycle production entirely in 1955.

1955 Harley-Davidson FLH "Panhead"
Harley-Davidson introduced the "Panhead" in 1948, so named because its stamped steel valve covers look like cooking pans. Year-by-year, the Panhead was improved as a luxury touring motorcycle. Its engine was increased from 1,000 to 1,200cc in 1953, and in '55 compression was raised to produce 60 horsepower. It was available in five standard colors that year, including the brilliant Canary Yellow seen here. This motorcycle, which John Parham purchased in 1978, was his first collectible motorcycle. Once, during hard times, he was forced to sell it to make payroll, then later he bought it back. For both beauty and sentimentality, it is still his favorite motorcycle, and now stands in a place of honor at the National Motorcycle Museum.

1956 Rumi Scooter
Rumi is an old Italian company that originally provided metal castings for textile machinery. In 1949, Rumi moved into the production of small motorcycles and scooters, and though all of its engines were small, it became a force to be reckoned with in racing. Its Formichino scooter—meaning "little ant"—was introduced in 1954, and reveals the company's metallurgical expertise. Whereas most scooters have sheet metal or plastic panels, the Formichino's body is made up of three aluminum castings (you could even say it has an exoskeleton, like an ant), and its smooth, twin-cylinder engine functions as a structural unit. Based on its fine quality and style, the Rumi Formichino is one of the most desirable vehicles among scooter collectors.

1957 Harley-Davidson KR Road Racer
Responding to the postwar popularity of British motorcycles, in 1952 Harley-Davidson introduced its all-new Model K, featuring foot shift, unit-construction engine, and swinging arm rear suspension. While the road-going Model K was not especially successful, a racing version, designated the KR, had a spectacular career, dominating American competition into the late 1960s. With accessories supplied by Harley-Davidson, the KR could be set up for dirt track racing or road racing, as seen here. Whereas modern racing motorcycles rarely last more than one season, this motorcycle speaks to the remarkable longevity of the Harley KR. It was raced in the Daytona 200 from 1957 through 1964. During that period, it was ridden by Tony Murguia, Bobby Hill, and Dave Estep who ultimately restored the motorcycle before it was acquired by the National Motorcycle Museum.

1958 Ariel Square Four
Ariel, a British firm that dates back to the production of three-wheelers in 1898, is best known for its Square Four, designed in 1931 by Edward Turner, who went on to become Managing Director at Triumph. The Square Four, featuring two cylinders behind two cylinders, was exceptionally smooth, and over time was redesigned from a 500cc to 600cc, then eventually to 1,000cc. In this final configuration, it was smooth, powerful, and very compact, and became popular in the United States as a fast touring machine. This is an example of the Mark II Square Four, built from 1953 through 1959, and was capable of 100 mph in standard trim.

1959 Triumph, Von Dutch Custom

This customized Triumph motorcycle belonged to Bud Ekins, and was given its flame paint job by the iconic hot rod painter and pin-striper Von Dutch while he worked at Bud Ekins' shop in Sherman Oaks, California, during the 1960s. With its bobbed rear fender, "frenched" tail light, small gas tank, no front fender, and flamed paint, it is a classic example of the "Kustom Kulture" of the period. In October, 2005, this motorcycle was selected for an exhibition entitled "Wheelz: The Art and Design of the Customized Ride" at the Columbus College of Art and Design in Columbus, Ohio. Even among cars and motorcycles by the nation's top builders, including Arlen Ness, Eddie Trotta, Paul Yaffee, the Barris Brothers, and Boyd Coddington, this Von Dutch-painted Triumph was declared by a *Columbus Dispatch* reviewer to be the "best of show." In addition to this motorcycle, John Parham owns and has placed on display at the National Motorcycle Museum a significant collection of unusual artifacts once owned by Von Dutch, including a hand-engraved aluminum helmet and a desk sculpture of his famous flying eyeball insignia.

1961 Triumph Thunderbird

The British Triumph 650cc Thunderbird, introduced in 1950, was the first foreign-made motorcycle designed specifically for the U.S. market. Its more powerful engine and stylish lines were immediately popular. Triumph's director, Edward Turner, chose its name from Native American lore, for the mythical bird that has the power to bring on the storm. (In 1955, the Ford Motor Company had to execute an agreement with Triumph to use the name on its new Thunderbird sports car.) In 1960, the rear-wheel enclosure and a valanced front fender were added to the machine. This kind of styling was gaining favor in England, but was very unpopular in America because it made the motorcycle look heavy and "less masculine." Many American dealers and owners quickly removed these panels, which were discarded as worthless. The factory tried to sell the idea by calling the styling "streamlined," but Americans derisively referred to them as "Bathtub Triumphs." Thus, an intact 1961 Thunderbird, complete with rear body panels, is a relatively rare and valuable collectible today.

1965 Harley-Davidson Sprint Road Racer
Seeking to expand its model line with middle and lightweight machines, in 1960 Harley-Davidson purchased a controlling interest in the Italian firm Aeronautica Macchi—called Aermacchi for short—which provided the Motor Company with both two- and four-stroke technology in small engines from 50cc to 350cc. Perhaps the greatest benefit from the venture was the Sprint CRTT, a 250cc four-stroke single that proved highly competitive in both dirt track and road racing until it was outgunned by the Japanese two-strokes. This is the Sprint CRTT in full road racing trim. John Parham acquired it after he spotted it in the back of a pickup truck at a vintage motorcycle event in Ohio in 2001. He placed his business card on the motorcycle with a note expressing interest, and the owner responded.

Harley-Davidson Captain America Chopper

For the 1969 motion picture "Easy Rider," two examples of the famous Captain America Chopper, ridden by Peter Fonda, were constructed by Cliff Vaughn from 1951 ex-police motorcycles. One of these machines was destroyed during filming, and its wreckage was given by Fonda to Dan Haggerty, who had a bit part in the movie and later became famous as "Grizzly Adams." The second motorcycle was placed in storage and subsequently stolen. It has never turned up, and it is presumed that it was broken up for parts, since at the time it would not have been recognized as having any special value. This is the actual remaining example from the motion picture. Haggerty began to reassemble it, but never finished. Later, it was fully restored by Dave Ohrt, and has been authenticated by Haggerty and Fonda. Due to the historic reputation earned by "Easy Rider," it has become the most widely-recognized motorcycle on Earth, and hundreds of replicas have been fabricated by fans all over the world. This, of course, makes the "one-and-only" even more valuable.

Signature ______ Date 8/28/03

Peter Fonda

Witness ______ Date 8/28/03

CERTIFICATE OF AUTHENTICITY

I, **PETER FONDA**, 100% guarantee this to be the only, last, original, authentic **"CAPTAIN AMERICA"** motorcycle from the 1969 movie ***"Easy Rider"***.

This bike was built and ridden in order to switch back and forth due to the rigors of film production.

This bike was also used in the crash sequence at the end of the movie. When filming was done, I gave the motorcycle to Dan Haggerty as a momento of his work on the film ***"Easy Rider."*** Dan later reassembled and restored the bike at his Woodland Hills, California home. No other authentic Captain America motorcycle exists.

Signature ______ Date 8/28/03

Peter Fonda

Witness ______ Date 8/28/03

1974 Benelli Customized Art Bike

Motorcycle owners have always seemed to enjoy customizing their rides. Over time, styling treatments have fallen into categories, such as the "chopper" or the "bobber." But there is another unusual category called the "art bike," where the motorcycle itself is treated like an artist's canvas to which its owner applies various objects to create an overall affect that is often outrageous, quirky, and amusing. This 1974 Benelli, built by Felix Predko of Felix's Chopper Shop in Windber, Pennsylvania, is a superb example of the type. While the chassis and sheet metal of the motorcycle have not been modified—as is always the case with the chopper or bobber—it has been encrusted with an incredible array of badges, accessories, tooled metal, stickers, and other ephemera. On this motorcycle, one can find a ship's bell, bits from a silver tea set, Cadillac tail lights, ornamental tassels from a lamp, and various bits and pieces that defy identification. Whereas one can step back to enjoy the overall profile of the chopper or bobber, the art bike requires close and careful study, and the more you look, the more incredible and astonishing the whole treatment becomes. John Parham owns three such motorcycles built by Predko, and they are considered by many visitors the most fascinating motorcycles at the National Motorcycle Museum.

1990 Harley-Davidson Sturgis 50th Anniversary Custom
This is a very special motorcycle built to celebrate the 50th anniversary of the Sturgis Rally and to raise funds for the National Motorcycle Museum. It was commissioned by Nace Panzica, the President of Custom Chrome, and built in 1989 by John Reed. Beginning with a 1986 Harley-Davidson Softail, Reed used a satin-like, cream-colored powder-coating and extensive gold plating to create a true work of rolling art. It was donated by Panzica to be raffled to raise funds for the Museum in 1990. Then, Panzica bought the motorcycle back from the raffle winner for $25,000 and later re-donated it to the National Motorcycle Museum in 1999.

Motorcycles surround John in every facet of his world. Here John in his home office with a few of his favorite motorcycle pieces. A 1905 Harley and his 1911 Flying Merkel.

Below: John's love of antiques goes beyond motorcycles, here he is seen with his two prize antique automobiles. His 1954 Chevy (left) is a car he drives daily, while the 1933 Roadster is saved for more special occasions.

Chapter Ten: Zachary, the Legacy

Zachary John Parham was born on July 23, 1984, a little over 60 days after the J&P Cycles building in Anamosa was destroyed by fire. John was trying to salvage his business, Jill was working full-time, plus part-time for J&P Cycles, and both were traveling to swap meets almost every weekend. Fortunately, both families were more than willing to pitch in with the care and rearing of young Zach. Jill's sister, Sue, and her husband Ralph, sometimes worked at the swap meets, and Sue could be counted on to baby-sit when necessary. But the greatest support came from John's parents, whose house at 106 East Webster became Zach's second home. John Parham, Sr. relates, "Anna had retired from her pre-school business and I was getting ready to retire. Zachary was a blessing for us. We had space at our house to give him his own room with a crib, then later a bed. He was very much at home with us, and we were in a position to adjust our schedules in any way to support John and Jill."

Not only were John and Jill on the road many weekends of the year, but after 1992 when Jill joined the company full-time, they were away at Sturgis two weeks each summer, plus gone a week

The legacy: John and Zach ride, with Zach aboard "Chaos," a machine of his own construction.

Jill and Zachary at Christmas, 1988.

Below: Zachary with the Easter Bunny. Zach had no idea that it was his mother Jill inside the bunny suit.

for the occasional motorcycle show in Europe. John Parham, Sr. states, "Sturgis time was a great time for us. We would plan a vacation with Zach, and in many ways these were a repeat of the early years with our own children. We took Zach to the attractions and vacation spots in Iowa and neighboring states that we had enjoyed 20 years earlier with our own kids." With Anna having been a lifelong teacher, and John Sr. a former teacher, they always emphasized educational opportunities during travels with their grandson. These included the Pony Express Barn and Jesse James's home in St. Joseph, Missouri, and President Lincoln's tomb and home in Springfield, Illinois. They also traveled to Omaha, Nebraska, where they visited the zoo, the Joslyn Museum where Grant Wood's famous painting of Stone City hangs, and saw the many aircraft on display at the Strategic Air Command Base and Museum. In Zach's recollection today, the most memorable trips were to Springfield, Illinois, and to Cameron and Shelby, Missouri, where he met many of his relatives. Zach recalls, "My grandmother and I would keep track of license plates on the road to see how many different states we could identify."

ଊ

When Zachary was eight, and his mother and father went to a drag race at Palmdale, California, promoted by J&P Promotions, arrangements were made for John Sr., Anna, and Zach to fly to the West Coast to meet them for a family vacation. John Sr. recalls, "We flew into Ontario, California, rented a car, and drove to our hotel at Laguna Beach. It was Halloween, because Zach wore his costume on the plane. We arrived late at night, and Zachary was sound asleep. The next morning he awoke to the booming surf of the Pacific Ocean right under the deck of our room, and when he went out to see it, he was swarmed by friendly gulls who even strolled into the room, looking for a handout. It was a new experience for a boy from Iowa." Zach confirms, "Although I had been to California before, this was my first time to see the ocean." After finishing their work in Palmdale, John and Jill drove to the coast to join the group and take a California vacation. The family relaxed at Laguna Beach and went to Knott's Berry Farm where Zach enjoyed the rides, including a memorable parachute jump.

Zachary's grandparents seemed to find an educational opportunity in most of the recreational and entertaining activities they provided for Zach. For example, while working the annual pineapple sale fundraiser at Camp Courageous, a charitable organization near Anamosa on whose board of directors John Sr. served, Zach was allowed to make change. His grandfather says, "He was only five, and it was his first opportunity to handle money in a business-like way." Not surprisingly, when Zach began elementary school, he did well in all areas, but excelled in math and science. John Sr. also got his grandson involved in growing giant pumpkins in anticipation of the Pumpkin Festival, a major annual event in Anamosa. Zach cultivated his own garden, put in next to his grandfather's garden, and learned to mix special fertilizers to make his pumpkins grow to extraordinary size. The youngster showed his pumpkins at the festival for six years—from his first through the sixth grades—and grew one to a weight of 550 pounds.

Not surprisingly, motorcycling and the world of swap meets also became a part of Zach's education.

John and Jill took him to nearby events, and on occasion even to some of the major shows, like the big ones in Milwaukee and Chicago. They also took Zach to a J&P Promotions show at the Meadowlands, in New Jersey, when "Home Alone" was a hit movie. Jill recalls, "We stayed a night at the Plaza Hotel in New York City, just like in the movie, and we took Zach for a carriage ride through Central Park, and got to see the Statue of Liberty." Zach recalls, "At the swap meets and bike shows, I got to hang out with Uncle Doug and Rob DeSotel, and sometimes help Mom when she was selling tickets at the shows." Zachary also demonstrated early that he had some of his father's entrepreneurial skills. He recalls, "The first time I remember selling something was when I was in about the fifth grade at a race where we had stickers that said, 'Friends don't let friends ride Rice Burners.'" The term "Rice Burners" was a pejorative reference to Japanese motorcycles, and Zachary found himself in a crowd of fiercely loyal Harley-Davidson enthusiasts who could appreciate the sentiment. He says, "Despite the fact we had been giving the stickers away for free, I went around and started selling them for 25 cents. I made $130!" Furthermore, when John was offering collectible toys and banks through Nostalgic Toy Creations, the Parhams rented a booth at the Chicago Antique Toy Show, and Zach came along. John says, "Zach was only about seven or eight, and I told him that he could have a dollar for every toy he helped us sell. I taught him how to watch people and detect the behavior that reveals they are interested. I taught him how to talk to people and listen and understand what they are looking for, and I explained that you can't sell anything sitting down. He really got into it. He got right out in the aisle and talked with people. He was quite a little businessman, and at the end of the weekend he had earned over $50."

ᘓ

Zachary also demonstrated competitive and athletic ability early on. At age eight he started taking Tae Kwon Do classes, and continued until he was 11, advancing to the level of Brown Belt. Don Fleming, his coach and a marshal arts teacher for 26 years, says, "One of the purposes of Tae Kwon Do is to teach discipline. Zach was well-disciplined when he arrived. He paid attention, was courageous, and would try anything. He was an inspiration to the other kids in the class." Through middle school and his first year of high school, Zach participated in football, baseball, basketball, and track. His idol was Michael Jordan, and on three occasions the whole family went to Chicago to watch Jordan play with the Bulls at the United Center. Zach says, "I would watch every game Jordan played on television if mom would let me, and I collected over 300 Michael Jordan playing cards. I still have them." However, Zach dropped out of basketball and baseball after his sophomore year. He explains, "You had to attend summer training camps to make the varsity squad, and I had begun to travel a lot during the summer. I was not as good at those sports as I was at football, so I gave them up to concentrate on football and track."

Zachary was good enough at football that he planned to attend Wartburg College in Waverly, Iowa, for its athletic

Zachary gets a mini-cycle for Christmas, 1992.

Below: John and Jill with Zach, age 8.

Zachary is greeted by gulls during his first visit to the Pacific Coast.

Below: Zach practices Tae Kwon Do, age 7.

program. Wartburg, which ranks at the top of its conference in athletics, is also one of the top liberal arts schools in the nation, known as well for its high academic standards. Zach did indeed attend Wartburg, but not for its athletic program. While playing defensive end against Anamosa's great rival, Monticello, Zach took a hit that resulted in a Grade Two concussion. He explains, "From about 3 p.m. on the afternoon of game day until midnight that night, I have no memory whatsoever. Even after viewing the films of the game, I still cannot remember anything." John recalls, "When we brought him home, he kept repeating himself. He knew us, but he had no idea who his girlfriend was. He did not recognize her at all." Zach also temporarily lost his memory for a full three months prior to the game, but that has returned. He says, "I was told the next time it could be worse, so that was the end of my football career." John adds, "He was on his way to becoming All-Conference, but that was the end of it. There were two more games that season, but Zach decided not to play." Later, however, missing the action of contact sports, Zach took up rugby at Wartburg College, much to his mother's chagrin. Jill rolls her eyes and says, "Rugby! I hate it! No helmets!"

During high school, Zach also got involved in paintball combat, and played on a semi-pro regional team his junior and senior years, traveling throughout the Midwest for weekend tournaments. He explains, "It is a very expensive sport. My tournament gun was worth $1,500, and you could easily consume $100 worth of paintballs during a weekend of practice, and as much as $200 during a tournament." To fund his paintball competition, Zach began to supervise the sale of off-catalog stock at J&P Cycles on eBay. He explains, "Dad would come upon and buy odd stocks of parts that were not compatible with the J&P inventory and catalog system, and I would liquidate these through the Internet." John confirms, "He got quite a business going. I would give him 10 percent of whatever he sold, and it was his responsibility to take the photos, write descriptions, post the products on eBay, handle the correspondence, take care of the shipping, and do the accounting for the program." John adds, "He made a steady income at it. Zach always found a way to earn money, and we never gave him an allowance. He bought a moped with his eBay earnings."

ଊ

Academically, Zach did well in high school, maintaining a 3.9 grade-point average while participating in both football and track. By the time he was 14, J&P Cycles' difficult years were behind it, and the Parhams were earning enough to supplement Zach's formal education with international travel, some of which was related to the company's business. For example, in the summer after his eighth grade, Zach went to Austria and Germany with his father and George Barnard, who were displaying for J&P at the European Super Rally, where Zach worked the booth. In the ninth grade, he made a similar trip to Denmark and Finland, again to attend motorcycle events where J&P was promoting its business. In the tenth grade, Zach went to Australia for three weeks, this time with People-to-

People, a cultural student exchange program. He saw Sydney, Ayres Rock, and got to snorkel off the Great Barrier Reef. After his junior year, he spent three weeks in France, studying French, taking historical tours, and living for a week in wine country with a French family. The summer before he went to Wartburg, Zach joined another People-to-People foreign exchange group to Italy, Austria, Germany, the Czech Republic, and Great Britain. During the May term of his sophomore year in college, Zach traveled to China and Taiwan on an internship with his father and Tom Ellsworth, an employee of Küryakyn, one of J&P Cycles' product suppliers. Zach says, "We toured factories and learned about overseas manufacturing. My grade for the term was based on a paper I wrote about this trip."

There was never a time when motorcycles did not figure prominently in young Zachary's life. His first motorcycle rides were aboard his father's beloved Harley Panhead. He recalls, "I got to ride with dad on his '55 Panhead when I was only about three. He would put me on his lap and ride around at J&P where there was no traffic." When he was just nine years old, Zach reviewed a children's book about motorcycling for his father's *Motorcycle Dispatch*. As he came of age, he became a rider and began to travel with his father. Zach had informally learned to ride off-road with a little Honda CT70, but when it came time to go on the road, Jill insisted that he get proper training through a Motorcycle Safety Foundation course. At age 18, Zach got a Harley-Davidson Sportster and completed a rider education course at Kirkwood College in Cedar Rapids. The Harley Sportster was a motorcycle that other high school kids would kill for, and that, indeed, his own father would have killed for at his age! Zach laughs when he remembers, "Everyone at school began to give me crap about being 'the rich kid,' but it was just good-natured ribbing." He adds, "It was good that the business had begun to perform well enough that Dad could throttle back a bit and begin to enjoy himself." One of the ways John began to find enjoyment was through long motorcycle trips with Zachary. Zach had been working on J&P's Sturgis crew since the age of 13, and in 2000 and 2001, he rode to Sturgis as a passenger on his father's motorcycle. In 2000, they set off early and made a big loop through Colorado and Wyoming before arriving in Sturgis from the west. Though John had been riding motorcycles for more than 30 years, he had focused so intensely on building his businesses that he had never taken the time for an extended motorcycle tour. This was his first long-distance ride, and he enjoyed sharing it with his son. In 2001, John and Zach rode to Minnesota, then across South Dakota to Wyoming, making a

Zach and his grandmother explore a covered wagon during a visit to St. Joseph, Missouri.

Below: Zach and his parents go to Chicago to watch Michael Jordan play with the Chicago Bulls.

Zach's grandfather teaches him the art of growing monster pumpkins.

Below: Zach rode on the back of John's motorcycle to Sturgis his senior year of high school. (2002)

big 2,000-mile loop before they returned to Sturgis. In 2002, Zachary was at the controls of his own motorcycle for the first time. This time the trip was not a multi-state loop since it was Zach's first solo road-riding experience. The two traveled across Iowa on Highway 18 into South Dakota, where they continued across the state to Sturgis, making a trip through the Black Hills before their arrival. Under any circumstances, the Sportster is not the best motorcycle for touring. Its seating position is a bit cramped, its fuel range is short, and it has limited luggage capacity, so Zach celebrated his achievement by wearing a T-shirt that said, "I rode my Sportster to Sturgis." In 2003, Zach graduated to a new Dyna Glide, a motorcycle built on Harley-Davidson's big twin engine that is much more suitable for long-distance travel. Zach recalls, "I got my first 1,000-mile oil change in Rapid City, then Dad and I continued on west to Gillette, Cody, and Yellowstone, then south to Jackson Hole where we went whitewater rafting before returning to Sturgis." Zach was so taken with Jackson Hole that later he decided it would be where he would honeymoon with his new bride in 2008.

In 2004, John and Zach had their bikes shipped to Seattle, to the motorcycle museum of a friend named Frank Mason, then flew out to pick them up. They rode Highway A1A down the coast of Oregon, then returned to Portland and went east, past Bridal Veil Falls and along the scenic Columbia River. Zach recounts, "It was cold along the coast. We had not expected this, and we had to stop to buy chaps to wear over our jeans." The pair crossed the Snake River and continued east on Idaho's scenic Route 12, through Glacier National Park, then into Alberta, Canada, before riding south to Sturgis. Again, they took a break at Glacier for some whitewater rafting. John reports about the ride, "Route 12 is one of the most beautiful roads I have ever ridden." He adds, "When Zach and I travel, our goal is to see America on two-lane roads, eat at mom-and-pop cafes, and stay in local motels." By the time they reached Sturgis, they had ridden 3,000 miles.

In 2005, J&P Cycles had a new show truck heading to the West Coast, so John and Zach put their bikes aboard the truck and had them dropped off in Las Vegas, where they flew out to collect them. Zach had just turned 21, so they spent the evening in Vegas where he could experience the casinos, then the next day they rode their bikes to the Grand Canyon, where they took a helicopter ride. Leaving Las Vegas, they traveled through Utah and visited Zion and Bryce National Parks, then visited artist Jeff Decker at his sculpture studio in Springville. Then they visited Estes Park, Colorado, before riding on to Sturgis, logging 2,200 miles for the trip.

After the J&P Cycles Open House in 2006, John and Zach's bikes were hauled to Los Angeles in the Vance & Hines truck. When they picked them up a month later, they found that Vance & Hines had installed new state-of-the-art exhaust systems on both machines. Traveling north on Highway 395, they rode through Death Valley and Hell's Canyon, Idaho. Zach says, "It was 125 degrees, and we put AC/DC's 'Highway to Hell' on the sound system and cranked it up loud. It was like riding in a furnace." They stopped in Butte, Montana, to take in Evel Knievel Days, then went into Yellowstone through the north entrance. There they did some white-water rafting, then rode on to Cody, Wyoming. John recalls with a laugh, "We arrived in Cody to find ourselves in the middle of a Hell's Angels convention." By the time they arrived in Sturgis, they had covered 3,000 miles. For 2007, John had other business and was not able to take an extended ride prior to the Rally, so Zach and J&P Cycles employee J.D. Denison mounted up and rode out. Zach recalls, "We left early and did an 800-mile day, straight through to Sturgis."

These days, Zach has a new riding companion, having met Brianna Johnson at Wartburg College. They were married July 12, 2008, and now live in Anamosa where Zach works full-time at J&P Cycles. Bree does not yet own a motorcycle, but enjoys riding passenger.

ƆR

Zachary Parham continued his outstanding academic performance at Wartburg, studying accounting and business finance, and graduated magna cum laude in the top 20 percent of his class of 500 students. He established his record as a superior student his freshman year, earning admittance into Phi Eta Sigma, America's oldest and largest honorary society for the encouragement and recognition of academic achievement. During his sophomore year at Wartburg, Zach had Tuesdays off, and he used the open day to build a motorcycle from the ground up, traveling to Cedar Rapids every week to work with Kody Wisner, a bike designer and builder who worked at Precision Performance and has since joined the staff at J&P Cycles in Anamosa. Zach undertook the project as an experiment to see if a complete machine could be assembled from parts sourced entirely through the J&P catalog, and as a learning experience to improve his technical understanding of motorcycles and the challenges J&P customers might face in building one. Zach knew that an accounting degree would give him professional skills to fall back on in any industry, but he had already decided he would like to carve out a career in his father's company, if possible. Zach explains, "If I am going to be in the motorcycle industry, it's important that I learn what it takes to actually build a motorcycle." Zach also knew that this kind of deep understanding of the product, the industry, and the needs of its customers was exactly what had enabled his father to build a multimillion dollar corporation that serves as a benchmark in the retail accessory segment of the industry, and a similar deep understanding would be required if he were to carry on that success.

The first thing Zach learned is that the popular television shows, such as "American Chopper," do not depict a real-world build. He says, "Those shows make it look way too easy. What they don't show is how often parts don't fit when you are building a custom motorcycle, and how much work and time it takes to make things right." Zach continues, "I worked on it all day once a week for a year, and it probably took about 500 hours." He named his motorcycle "Chaos," joking that the name often reflected how he felt about the organization of the job. However, the end result was anything but chaotic. Rather, it was a sleek and artful chopper, ten feet long, with a gorgeous silver paint job with black and red tribal flames. Its

Zachary gets his first true road-going motorcycle, a Harley-Davidson Sportster.

Below: Zach begins to travel with his father and graduates to a bigger Harley, seen here at Bear Butte on the way to Sturgis in 2004.

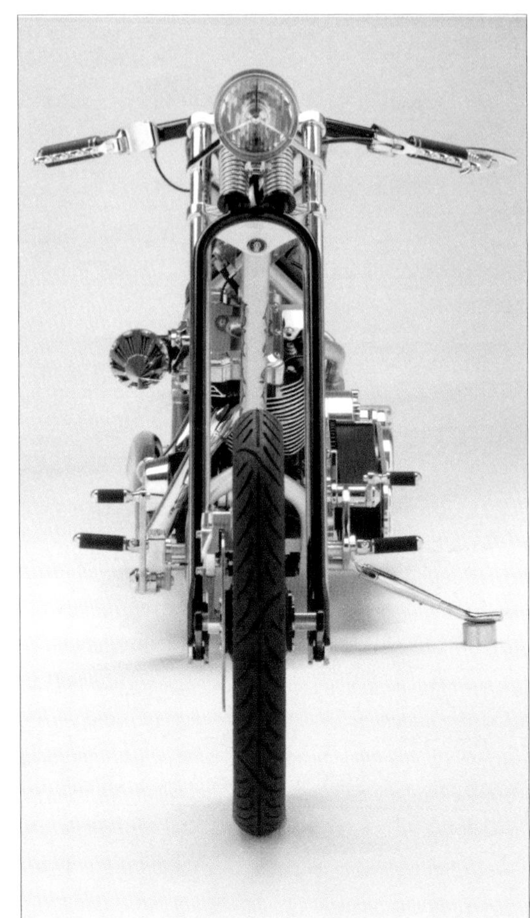

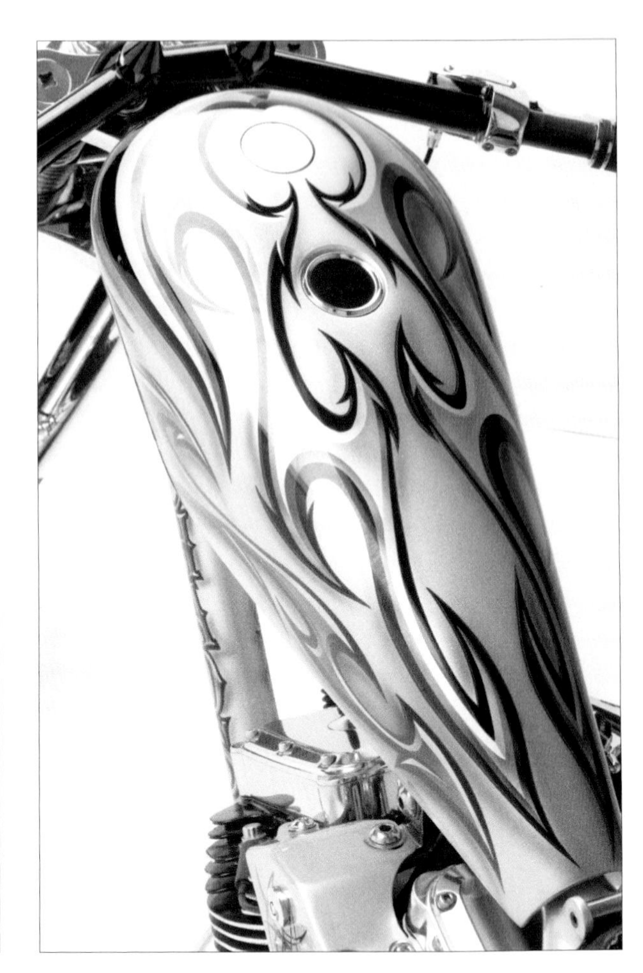

PRECISION

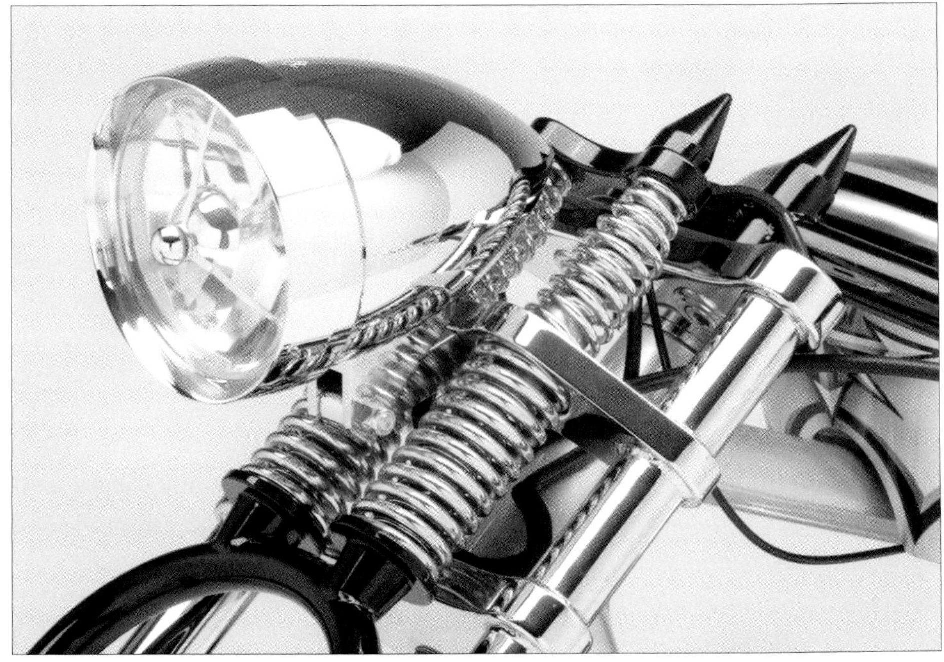

While at Wartburg College, Zachary creates Chaos, his hand-built custom chopper. The project nets him a cover story in the Wartburg magazine, pictured at right. The motorcycle is later featured in "Easyriders," the nation's largest custom motorcycle magazine.

Zach graduates with honors from Anamosa High School in 2003.

Below: John and Zach in front of the Venetian Hotel in Las Vegas, just after Zach turned 21.

frame, fuel tank, and oil tank were from Redneck Engineering. The engine is a 92-inch S&S Indian power plant with a Twin Tech ignition, five-speed RevTech gearbox, and Martin Brothers exhaust. It has a Paul Cox Rigid Air seat system, Billet Concepts controls, Paul Yaffe Originals footpegs and mirrors, and an Arlen Ness headlight. The forks are raked at 48 degrees and a 200 millimeter Avon tire was selected for the rear. The elaborate paint was done by Scott Takes of Underground Art Studios in Cedar Rapids. Parham appraises the bike at $50,000, but does not seem inseparably attached to it, despite the time and effort he put into the project. He says, "I may just sell it and use the money to build another." Zach and Chaos became the cover story, entitled "Mind Over Motor," in the Summer 2007 issue of the Wartburg alumnus magazine, and the motorcycle was also featured in the July 2007 issue of *Easyriders*, a leading national magazine for custom motorcycle enthusiasts.

In the spring of 2004, Karris Golden, Assistant Director of Communications and Marketing at Wartburg, floated the idea of creating an alumni motorcycle club. Karris rides a 2003 Harley-Davidson Springer Softail and her husband, Josh Neesen, has a 1994 Fat Boy. They were sure there were others in the academic community who might enjoy getting together to ride their motorcycles. They called their club the Knight Riders, since the knight is Wartburg's mascot. Golden sent out an e-mail to solicit interest, and as a student with a motorcycle registered on campus, Zach was one of the recipients of the message. He made an appointment with Golden to offer his support, including the support of his parents and J&P Cycles. As a result, John and Jill both attended Knight Riders poker runs at Wartburg, and brought a nice selection of prizes from the J&P inventory. Golden says about Zach, "He was a stellar student; one of our best. He is genuinely nice, humble, helpful and intelligent, and I know many of our professors were very excited about his potential." Golden adds, "Many people think Zach is shy, but he is not. He is thoughtful and respectful, and listens to other people, and I think some mistake that for shyness." In this respect, Zach is similar to his father. Gloria Campbell, Associate Professor of Business Administration, voices a similar view, stating, "I have a great deal of respect for the business that the Parhams have put together, and for their parenting skills. I found Zach to be an amazingly down-to-earth young man who was a great addition to our program. I'm sure he will be important in the long-range planning at J&P Cycles."

During his freshman year at Wartburg, Zachary met and fell for Brianna Johnson, a native of Wasilla, Alaska. Bree, as she is called by friends and family, was awarded an academic scholarship to Wartburg and earned a degree in English Education. She now lives with Zach in Anamosa and teaches English and Second Chance Reading for ninth to twelfth-graders in the Marion Independent School District in Iowa. Like Zach, she also excelled at athletics, earning a position on a high school volleyball traveling team that played throughout the United States, then for two years at Wartburg. In addition to their affection for each other, the two students found they could benefit from their complementary aptitudes and skills. Brianna explains, "I do words and Zach does numbers. I edited his papers and he helped me with my math." After their graduation from Wartburg, Zach and Bree returned to Anamosa where he went to work full-time for J&P Cycles. Wartburg communications officer Karris Golden says about Johnson, "She was a great student and has a bright personality and a million-dollar smile. We used her as a model in some of our Wartburg admissions literature because she fairly projects vitality and excitement. When Brianna is in a room, other people want to be in the room with her."

ଓ

Zach's position at J&P has not been an entitlement. Since he began working there, his parents have systematically positioned him to learn every aspect of the business, and it has been clear from the outset that he has no privileges over other employees. Zach says, "I started working part-time in the warehouse when I was 12, sweeping the floor and shredding paper. One of my jobs was to take a yardstick and drag out parts that had rolled under the shelves, then I would clean them up with a rag and return them to stock. When I was 14, I started parts picking, and at 17 I was moved to sales in the showroom. While attending college, I spent my summers working in the purchasing department so I could learn that side of the business." When a new J&P store was opened at Destination Daytona at Ormond Beach, Florida, early in 2007, Zach became responsible for all of its purchasing and inventory. Later that summer, he was made manager of the retail store in Anamosa while still retaining his purchasing responsibilities for the Florida store. Then, early in 2008, Zach was named Operations Manager, and his responsibilities were expanded to include management of both retail stores, the call centers in both Iowa and Florida, and both warehouses. Again, this was not an entitlement dictated by John and Jill, but rather a promotion recommended by a group of senior staff with whom Zach was required to interview. One of these said, "He knows every aspect of the company inside and out, he understands the industry and its customers, he is smart and well-educated, and is energetic and aggressive about improving the company." Jill observes, "Zach actually handles some situations better than John and I because of his accounting background, his technical background, and the knowledge he has gained from growing up in the industry." She continues, "He is not scared to make a decision, and he communicates very well with others. He has my sense for people, John's sense for challenge and opportunity, and he is open and hungry to learn. Obviously, John and I are very proud of him." In addition to his responsibilities with the Anamosa and Destination Daytona stores, since graduating from college Zach has been put in charge of the Sturgis operation to make sure that it runs properly.

About his future at J&P, Zach says, "I would like to go into the marketing side of the company. It is exciting, and think I would be good at it, and I have some ideas about how to make the company grow." Then he adds, "But my training is in the accounting and business management side, and that is probably the direction I will go. I am a lot like my mother. I am a numbers person, and she may be

As he officially moved into the business, Zach began to travel more with his father. Here they are seen crossing Death Valley, 2005, and in the Canadian Rockies (below) on their way to Sturgis in 2004.

Zach in Las Vegas, just after turning 21.

Below: He joins his parents in keeping the world on two wheels.

relying on me to work in her areas of responsibility so she can retire in a few years." Still, if Zachary ends up in the personnel, information processing, and business controls side of the company, there is little doubt he will have strong advice for sales and marketing. He says, "We have plenty of room for growth in Internet sales. At present, the Internet provides about 25 percent of our sales, and we should push that to 40 percent in two to three years. We should be well positioned to do that because we are currently undertaking a major upgrade in our website that will improve interactivity and catalog search capability, and come online soon." Zach predicts, "There will be growth in the sport bike market, but this will happen mostly through our Florida store." He continues, "Unless Harley-Davidson can appeal to younger riders, the metric cruiser is going to gain market share, and this is a change we need to be prepared to respond to." Zach says, "Our catalog will always be our mainstay, but we should look for ways to more aggressively distribute it on CDs and expand our use of the Internet." And about the future in general, he says, "The market is not going to continue to grow the way it has these last 20 years. There are not going to be more customers, so we need to find ways to attract customers away from our competitors." This can be done, Zach feels, if J&P continues to maintain its high standards of customer service.

When J&P veteran employees and associates throughout the motorcycle industry are posed the question, "Is Zach more like John or more like Jill?," they usually break into a bemused smile. Few answer quickly, and most give the question a lot of thought. Typically, they will respond with something like, "In personality and aptitude, he is more like Jill. He is personable and outgoing, relaxed, and quick to laugh or break into a smile." They acknowledge that he does not have John's serious intensity, but almost always they begin to backpedal from any suggestion that he is cast entirely in the model of Jill. Often, one who knows them well will say something like, "John's success has come from his incredible grasp of the product, his empathy for the customer, and his uncanny intuition about where the market is going. Zach has that. He has an incredibly deep knowledge of the industry for a man his age, and he has his father's understanding of the product, the customer, and the market." For example, J&P's Anamosa Warehouse Manager Matt Ahrens states, "Zach is down to earth. He is a cross between John and Jill, but probably has more of Jill's personnel management skills. He is an impact player who is going to make a difference at this company." Tom Ellsworth, who is in charge of product development for Küryakyn and has traveled with John and Zach in Asia, says, "Zach has a lot of his mom, but he has the vision of his dad. Zach catches problems before they hit the floor, and fixes them. With John and Jill, he forges ahead and she takes care of details. Zach can define the direction also, but mops up the details as he goes."

Jeff Decker, the Parham's good friend, says about Zach, "He is not a trust-fund kid. He could have gone off to Harvard and spent his daddy's money, but he didn't. He stayed in Iowa because that's who he is. He has, and he will always have that Iowa work ethic that he learned from his parents." Decker continues, "I can recall when I was displaying my art in Davenport, and Zach was still a kid. There he was, sweeping up cigarette butts in front of the booth, and when I gave him a T-shirt he was genuinely excited. He was a down-to-earth kid, and he still is, just like his folks." Decker adds, "I think Zach looks at his parents and sees proof of the American Dream, not a silver spoon." Mike Buettner, former CFO of Motorcycle Aftermarket Group, an investment company affiliated with many of the motorcycle industry's leading aftermarket brands, echoes Decker's sentiments. Buettner got to know Zach when he served an accounting internship with MAG in 2006, and he says, "Here's a kid who has not had to want for anything, but he has good values and works hard, just like his parents." He adds, "Zach has traits of both. He has Jill's grasp of systems and numbers, and he has an unbelievable understanding of the business and the industry." Tom Hinderholtz, a designer and supplier of lighting accessories, adds, "Success has not spoiled Zach. He is extremely mature and impressive in his own right. He will do good things and is capable of carrying on the work of the company."

About Zachary's desire to make his career in the family business, John and Jill's longtime friend Mike Corbin says, "That in itself speaks volumes about the wonderful balance that exists in this family." He explains, "Many of us who have worked with the intensity of John and Jill end up driving our kids away from the business we love. Our dedication seems obsessive, creating a model that our own children might want to run from." He concludes, "Somehow John and Jill have worked 25 hours a day for their dream, but they have still found the time to be good parents in the process. They have raised a son who has their best qualities and understands and admires their work enough that he wants to continue building the family dream."

It has been observed elsewhere that John and Jill are more than a husband and wife, but also a Yin and a Yang that, together, have created the success of J&P Cycles. They are utterly different, but they complement each other in ways that create a whole that is greater than the sum of its parts. Many who know Zachary Parham believe he is a literal flesh-and-blood personification of this idea.

Zach and Brianna, married July 12, 2008.

Zachary & Brianna Parham
Married July 12, 2008

Chapter Eleven:
J&P Cycles in the New Millennium

The 1990s, which had opened with J&P Cycles on the verge of bankruptcy, turned into a decade of success, growth, and achievement for the little motorcycle business on the outskirts of Anamosa. J&P Cycles emerged from the decade as an internationally recognized brand that was now being hailed throughout the American motorcycle industry as an "overnight success," recognized by *Dealernews* as one of the nation's Top 100 independent motorcycle dealers. But John and Jill Parham, and many of the 90 individuals they now employed, knew that sacrifice and 20 years of hard work had gone into earning this recognition. There was nothing "overnight" about it. Since the mid-1980s, opportunity had presented itself with the resurgence of Harley-Davidson as a spectacularly popular brand, and J&P had seized that opportunity by sharpening its focus on serving the ever-expanding market of Americans who wanted to improve and customize their motorcycles. The Parhams began to sell off their shows and swap meets, retreat from the collectible toy and bank business, and wind down the work of their publishing company while they directed their time and resources more narrowly toward their motorcycle parts

In October 2007, John, Jill, and local dignitaries cut the ribbon to celebrate the opening of J&P Cycles Destination Daytona Super Store, the emblem of the company's spectacular success in the new millennium.

J&P CYCLES

As the new millennium arrived, J&P again expanded its warehouse. Shown here is an aerial view taken at the company's open house in 2004, on the occasion of its 25th anniversary.

Below: By 1999, catalog sales had become the mainstay of the business.

and accessory business. By 1999, annual sales had grown to $18 million, and they looked forward with optimism as they broke ground for a second expansion that would more than double the size of the J&P sales and warehousing facility. Jill recalls, "When we hit $18 million in sales, it seemed inconceivable. I simply could not get my mind around it. I never imagined our motorcycle business could reach that level of sales." Clearly, those who had worked so hard to build the company, including both John and Jill, could not envision the continued growth and spectacular success that lay in their future as the new millennium arrived.

In 2000, staffing grew by nearly 50 percent over 1999, with payroll increasing to 132 employees, which represented a 150-percent increase over the last five-year period. And for the second time, *Dealernews* named J&P Cycles a Top 100 dealer. The following year—in 2001—Memphis Shades, a manufacturer of motorcycle windshields, designated J&P Cycles its "Retailer of the Year," and for the third consecutive year J&P was named a Top 100 dealer. Growth was coming from catalog sales and greater exposure at motorcycle rallies throughout the nation. With John no longer putting time and resources into the organization of shows, swap meets, and drag races, J&P Cycles could attend more events as a vendor, so the company increased its outreach and visibility by putting a big-rig "mobile showroom" on the road. It was a 30-foot tractor complete with living quarters for the crew, and a 40-foot trailer that opened out into an attractive, awning-covered sales area, all done up in an eye-popping yellow livery with red and blue graphics, consistent with the color scheme of the J&P Cycles logo.

Finally, with industry-wide recognition for its remarkable success, J&P Cycles began to attract the attention of investment groups looking at the high-flying motorcycle industry as a whole. One of these was the Motorsport Aftermarket Group, which was created for the purpose of investing in a range of accessory manufacturers and suppliers in both the road and off-road segments of the American motorcycle market. The companies within the group include Küryakyn, Vance & Hines, Mustang, Renthal, Performance Machine, Progressive Suspension, and White Brothers. J&P Cycles is unique as the only retailer in the family of branded aftermarket suppliers. This in itself is a testament to how important J&P had become as the world's largest motorcycle aftermarket retailer, which appealed to MAG because it would provide a channel for retail sales of the products of most of its other companies. Tom Ellsworth, director of product management and development for Küryakyn, explains, "John has benefitted by networking with the other companies to learn more about how they design products and bring them to market, but it is J&P that has led to MAG's success. Their desire to have the ultimate in customer service has led to greater sales for all of the companies and to higher standards of performance throughout the group. They have helped the companies get closer to their customers."

It was a significant development that went practically without notice in the motorcycle industry, consistent with the policy to maintain a low profile by keeping their successful brands under the leadership of those who had made them successful. As a result, day-to-day business, managed by John and Jill, continued as usual at J&P Cycles, but behind the scenes the new arrangement resulted in a source of capital and improved synergy with leading brands that would contribute to even more rapid growth at J&P Cycles. Thus, as the third millennium dawned, J&P Cycles stepped up to an opportunity for performance that would simply eclipse its widely-acclaimed success of the 1990s.

ಌ

In 2000, J&P Cycles launched a separate catalog for antique and vintage Harley-Davidson motorcycles. Not only did this initiative appeal to John's heart as a motorcycle collector and the patron of the National Motorcycle Museum, which had recently reopened in Anamosa, but it made good business sense as well. The Antique Motorcycle Club of America's rules provide that motorcycles must be 35 years old or older to be recognized as "antique" and eligible for club judging and awards. By the 1990s, a great number of post-war Harley-Davidsons had fallen into this category, making them desirable as collectible motorcycles. Not only were these motorcycles plentiful, but they appealed to Baby Boomers, just as John's beloved yellow 1955 Panhead appealed to him. As a result, restoration and collecting of Harley-Davidsons up to late-1960s models became very popular, contributing to a boom in AMCA membership.

The trend created enough demand for period parts that specialty shops throughout the nation began to manufacture and sell reproduction parts, what the collectors call "repops."

In the past, restorers and collectors had prowled the aisles of swap meets, looking for incredibly rare and valuable original parts, and a restoration project might languish for years while a key part was sought. Or, the owner might resort to the very expensive alternative of having that single part machined or fabricated. With more demand, what had once been a "one-off" part could now be reproduced in quantity, justifying the cost of patterns and dies. Suddenly, AMCA swap meets became places where a new class of vendors offered a wide array of aftermarket parts. This parts supply made restorations easier, quicker, and less expensive, resulting in increased interest and involvement in the whole enterprise. As more good replica parts became available, including complete reproduced engines, frames, and sheet metal for favorite vintage Harley models, John did exactly what he had done when he turned J&P Cycles into a mail-order catalog business in the mid-1980s. Rather than requiring customers to come to the parts, Parham took vintage Harley parts to the customers through a catalog and mail-order sales. And, as growth of the AMCA made replica part manufacturing more viable, suppliers began to offer parts for even

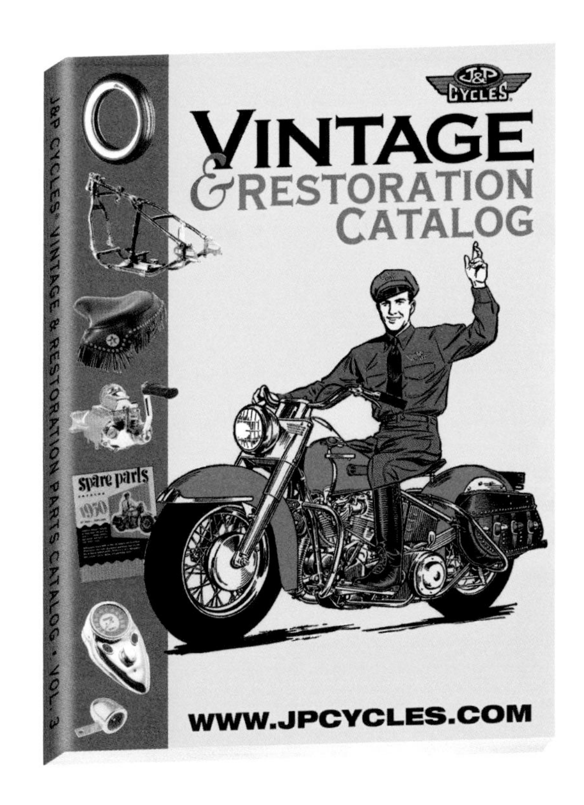

In 2000, J&P launched a separate catalog for vintage Harley parts. Though the vintage parts sales are barely a blip on the J&P Cycles radar, the company still continues to display at Antique Motorcycle Club of America meets because the vintage cycle scene remains close to John's heart.

Below: J&P Cycles uses its catalogs to build a raffle bike each year for the National Motorcycle Museum to use as its main fundrasier. Pictured here is the 2008 Museum raffle bike.

Despite growing catalog sales, J&P Cycles in Anamosa remains a busy point-of-sale dealership. Many customers who have received good service through the catalog travel to Anamosa as a destination.

Below: A huge clearance sale is conducted each year during the annual open house at the Anamosa store.

earlier periods, redoubling the whole business and hobby of collecting and restoring old motorcycles. Just as one example among many, John Parham's good friend Lonnie Isam offers more than 1,600 reproduced parts for Harley-Davidsons dating 1905 to 1929. Catering to this trend, J&P's Vintage Harley Catalog, launched in 2000, has since grown to 336 pages containing more than 10,000 parts for Harley-Davidsons, 1929 up to the 1984 model year.

ω

J&P Cycles would also find opportunity in a new class of Japanese-made motorcycles. For their first 30 years in the American market, the Japanese manufacturers followed an entirely different path from Harley-Davidson, which had been for many years the sole remaining American motorcycle manufacturer. As early as the 1970s, the Japanese brands had begun to cut deep into the Milwaukee brand's sales in both the street performance and heavyweight touring segments of the market, but they built nothing that looked or sounded remotely like a Harley-Davidson, and apparently had no desire to do so. But in their intense rivalry with one another, they practically drove Harley-Davidson into bankruptcy. The boom of the 1960s had slowed down by the mid-1970s, but Honda, Yamaha, Kawasaki, and Suzuki refused to scale back their production. Rather, they flooded their American dealers with motorcycles, and started discounting in an effort to move excess inventory. Their pricing practices were so extreme that they ran afoul of U.S. "anti-dumping" regulations, which prohibit importing companies from strategically selling their products below fair market value. Harley-Davidson filed a suit against the Japanese manufacturers in 1978, and they were found guilty of dumping their products on the American market.

As a result, the U.S. government applied a stiff tariff on all Japanese-made motorcycles over 700cc, the segment of the market in which Harley-Davidson was trying to compete. The Japanese argued that the designs, styling, technology, and performance of their bikes were not similar to Harleys in any way, but they nevertheless were forced to significantly increase the prices of their larger models. Without a doubt, this government intervention saved Harley-Davidson. It gave the new owners of the Motor Company breathing room to improve the quality of their products and develop the Evolution engine, which endowed the brand with a reputation for reliability like it had never before enjoyed throughout its history. In fact, Harley-Davidson righted itself and improved its sales so quickly, it actually petitioned the government to cancel the tariffs against its Japanese competitors a year before they were scheduled to expire.

In addition to offering better quality, Harley-Davidson can attribute its resurgence and eventual dominance of the heavyweight segment of the U.S. motorcycle market to its uncanny ability to tap into the nostalgic tastes of the Baby Boomers. Harley-Davidson began to deliberately build motorcycles with the silhouette, color schemes, and styling details of the pre-war Harleys of yesteryear. They brought back their classic "springer" front suspension and "tombstone" taillight. It was a gambit that the Japanese—coming from a different cultural perspective—could never have thought of, and for quite some time their dealers and the press continued to ridicule Harley-Davidson as behind the times and incapable of building a modern motorcycle. But Harley-Davidson's sales continued to grow, at a surprising rate, and by the mid-1990s, Harley-Davidson was building more than 100,000 motorcycles a year and making enormous profits from accessories, apparel, and the licensing of its logo. For those who could not own a Harley, wearing the Harley logo had become the next best thing, and this popularity drove a steadily upward sales trend, unabated for nearly two decades.

There had been a time when the technologically-oriented Japanese brands would never have stooped to build something "low-tech" like a Harley-Davidson. However, tweaking the nose of the Japanese companies with its anti-dumping suit would eventually bring the Motor Company more intense and direct competition than it had seen since the days of its great rivalry with Indian during the 1920s, '30s, and '40s. The Japanese manufacturers could not ignore the sales phenomenon unfolding before their eyes in the American market, and, besides, they owed Harley one for its dumping suit against them. They decided to go head-to-head by entering the heavyweight market with motorcycles that looked like a Harley-Davidson, especially its FX models referred to generically as "cruisers." Their first attempts were clumsy, almost laughable. But soon they began to get it right. They started producing cruisers that were more appealing to the American eye, and usually they could deliver them at a price lower than a Harley-Davidson, especially since Harleys were so popular that dealers had long waiting lists and often tacked on surcharges.

The first to get it right was Kawasaki with its 1,500cc Vulcan. It had styling that was more Harley-like than any previous Japanese attempt, and it even offered modern technology in a liquid-cooled, overhead-cam V-twin that was disguised to look like the traditional air-cooled technology of a Harley-Davidson. Then Yamaha came with its Touring Star. It was so close to Harley in appearance that it was indistinguishable to the untrained eye. As a result, with all five leading brands in vigorous competition, the cruiser segment of the American market became the most popular product niche, with all four of the Japanese brands trying to out-Harley Harley.

Over time, the Japanese brands developed their own identities and styles, eventually producing cruisers that did not look so much like a Harley, but were nevertheless very popular. These included the 1,800cc Honda VTX, a true muscle bike that appealed to riders who wanted more brute power and quicker acceleration than a Harley could provide, and the Suzuki Boulevard, which departed from the norm with its own somewhat unorthodox styling, with sport bike features that broadened the concept of the cruiser niche and brought a younger demographic into the

With all Japanese brands beginning to build cruisers competitive with Harley-Davidson, J&P Cycles moved into the Metric Cruiser market, launching a separate catalog for Metric Cruisers in 2004.

Below: The 2007 Metric Catalog. Adorning the cover is Baron Custom Accessories owner and president John Vaughn-Chaldy. John has been a huge supporter of J&P Cycles over the last several years and has participated in many collaborative projects including building this Honda VTX for J&P Cycles 2007 Catalog Cover.

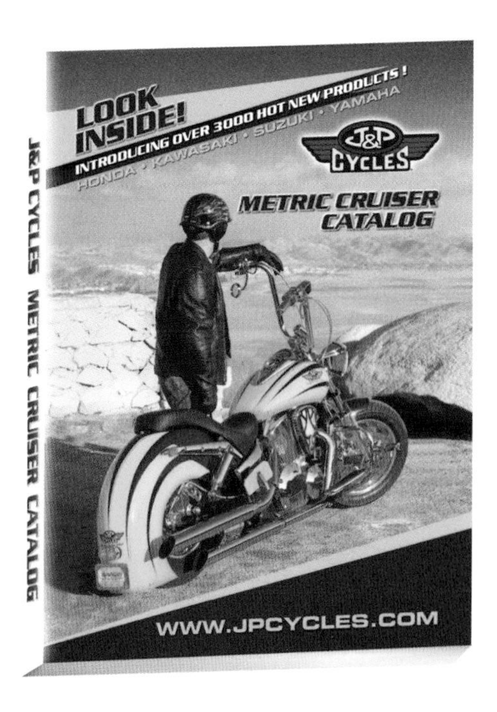

In 2003, J&P Cycles became a regular presence on national television. Pictured here are John and Jill filming for "Corbin's Ride-On," carried on SPEED Channel. The same year, another 45,000 square feet were added to the warehouse and a million dollar computerized conveyor system was installed (below), increasing productivity by 80 percent.

market for this category of motorcycle. Because these bikes are engineered on the metric system, as are all Japanese vehicles, they earned the generic name of "metric cruiser." Like the owners of Harley-Davidsons, buyers of metric cruisers are the kind of people who love to customize and personalize their motorcycles with special paint, graphics, accessories, and performance enhancement.

With a keen eye on the market, John Parham had not failed to notice this trend. J&P began to stock aftermarket parts for metric cruisers, and in 2003 came out with a separate catalog with over 300 pages aimed exclusively at owners of the Japanese brands, including the Honda luxury touring Gold Wing. By J&P Cycles' 25th anniversary year, 2004, the Metric Catalog had grown to over 400 pages, and would continue upward in size to just under 500 pages as J&P's metric product line grew and more metric cruisers were sold. The growth of the metric cruiser market has brought new suppliers, such as Baron Custom Accessories, into the J&P product line. Those who are watching this market trend closely speculate that the appeal of Harley-Davidsons may wane as the Baby Boomers pass into history, while the more powerful metric cruisers may maintain their appeal to a younger generation, thereby playing a greater role in upholding sales in the aftermarket. Significantly, Zach Parham is a member of this younger generation, and though he loves Harley-Davidsons as much as his father does, he believes in positioning J&P to expand in the metric cruiser aftermarket as buyers his age and younger become a larger demographic segment among American motorcycle owners.

With its official entry into the growing metric cruiser aftermarket, 2003 proved another banner year for J&P Cycles, which continued to grow while earning both local and national recognition. For the fifth consecutive year, J&P garnered a Top 100 dealer award. In addition, John and J&P Cycles were featured on the cable television show "Corbin's Ride-On," distributed nationally on SPEED Channel. And while most people in the little town of Anamosa still had no idea what was going on with all the UPS trucks arriving and leaving daily at the big warehouse out on Highway 151, the impact of J&P Cycles on the local economy had become impossible to ignore. In 2003, the Anamosa Chamber of Commerce created

a new top honor entitled "The President's Award," and J&P Cycles became its first recipient. Outreach to customers was improved during 2003, both through cyberspace and in the real world. The J&P Cycles website was redesigned to give customers quicker access to special prices on clearance items, and the big, yellow mobile showroom tackled an exhaustive schedule that included appearances at 34 special events from coast to coast.

☙

J&P Cycles had a lot to celebrate upon the arrival of its 25th anniversary in 2004. Its Harley-Davidson catalog was now 884 pages, and its metric catalog had grown to 432 pages. In fact, the metric market had become so strong that J&P opened a new metric-only showroom at its Lazelle Street facility in Sturgis for the 2004 Rally. In Anamosa, another 45,000 square feet of warehouse were added, bringing J&P's total floor space up to more than 150,000 square feet. With this warehouse expansion, a million dollars were invested in a sophisticated, computer-driven conveyor system that sped up fulfillment operations and tracks orders, returns, and inventory through bar-code scanners. Matt Ahrens, who was hired as distribution center manager shortly after installation of the system, says, "We have improved productivity by 80 percent with the new system, and are handling 4,000 orders a day." Assistant Distribution Center Manager Paul Gabriele explains, "Warehouse efficiency is as critical to customer service as any other function of the company. For example, our damage claim rate is down to only one in 10,000 packages." In addition to warehouse improvements, a 26-person technical services call center was set up in Ormond Beach, Florida, and even bigger plans for a new Florida retail store were on the drawing board. The Ormond Beach call center location was chosen for its proximity to Wyo-Tech in Ormond Beach and the Motorcycle Mechanics Institute in Orlando, both sources of technically-trained people capable of maintaining J&P's high standard of technical support for its customers. With the addition of staff in Florida, J&P's payroll increased to 200 people, amounting to a doubling of staff in just five years.

Arlen Ness autographs the shirt of one of his many fans at the J&P 25th Anniversary Open House in 2004. As seen below, the annual event had become a significant industry trade show, bringing out the big rigs of many of J&P's top brand suppliers.

Not only did J&P Cycles earn Top 100 Dealer status for the sixth consecutive year, but it was named the nation's best independent dealer by *Dealernews*. Likewise, Custom Chrome honored the company as its top retailer in the nation. In the meantime, the company profile that had appeared on the "Corbin's Ride-On" television show proved so beneficial that John decided to get more deeply involved in television. As a result, J&P Cycles became the sponsor of six segments about the do's and don'ts of customizing a motorcycle. The shows were filmed at J&P's

The J&P Cycles open house always draws motorcycle industry celebrities. Above, national road racing champion and custom bike designer Roland Sands. (Ed Youngblood photo)

Below: Keith Ruxton and Dave Campos, members of the Easyriders streamliner team who held the world speed record of 322.16 mph for 16 years. (Ed Youngblood photo)

shop in Anamosa, and featured John assisting "Corbin's Ride-On" host Brian Jackson. The idea worked so well on television that J&P created on-site at Anamosa a winter workshop series where customers could come and learn about building, customizing, and maintaining motorcycles.

J&P Cycles had been hosting an annual open house for many years, but its 25th anniversary event, scheduled for June 26, 2004, was something special. Arlen Ness, known as the King of the Customizers, was the guest of honor, and brought with him some of his most famous creations, including "Nesstalgia," a striking yellow creation reminiscent of the lines and styling features of a 1957 Chevy. A veritable trade show of product pavilions and big rigs included participation by Custom Chrome, Drag Specialties, Arlen Ness, Corbin, Küryakyn, Samson, S&S Cycle, Bikers Choice, Memphis Shades, MBNA, Midwest Motorcycle Supply, Mid-USA, Mustang Seats, Baron Custom Accessories, and Bassani Exhaust. More than 50 beautifully-customized motorcycles arrived for a ride-in bike show, and the Easyriders Joe Teresi Dyno Drag Semi was there to entertain riders and test their reflexes with a simulated drag race. More than 8,500 J&P Cycles customers arrived to enjoy free food and entertainment that included a biker rodeo, stunt riders, and a wall of death thrill show. More than $4,000 in door prizes were given away, a silent auction raised over $3,000 for the National Motorcycle Museum, and an industry charity golf tournament on the day prior to the open house raised nearly $4,000 for Camp Courageous of Iowa. John Parham said, "With perfect 80-degree weather, it was a spectacular day for J&P Cycles, its suppliers, and its customers. We just can't believe it! This milestone is really a dream come true for us. In the early years, we never thought we would make it this far. Our thanks to everyone who supported us over the years. You have helped make J&P Cycles what it is today."

Growth continued in 2005. Payroll increased to 279 employees and additional property was acquired in Sturgis, bringing the J&P site up to a full city block. The Harley-Davidson catalog went beyond 1,000 pages, featuring more than 35,000 products. The Metric Catalog grew to 536 pages, including a new section for the owners of American-made Victory motorcycles. The Anamosa store was reconfigured to add another 2,000 square feet of retail space, and for the seventh time *Dealernews* named J&P Cycles one of the nation's Top 100 dealers. In addition, Samson Exhausts honored J&P as its top-selling dealer. A six-week winter workshop series, begun the previous year, was continued, and more than 150 customers braved the Iowa winter weather to learn from J&P staff about maintenance, bolt-on accessories, tires, wheels, brakes, engine performance, and exhaust systems. Photographer Pam Proctor, who documented the seminars, said, "Whether they were new or seasoned riders, the attendees really appreciated the visual displays of parts, product samples, and great technical knowledge that the staff was able to provide."

The June open house featured Biker Billy and his "Cooks with Fire" show, as well as the Globe of Death motorcycle stunt team. More than 8,000 customers turned out for the day to enjoy free food, entertainment, and special discount prices throughout the store. SPEED Channel and Bradley David Productions brought "Corbin's Ride-On" to Anamosa twice to shoot segments for its 2006 shows. These included complete custom bike builds of a Harley-Davidson and a Kawasaki Vulcan. J&P Cycles and the National Motorcycle Museum also earned national television exposure when John and his friend David Ohrt staged vintage bike racing for the History Channel. Using the 3/8-mile dirt track at the Monticello fairgrounds, Parham and Ohrt cut exhibition laps for the camera aboard a 1912 Indian single and a 1914 Harley-Davidson twin. Parham relates, "The Indian was David's and the Harley was mine, but we rode each other's motorcycles. We started out easy, but as racing always goes, pretty soon we were probably running way to fast. But we were having fun." Later, artist David Uhl would use photographs taken that day as inspiration for his oil painting of John Parham, dressed as a mid-teens Indian factory team rider.

Construction was begun for another 15,000-square-foot addition to the Anamosa warehouse, and it was announced that ground would be broken soon for a new year-round retail store in Ormond Beach, Florida. With more warehousing added, J&P Cycles' facility grew to over 165,000 square feet, necessary for keeping up a high level of customer service for a business that reached sales of $75 million in 2006. Again, the Harley catalog grew in page count by another 10 percent, up to 1,192 pages. J&P also stepped into the sport-bike market, developing a line of parts offered through a new and separate sport bike catalog. For the eighth time, J&P Cycles was named a *Dealernews* Top 100 dealer, and John was inducted into the Sturgis Motorcycle Hall of Fame. During the 2006 season, J&P Cycles appeared on 10 segments of the television show "American Thunder," seen on SPEED Channel. Filming took place in Anamosa, at the J&P Sturgis store during the Rally, and at J&P's seasonal store in Daytona Beach, Florida. Attendance at the June open house in Anamosa, which featured an appearance of bike builder Eddie Trotta and a collection of Indian Larry choppers, grew to more than 10,000 customers. However, perhaps the most exciting event of the year was when the newly-christened "J&P Cycles Express" streamliner set a national speed record of over 178 mph at the Bonneville Salt Flats. This beautiful machine, built by Bonneville legend Bob George, was originally acquired for display at the National Motorcycle Museum. However, former J&P technician Jeff Wiley thought it could be refurbished to a competitive standard, which proved correct when it appeared at Bonneville in September in its new J&P Cycles yellow, red, and blue livery and was piloted to the record by veteran speedster Leo Hess.

J&P's 35,000 square foot Destination Daytona Super Store facility opened in June 2007.

Below: 15,000 square feet of tires, clothing, parts and accessories are available to J&P's customers at the Destination Daytona Super Store.

John, Bruce Rossmeyer and Ormond Beach Director of Economic Development Joe Mannarino stop for a photo at the Destiation Daytona grand opening celebration.

Below: John and Jill overlook the store from its second-story mezzanine. (Buzz Kanter photo)

☙

The spectacular success of Harley-Davidson since 1990 has attracted big money to the motorcycle retail industry, and led to a sea change in the quality and character of motorcycle dealerships. Once grubby storefronts and garages run by enthusiasts who had no ambition beyond selling an occasional motorcycle to another hardcore biker, motorcycle dealerships have become megastores in high-traffic locations, offering a wide array of products and services, including food and entertainment, to an ever-broadening demographic. They are designed with products and ambiance to appeal to women as well as men, and they have moved from the inner city to suburban freeway interchanges. It has become a powerhouse business that has attracted entrepreneurs as interested in their return on investment as they are in motorcycles.

Bruce Rossmeyer has become legendary as a leading power in this powerhouse industry. As a principal in at least 14 Harley-Davidson dealerships, he took over a Daytona Beach, Florida, location in 1994, where it is rumored that he has sold as many as 300 motorcycles during the annual Daytona Bike Week celebration in March. But one location in the world center of motorsports was not enough for Rossmeyer. In 2004, he broke ground for Destination Daytona, a 150-acre, $50 million complex at the intersection of I-95 and US1 that, when completed, will include two hotels, two strip malls, seven restaurants and bars, condos and apartments, and an amphitheater. Anchored on the south end of the property at the intersection of the two busy highways is Rossmeyer's latest Harley-Davidson dealership, a 105,000-square-foot store featuring two levels of motorcycles, apparel, and accessories. The anchor at the north end of the complex, also facing I-95, is the new Destination Daytona store of J&P Cycles, the world's largest retailer of motorcycle aftermarket products. Between Rossmeyer's and J&P Cycles is an Arlen Ness store and three other motorcycle dealerships. It has been Rossmeyer's policy to retain ownership and build to suit for his tenants. However, in the case of J&P Cycles he made a unique exception. He explains, "When I started the project, John contacted me, but he wanted to buy the land and build his own store. I made the decision to sell to John, and he is the only one I have done this with. I felt that J&P Cycles brought so much credibility to the project, I was willing to make this exception in our policy." Rossmeyer adds, "It was a win/win situation because in this industry John is known for his professionalism and credibility."

The J&P Cycles Destination Daytona Super Store opened in June 2007. It is a two-story, 35,000-square-foot facility in a Spanish Colonial style that includes 15,000 square feet of showroom and 9,000 square feet of warehouse on the ground floor, plus 11,000 square feet for offices and a call center on the second level. Around the expansive showroom is a mezzanine displaying twenty-five of John Parham's rare antique motorcycles, and the walls behind are covered with giant canvas prints. J&P was assisted with its interior design by Steve Wierzbowski, a strategic project planning and retail design consultant with the Dobbins Group, who worked with Harley-Davidson on its modern dealership prototype in the 1980s and was involved with the design of the visitors' center at the Motor Company's Capital Drive facility in Milwaukee. Wierzbowski says, "I like doing motorcycle dealership design, so we took a booth at the trade show in Indianapolis in 2005. John Parham was one of the first people to walk up to our booth. I knew who John was—there's no one in the motorcycle industry who doesn't—and I got really excited when he started describing what he wanted to do at his new Destination Daytona store." Wierzbowski adds, "Coincidentally, at the time I was working on the interior design at the big Iowa 80 truck stop just south of Anamosa, so it was convenient to start working with J&P right away."

Wierzbowski learned that John and Jill wanted the store's interior designed to very high standards. It was going to be everything that the Anamosa store could not be, since it had always been a compromised design, starting as an implement dealership and expanding piecemeal over the years, as growth demanded and resources would allow. Destination Daytona was their opportunity to begin with a clean slate and do it right. Wierzbowski explains, "The Florida store had to epitomize their ideas of quality and service. The color scheme, the fixtures, and the traffic pattern were all designed to make the customer feel welcome, to make merchandise easy to locate and examine, and to give customers ready access to the personnel who can help them. The service desks are set up so the salesperson never has to turn away from the customer. There are moveable information kiosks that can be moved to different locations throughout the store and plugged into data jacks in the floor. Display fixtures are no taller than 60 inches so that the customer can see from one end of the store to the other and never feel like he or she is in a maze. Everything addresses J&P's demand for customer service, friendliness, and accessibility." Wierzbowski concludes, "And although everything looks very opulent, we have applied what I call 'value engineering,' which creates the best appearance for the lowest price. For example, the stands on which custom motorcycles are displayed were salvaged from the Guggenheim's Art of the Motorcycle Exhibition in Orlando. They are beautiful, quality work, but John got them at the right price." The result is a motorcycle aftermarket retail store that has no parallel in the United States, and possibly the world. As one awestruck visitor at its grand opening in October 2007 said, "This place is the Cabela's of motorcycle stores!" During the Biketoberfest week, 35,000 customers visited the store!

For the grand opening of J&P's new Destination Daytona Super Store, John and Jill celebrated the occasion by riding John's Harley-Davidson from Anamosa, Iowa to Ormond Beach, Florida. On the way they stopped in Montgomery City, Missouri, to visit with Kenny John, one of their oldest friends and the designer of the J&P Cycles logo. Then, they rode on to Nashville where they spent the night with Somer Hooker and his wife Loyce. Hooker is a motorcycle collector and broker who has advised John on the development

In 2007, J&P Cycles again expanded its product line by creating a sport bike catalog. In the mean time, its Harley-Davidson catalog has grown to a thousand pages. By 2008, J&P's four catalogs combined contained more than 63,000 items on more than 1,900 pages.

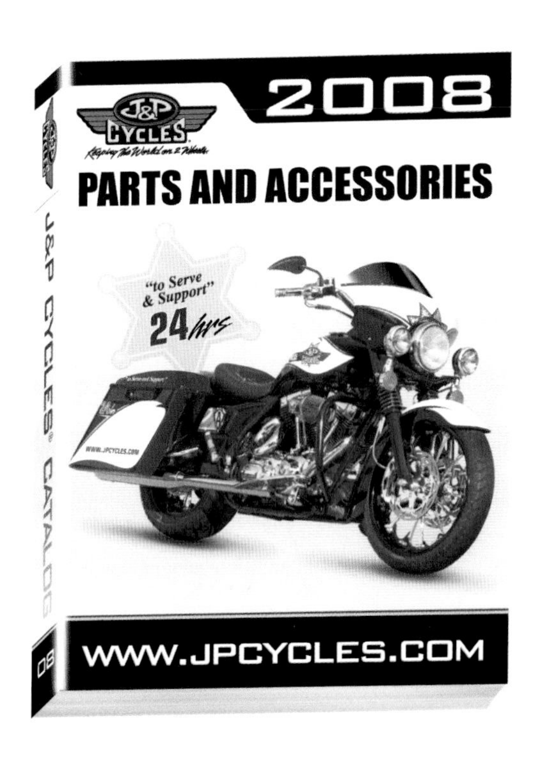

The story of J&P's success and leadership in the industry earns a Dealernews cover story.

of his collection. From Nashville, they traveled east to Maggie Valley, North Carolina, to visit their friend Dale Walksler, the founder and curator of the Wheels Through Time Museum. From Maggie Valley, they traveled on to Ormond Beach for the Daytona Beach Biketoberfest and to join local dignitaries for the ribbon cutting at their new store. It was the first time in their 33 years of marriage that John and Jill had found an opportunity to take an extended, multi-state motorcycle tour together. Though John had taken many trips with Zach, Jill had previously stayed home to manage the company.

☙

At the big annual dealer expo in Indianapolis, you will occasionally see people walking around with a lapel button that says "Mail Order," with a diagonal bar across it, meaning "No Mail Order." These are local retailers who hate and militate against businesses like J&P Cycles that sell and ship products to an international clientele. Those who oppose mail-order retailers will tell you that they provide unfair competition because they can discount deeply through volume, or that they lack the overhead of local retailers who must maintain and staff a presentable facility. They envision a mail-order retailer as a company with a vast warehouse, no showroom, low-paid workers not qualified to deal with the public, and a website or phone room of people who anonymously process orders with little or no accountability for their performance. Although J&P Cycles has been the target of such anti-mail order feelings, none of these arguments apply.

J&P Cycles began 30 years ago as a local dealer, just like those who object to mail-order retailers, but John Parham was not satisfied to stand and wait for customers to walk through his door. In fact, he could not afford to wait for customers, because his tiny rural market could not deliver them in sufficient numbers to survive. Parham never set out to be a mail-order giant. He moved into the field on a small scale out of necessity, and what J&P Cycles has become evolved over a period of nearly three decades. Still, once his bread and butter lay in mail order, he maintained a conventional retail outlet, and, in fact, made a multi-million dollar investment in the Destination Daytona Super Store and a full city block complex in Sturgis, SD. Volume sales were clearly one of Parham's objectives since the early 1990s, but discounting has never been the method through which he achieved high volume. Instead, J&P Cycles has always based its relationship with its customers on quality service, not price. Discounters can create problems at both ends of the market, not just among fellow retailers, but also among suppliers. Hector Melendez of Daytona Twin Tech, one of J&P's suppliers, says, "J&P maintains price integrity. This is important to and appreciated by a supplier." And anyone who has seen the capital investments in both Anamosa and Ormond Beach will realize that J&P does not beat its competition through low overhead. Quick and consistent customer service requires a significant investment, which J&P has and continues to make as customer expectations rise and retail becomes more competitive.

Furthermore, a review of the direct-mail retailers who have come and gone in the motorcycle industry will reveal that the whole concept of the low-overhead discounter does not work, at least not for long. Those who do not make the investment and commitment in a full-catalog inventory, swift response, a liberal return and refund policy, and superior customer service do not last very long. In fact, it could be argued that a company like J&P Cycles must invest much more in human resources than a local dealer because it must in order to survive. And consider the cost of printing and distributing more than a million 1,000-page catalogs a year for free. How many of these never yield an order? No one will ever know, but it is clear that J&P Cycles does not succeed by skimping on costs. And dealers who want to complain about direct-mail discounters do not have a complaint against J&P, which has never competed on the basis of price. Ted Sands of Performance Machine, one of J&P's suppliers, states, "I am constantly surprised by what J&P has achieved. It has gotten big without being a discounter. Instead, its business is built on outstanding and consistent customer service. Rather than always focusing on what his competitors are doing, John's focus is internal, always looking for ways to make his company better." The idea that J&P Cycles has become a benchmark success through some unfair competitive edge just does not wash, and any local retailer who feels resentful toward its success might consider that he or she could have done the same, given a willingness to sacrifice, work hard, and take risks equal to that of John and Jill Parham. George Munger, Küryakyn's director of dealer development says, "There are lots of dealers who would like to do what John has done, but they just don't have the drive to do it."

This debate over the role of mail order in the American motorcycle retail business was addressed by *Dealernews* in August 2007, when it devoted a cover story to John, Jill, and J&P Cycles entitled "The World According to John." The story declared, "Don't hate him because he's built a big business. John Parham and J&P Cycles are an integral part of the motorcycle culture." In this feature, Parham argues that J&P's success is derived from the simple principles that apply to any retailer, whether or not they are involved in selling by mail. He says, "This business isn't rocket science.

J&P Cycles Anamosa, IA showroom includes a specially designed 2nd story mezzanine which displays 12 of John's favorite vintage motorcycles as well as several pieces of motorcycle memorabilia.

Below: John, Jill, Doug Hessing, Rob DeSotel, and Nicole Ridge receive the Dealernews "Best Independent Dealer" award in 2004.

1996

1999

2003

2007

Here's to 30 years! John & Jill Parham - 2008

Customers can buy their products in a multitude of places, so when they come into your store they should be welcomed within their first 20 steps. Welcome them, show them you appreciate them, have a good presentation of the product, and have the product available." It has worked for J&P Cycles, whether through its catalogs, the telephone, and the Internet, or through conventional traffic coming through the doors of its Anamosa, Sturgis, and Destination Daytona stores. The Dealernews article explains that J&P Cycles has not succeeded by feeding at the table of other retailers, but rather, through aggressive promotion and excellent customer service, J&P has baked a bigger pie to the benefit of the whole motorcycle industry, including manufacturers, aftermarket suppliers, customers, and, yes, other dealers.

Küryakyn's Tom Ellsworth believes that the success of J&P has actually helped, not hurt, local retail. He says, "Direct mail enhances brand and exposure. It actually helps point-of-sale retail. I've seen people bring the J&P catalog to their local dealer to ask for specific parts. It is a bible for selection, like having an owner's manual for everything." Ellsworth makes a compelling argument in light of the fact that J&P's four catalogs represent over 1,900 pages containing more than 63,000 parts. By helping people get more enjoyment out of their motorcycles and raising customer satisfaction to a higher level, J&P Cycles has not just ridden the great motorcycle boom of the 1980s and '90s, it has contributed to it significantly, and, in a literal sense, helped keep the world on two wheels.

Chapter Twelve: Trouble on the J&P Cycles Express

Near the western border of Utah, a spur of pavement juts north off of Interstate 80, then turns eastward, like a road to nowhere. Those who use this road just call it "Where the Asphalt Ends." This morning, before dawn, they are lined up, awaiting daylight. The parking lights of box vans, rental cars, and sport utility vehicles shine dimly in the darkness. Among them are many trailers carrying motorcycles. All is silent except for the soft clatter of a couple of diesel engines, idling away. Slowly, a band across the eastern sky turns to peach then fades upward to black, silhouetting a range of jagged mountains in the distance. The brilliant white point of Venus–the Morning Star–penetrates the night sky as the peachy band of light grows and brightens when the Sun shows itself like a great orange thumbnail, emerging from behind the mountains. As it rises and grows into a bright sphere, its light diffuses through the atmosphere and reveals ahead of the awaiting vehicles a vast, white expanse, bounded to the right by Interstate 80 where the lights of tiny trucks creep along the horizon, and by great mountains to the left, illusively much farther away than they seem. The idling diesels clatter up, and other engines come to life as the waiting

Bonneville holds surprises, even for a team with top equipment and the experience of a national record. The J&P Cycles Express awaits its first run at Bonneville, 2007.

At the J&P open house in June, the Express sits with its sister ship, the twin-engine Easyriders streamliner that has held the world motorcycle speed record for 16 years. Soon the Express will leave for Bonneville to defend its national record. (Ed Youngblood photo)

Below: Zach Parham and Scott Holton examine the data-retrieval system that will later fail to perform.

caravan slowly moves forward, dropping over the edge of the pavement and proceeding out onto the huge white desert of Bonneville.

The Bonneville Salt Flats is an other-worldly place of nearly 160 square miles, the remnants of Lake Bonneville, which, 36,000 years ago, contained nearly 20,000 square miles of surface area; almost the size of Lake Superior and far deeper, covering portions of the states of Utah, Idaho, and Nevada in the North America Great Basin. Over the eons, some of the water drained off due to seismic action, and the rest evaporated, leaving behind several smaller lakes, including the Great Salt Lake, lying west of Salt Lake City. What remained of the ancient Lake Bonneville is a flat table of hardpan white salt, laid out so large that one can see the curvature of the earth, making the mountains in the distance look like they are floating in air because their bases fall beneath the horizon. So strange, uninviting, and eerily beautiful is this place, that some people compare it to the dark side of the Moon, not that they have the slightest idea what that might be like. The caravan of trucks and cars is here this morning–and about this time every year–because Bonneville is one of the few places on Earth where one can lay down a racetrack ten miles long, as straight and level as a ruler. Here the speedsters test their ingenuity and their nerve by pushing experimental vehicles to the outer limits of performance in pursuit of national and world speed records.

For these men and women and their amazing machines, Bonneville is a beauty, and Bonneville is a bitch. It has no mercy and plays no favorites. At a mile in elevation, its thin air punishes engines far beyond their design parameters, and it seems to be the home of gremlins that are dedicated to proving a Salt Flats' version of Murphy's Law: if anything can go wrong, at Bonneville it will! Land speed racing is, without a doubt, the most frustrating motorsport in the world. Because practically every part of many of the vehicles has been hand-fabricated, it is breathtakingly expensive. Because little meaningful testing can be done at any other venue, speed vehicle owners often come to Bonneville only to discover that they are woefully under-prepared or wrong-headed in their design decisions. Because of the remoteness of the place, large crews and great outlays of equipment must be brought in order to be prepared for every possible problem. And if this were not enough, then there is the surface itself, and the unpredictability of the Bonneville weather.

This place seems to follow its own meteorological rules, and within minutes a near-perfect day can be shattered by a thunderstorm, rolling in over the mountains; or a rising wind across the valley that makes it too dangerous to operate vehicles at high speeds. With rain, the salt immediately becomes sodden, then water will gather on its surface as Bonneville quickly reverts to its primal nature, the lake that it once was. When this happens, the day is done and everyone whiles away their time in an expensive hotel room in the small, nearby town of Wendover, Utah, or, worse yet, at the crap tables just across the state line in West Wendover, Nevada. It is suitable, perhaps, that the owners and teams have easy access to gambling, because gambling is what speed racing is all about. Bonneville can give the most haphazardly-prepared team a speed record, or the best-prepared team a disastrous defeat.

In the outer limits of land speed motorcycle racing, the machines have no resemblance to the motorcycles most of us are familiar with. Their kinship is little more than the fact that they contain an internal combustion engine (usually) and are limited to two wheels running in a single track. Otherwise, they look like projectiles, manned darts that skim across the surface of the salt. Because the key to speed is minimal frontal area, these motorcycles—called "streamliners," or "liners," for short—have the narrowest possible cross section, built barely large enough to hold a small man lying prone. In most cases, the engine compartment, containing one or more engines, is behind the pilot, and behind that, aft of the rear wheel are two parachutes that are deployed to slow the liner down at the end of the course. Its chassis, built to rigorous safety standards, is sheathed in a smooth skin made of aluminum, fiberglass, or more commonly today, carbon fiber. These machines resemble brightly-painted cigars as they speed across the salt, trailing a muted howl that seems to rise from the surface.

The pilots of these streamliners are an elite fraternity. It requires nerve to pilot any motorcycle across the flats of Bonneville above 200 miles per hour, but almost anyone with the will is capable of this aboard an open or partially streamlined motorcycle. Those who lie on their backs and allow themselves to be strapped into a tube more confining than a coffin that they will throttle to speeds approaching and surpassing 300 miles per hour are a whole different breed. Though they possess the reflexes of a cat, they seem to lack the central nervous system that lets the rest of us translate what is happening around us into fear. The noise and vibration inside a streamliner can be deafening and disorienting. Yet these pilots manage to ignore the din while they

J&P Express crew preparing for the day at Bonneville 2007.

Below: The J&P Express with the best of the best, world record holders Ack Attack and Number 7 at Bonneville, 2006.

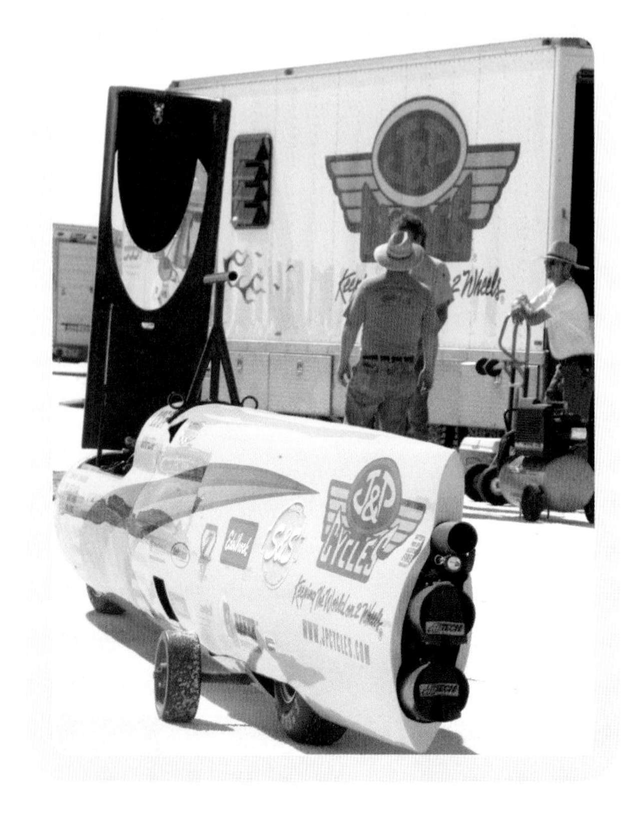

Above and below: with bodywork installed, the J&P Cycles Express is ready to receive its pilot, Leo Hess, and make its run.

carefully open a throttle just enough to maintain maximum traction on the hard salt surface, watch a tachometer needle rise, throttle back and shift gears, throttle up again, and concentrate on the mile markers as they flash by, faster and faster and faster, waiting for the moment when they will throttle down, activate their drag chutes, then lower air-driven skids at the right moment so their very expensive machine will not tip onto its side and leave the logos of sponsors scraped off on the salt. If this were not enough, a liner pilot must have the reflexes to react instantly to the slightest gust of crosswind, or a wobble caused by an irregularity on the course. And they must have the judgment and presence of mind to activate built-in fire extinguishing systems if something goes terribly wrong. In the event of a catastrophic engine explosion, the belly pan of the liner in which the pilot is lying may fill with super-heated oil, capable of bursting into flames and turning the insides of the machine into an inferno. These are men and women who must keep all of these factors present in their minds, yet be frightened by none of them. It is said that two-time world record holder Dave Campos would sleep in the cockpit of his machine as a kind of Zen exercise in psychological preparation for the rigors of his task. Any rider with the slightest tendency toward claustrophobia dares not attempt to pilot a streamliner.

The designers and builders of land speed streamliners are an elite fraternity as well. They are creative and ingenious men with a wide range of skills who have built their body of knowledge over decades of experience through trial and error. They include, among others, the late Don Vesco, current world record holder Denis Manning, Mike Akatiff, Sam Wheeler, and Bob George. George, born in Glendale, California, in 1939, made his first trip to Bonneville when he was 19. He became the first man to make twin-engine machines run effectively, and he was a mentor to Don Vesco and Dave Campos, both of whom became holders of the ultimate motorcycle land speed record. George designed the twin-engine streamliner sponsored by *Easyriders* Magazine that Dave Campos piloted in 1990 to a speed of 322.492 miles per hour, a record that stood for an astonishing 16 years! Using what he learned from the spectacularly successful *Easyriders* machine, George then built a similar twin-engine liner, utilizing more modern and lighter-weight materials. Later, this machine was shortened to become a single-engine chassis, and early in 2006 John Parham acquired it at a motorcycle auction in Las Vegas with the intention of adding it to his motorcycle collection, and placing it on display at the National Motorcycle Museum in Anamosa, Iowa.

ଓ

John Parham's streamliner never made it to the National Motorcycle Museum. On his staff at J&P Cycles was a technician named Jeff Wiley, a Bonneville veteran who raced open motorcycles with Leo Payne in the 1970s, and served for a time as an engine tuner on the crew of Bob George's Jammer streamliner, which later became the world-record-setting Easyriders streamliner. Wiley handled specialty work for J&P, building and maintaining its fleet of show bikes. He got his hands on the streamliner originally to detail it for display at the Museum, and he recalls, "The steering was frozen and the wheel bearings were shot," both of which are damage routinely caused by running on the corrosive salt. He adds, "All of the safety equipment, including harnesses and fire bottles, needed to be replaced." But as he cleaned and evaluated the liner, Wiley told John that it could easily be made race-ready. For Parham, this was just the type of challenge he enjoys, and at his direction, the motorcycle was stripped and rebuilt, and a 1,350cc Harley-Davidson Sportster-based engine was installed. Its carbon fiber shell was painted an eye-popping yellow with red and blue panels, and the logos of various J&P business partners were affixed to its sides. With a large logo of the National Motorcycle Museum mounted on either side of its nose, and a big J&P Cycles logo on its tail, the streamliner was rechristened the J&P Cycles Express and became a rolling billboard for Parham's various business interests, ready to make its debut at the 2006 motorcycle speed trials at Bonneville.

In retrospect, motorcycle speed enthusiasts have described Bonneville 2006 as the perfect storm. Departing from decades of Bonneville tradition, where cars and bikes have been run together, it provided a new format for motorcycles only, enabling more time on a motorcycle-friendly track that had not become rutted by the heavy automobiles. Furthermore, the salt was in better condition than anyone could remember, and an unprecedented field of top-tier equipment arrived with the intention of taking down Dave Campos's 16-year-old ultimate motorcycle speed record. The first to do so was Mike Akatiff's 1000 horsepower twin-Hayabusa Ack Attack, piloted by Bonneville veteran Rocky Robinson, which raised the world record to 343 miles per hour. That record lasted only 48 hours when dirt-track star Chris Carr, a Bonneville rookie, climbed into the cockpit of Denis Manning's Number 7 machine and upped the figure to 350 miles per hour. Then Sam Wheeler went onto the course and ripped off a run at 355 in his single-engine EZ-Hook liner. Wheeler, however, was unable to back it up with a two-way average because he shredded a front tire and damaged his machine at the end of his first run. For the E-Z Hook team, this made a new record impossible since the rules provide that the recognized top speed is based on a two-way average, with both runs being completed within a period of two hours. It was a good week also for the J&P Cycles Express team. Although they were not racing for the glory of the ultimate motorcycle land speed record, they succeeded in earning an AMA national record of more than 178 miles per hour in their 1,350cc engine class. Though not an ultimate record, this achievement was important for J&P Cycles, due to the fact that land speed racing for motorcycles has experienced a renaissance in recent years, capturing more media attention than ever before.

Motivated by the success of their 2006 performance, the J&P Cycles crew returns to Bonneville in 2007 with an ambitious plan. They have

Leo Hess, without his fire suit, tries on the liner for size.

Below: The week begins disastrously with a 300 m.p.h. crash for Ack Attack. The machine is irreparable and its 2007 speed trials come to a bitter end.

The J&P team runs into unexpected problems with the small 1350cc Sportster motor.

Below: The crew tows the Express down to the 10-mile course to the starting line for a run.

come with a rebuilt 1,350cc engine with the hope of beating their own national record, plus earning an FIM world record. In addition, they have brought a new S&S 1,650cc engine with which they hope to earn both national and world records. It features an S&S lower end, Red Shift cams, Axtell cylinders and Zipper's heads. Power is transmitted through a Primo-Rivera primary drive, Barnett clutch, and a Baker transmission. They start the week with what they call their "little engine," which they have souped-up even more, using a new crank, re-ground heads, new cams, and a redesigned exhaust system. The field of motorcycles is much larger than the previous year, but Sam Wheeler has not returned with his EZ-Hook, having been unable to acquire special tires rated for 350-plus speeds that will fit his machine. But the other over-dogs are there; Ack Attack and Number 7 are prepared to do battle. As the teams set up shop and prepare their motorcycles, the bright yellow J&P Cycles Express, with paint by Scott Takes at Underground Art Studios in Cedar Rapids, stands out as one of the most beautiful liners in the pits. It draws crowds equal to those visiting the pits of Ack Attack and Number 7. If show were all that counts, John Parham would have already met his marketing objectives. But you have to go, in addition to show, and that test will come the following day, in part because J&P's pilot Leo Hess has not yet arrived.

Bonneville 2007 begins badly. Ack Attack sets out to draw first blood, as it did in 2006, making its first run of the meet at just under 300 mph. Then, on its return run, accelerating across the salt at above 300 mph, the tail of the liner begins to yaw. Pilot Rocky Robinson lets off the throttle, and sensing that the machine has settled down, rolls on the throttle again only to feel the liner yaw into a wild fishtail, swinging from one side to the other. Then, completely out of control, it crashes onto its side, slides, then flips to its other side. The canopy flies off and sails a hundred feet into the air as the liner rolls onto its top, scooping salt into the cockpit around Robinson and even into his helmet. By now the chutes are out, slowing the liner down and pulling it out of its roll. Owing to the structural integrity and safety equipment of the machine, Robinson is unhurt, but Ack Attack proves a near-write-off. Back in its pit, workers begin to rip away body panels because their fasteners are ground over and impacted with salt. What they find is irreparable, and Ack Attack's week has quickly come to an end. Wrapped with tape to keep it from littering pieces of its shattered body panels on its way home, Ack Attack is loaded onto its trailer as a pitiful commentary on the merciless nature of Bonneville. Other speedsters listen carefully and heed Robinson's warning that there seems to be a soft spot on the course at the sixth mile. This is a portent of things to come as many teams will discover that the condition of the course is far inferior to that of the previous year. There will be more crashes during the week.

The next day, J&P's pilot, Leo Hess, arrives. Hess is a 58-year-old hot rodder from South Dakota who has been building and piloting fast cars and motorcycles since the age of ten. He is another protégé of Bob George and once piloted his twin-engine Jammer to a speed of nearly 238 miles per hour. With a physique like Rudi Nureyev and an attitude like Cool Hand Luke, he is a classic streamliner pilot, which journalists have often compared to Wild West gunfighters for their nerves of steel and lightning reflexes. In the case of Hess, it is more than just a comparison, since he is one. When not racing motorcycles or building fast engines, Hess is active in competitive shooting and quick-draw contests, able to pull from his holster and bullseye a target in 0.27 seconds. You look into his eyes as he is being strapped into the coffin, and it is clear that his pulse rate barely elevates, as if this were just another day at the office. The engine is brought to life, the canopy closed, and the liner is towed up to a speed of 50 or 60 miles per hour where its engine can get a grip on its tall gearing. Hess raises the skids, releases the tow rope, and rolls on the throttle. The engine sputters and struggles, then clears out and revs up toward full song. Then suddenly its tone goes flat, refusing to rev any higher, and Hess is forced to shift prematurely into second gear. Again, the sound rises then flattens out as the liner disappears over the horizon. John Parham, standing in the wake of its sound, says, "Something's wrong." Minutes later, a speed is announced over the radio: barely 150 miles per hour. John says impassively, "That's a disappointment," and the crew loads up to race to the other end of the course to retrieve Hess and the Express.

At the eight-mile marker, Hess is already out of the machine and walking around. "I couldn't get it over five grand," he says. "It would rev up, then just quit, and not rev any faster." He adds, "It wouldn't even pull top gear, and I had to downshift to keep it running." Knowing there was no hope to break the record, he shut off early and let the Express coast to a speed where he could stop with its brakes alone, saving its crew the bother of repacking its chutes. Everyone is confounded, and Express is loaded up to return to the pits for a diagnosis of the problem. Bonneville liners contain sophisticated data retrieval systems where all kinds of information is collected from sensors on the engine, clutch, exhaust, and other critical components throughout the machine. This information is stored in memory, and can be downloaded to a laptop after the run. The shell is pulled off the Express and a laptop plugged in. Inexplicably, the screen indicates that no information has been retrieved. Frustration goes off the scale as team members begin to question who didn't do his job, and Wiley announces angrily that he is prepared to yank this data-retrieval system off the machine and throw it in the trash.

As the team falls to bickering, John Parham seems oblivious to the storm. If there is consternation

Leo Hess is strapped in for his first run, but the liner underperforms. (Ed Youngblood photo)

Below: Later a storm arrives and crew members must hold the awnings down with an engine change underway. Nothing is easy at Bonneville.

John, on the salt after a difficult week. There is always next year.

Below: John talks with legendary drag racer Pete Hill.

on his face, it is well hidden by his mustache, dark glasses, and flat-brimmed straw hat. While others rant, he sits quietly on a stool next to the trailer, rapidly jotting notes into a small spiral notebook, refusing to let the chaos penetrate his concentration. This is definitive Parham. In his long career he has experienced losses, made mistakes, seen his property burn up, and watched biker gangs ruin his best swap meets, but he is not a man to put energy into retribution and recrimination. He dwells on the past only so long as it will yield its lessons. Then he moves on. In this case, the copious notes he is making in his small book will become a formula that he will later work to find a solution. Having jotted down everything he thinks is important, he suddenly stands up and announces, without raising his voice, "That's enough! You're wasting time and energy. Let's open that engine and find out what is wrong." The team falls silent and begins to gather the tools and equipment that will be needed for the job.

In the meantime, a spectator who was standing by the course when the Express sped past comes over and reports that it sounded like an air compressor. He says, "The exhaust note wasn't clean. I could also hear it going chuff-chuff-chuff as it came by." This is a clear indication that a head gasket is leaking, and, sure enough, it is what Wiley discovers as he removes a cylinder head. The surfaces are cleaned, the valves are lapped, and the head is reinstalled. Still, a compression check reveals that the offending cylinder remains 50 pounds below spec. The connecting studs may be pulling away from the engine case, and this is fatal damage that cannot be repaired in the field. Parham recognizes that the "little engine" is done, and instructs the crew to pull it out and install the big engine. It is only four o'clock, and there should be plenty of time to get the liner ready to run the following morning in the 1,650cc class. But Bonneville has not finished tormenting the J&P team.

From the west there is a storm approaching. Still miles away, it looks like a huge, gray dome, blotting out the mountains behind it. Two Easy-Up tents are lashed together over the liner to provide protection, and from their corners hang 20-pound weights to keep the awnings in place. As the storm approaches and the wind begins to rise, crew members attach additional weights to the frame. The Küryakyn team in the next pit over even moves its motorhome in close to create a better wind break for the J&P crew. Wiley works feverishly to remove the engine, knowing he should have the job done and the vehicle covered before too much salt starts flying around. But the storm is too strong and too fast, and as the wind rises to gale force, the awning's legs begin to dance on the salt. Team members not involved in the engine change leap up and grab the frame, applying additional weight. Nearby crews see the crisis and rush over to help, grabbing the frame of the tent and hanging on. Soon there are eight or ten men hanging from the frame, and still the tent jumps and shutters like a giant sail, threatening to lift everyone off his feet. Now it is raining sideways, and the water that covers the team tastes like salt. Then enormous bolts of lightning begin to crack between the sky and the desert floor, and someone observes, "You know, we're all just hanging here from a lightning rod!" Nervous laughter runs through the crew, but no one lets go of the awning frame or abandons his post until the work is done, the Express covered, and the awnings collapsed and packed away.

ঔ

Sodden, the team returns to the hotel to await the morning and plan how to break in the new 1,650cc engine that has been run only briefly at the shop before leaving for Bonneville. Given the amount of rain dumped onto the salt, everyone wonders if there will even be a course to race on. The next day, though the course has dried out enough to resume racing, the J&P team never sets a wheel on the salt due to persistent oil leaks in the new engine that must be traced down and stopped. Finally, on Thursday, Hess manages to get in three runs. Still, even with the big engine, he is unable to get the liner up to a respectable speed, and later it is learned that the electronic rev-limiter is not working correctly. In fact, several unstreamlined production motorcycles have gone faster than the Express this week. If its record-breaking performance of 2006 represented beginner's luck, 2007 must be Bonneville's revenge. But it could have been worse. Hess has kept the rubber down, and the Express will return to homebase undamaged. Others have not been so fortunate.

In fact, this has been more like the typical Bonneville, unlike the perfect speed storm of the prior year. A few teams have had a good week, but for the majority it has been nothing but frustration. Ack Attack is destroyed, two other top streamliners have crashed, the J&P Express has failed in its mission, and Denis Manning's record-holding Number 7 has not even put a wheel on the salt. Everyone packs up to head for home. For the J&P Express team it feels like a defeat, but John Parham is taking away his little book of notes, and there's nothing that motivates him more than overcoming a problem. For the true devotees of Bonneville, there is always next year, and this is the case with the J&P team. John summarizes, "We just tried to change too many things. Every major component, including the exhaust system and the carburetor, was different from 2006, and we didn't leave adequate time for dyno testing. That won't happen again. While the J&P Express will be taking the year off in 2008 due to the press of business in opening the Destination Daytona store, Zachary's wedding in July, involvement in Harley-Davidson's big 105th anniversary celebration, and preparation for J&P Cycles' 30th Anniversary in 2009, you can bet we will benefit from our 2007 learning experience when we eventually return to Bonneville."

Pilot Leo Hess prepares to get into the streamliner on the final day of the 2007 Bub races. The J&P Express was the final bike to run at the 2007 event. Trying one more time to sort things out from what had been a very frustrating week.

Below: The 2007 crew poses with the J&P Cycles Express before leaving Bonneville, hoping for better luck next time. Left to right: John, Lonnie Isam, Jeff Wiley, Mike Shaffer, Zach Parham, George Barnard, Paul Gomez and Scott Holton

J&P Cycles® Express Streamliner Sportster® Sets AMA National Record of 176.805 MPH
In the 1350 CC Carbureted Gas Class - Piloted by Leo Hess - September 2006

2006 Express team (top photo) Harry Bunker, Scott Holton, George Barnard, Mike Shaffer, Jeff Wiley, John Parham, and Paul Gomez. Pilot Leo Hess not present.

Chapter Thirteen: Anamosa, *American Gothic*, And the *Vroom!mates*

Anamosa, Iowa, a small county seat of less than 5,500 people, was founded as the settlement of Buffalo Forks in 1838. Later, its name was changed to Lexington, then changed again to Anamosa because there were so many Lexingtons springing up throughout the country that they created postal delivery problems. According to legend, Anamosa—meaning "white fawn"—was the name of a Native American girl who, with her lover, threw themselves to their deaths from a bluff on the Wapsipinicon River near the site of the future town. Until recently, Anamosa's largest employer was the Anamosa State Penitentiary. Founded in 1872, it is a medium-security facility that houses around 1,500 inmates, which are included in census figures for the town's population. Built of white limestone quarried nearby, it is an impressive, castle-like complex nicknamed "The White Palace of the West." Today, Anamosa has only a slightly larger population than it had in 1956 when John Parham, at the age of two, moved there with his family. Bertha Finn, who co-authored a history of the town published in 1988, is fond of saying, "Everything has changed in Anamosa except the noon whistle." And much of that change, at

John and Jill Parham on the J&P 30th Anniversary Harley-Davidson Street Glide. (Michael Lichter photo)

Small town life means things like the local Christmas tree walk in Anamosa. J&P Cycles puts on a display each year saying thank you to the community that supports them and has helped them grow. (2002)

Below: Christmas. 2004.

least in recent years, can be attributed to the growth of J&P Cycles and development initiatives undertaken by John Parham Enterprises, or John Parham individually or in partnership with other local citizens.

In terms of population growth, Anamosa has remained stagnant in part because its banking institutions would not look beyond agriculture during the 1970s and '80s. This was the same mentality that almost brought J&P Cycles down and nearly left John and Jill homeless in 1987, sending the Parhams to lending institutions in other eastern Iowa cities in search of capital. As a result of this past limited vision toward investment, Anamosa has very little light industry, most of which found a more progressive and welcoming community in nearby Monticello. An editorial that appeared in the *Cedar Rapids Gazette* in 1962 would seem to aptly describe a town like Anamosa, stating, "A small town may suggest boredom, a certain stagnation, a limitation of ability, a complacency that results from not caring to better oneself, a need of growth and development." All of which begs the question, "Why would a man as driven, creative, and progressive as John Parham have kept his business in Anamosa?" Why would he not relocate to Chicago where there would be a larger pool of artistic, communications, and business talent? Chicago, after all, is a stone's throw from Milwaukee, the center of his Harley-Davidson world. Or why would he not relocate to California, which—so say Californians—is on the cutting edge of everything? Los Angeles, after all, is the heart of the modern American motorcycle industry, and the West Coast, from San Diego to Oakland, is the crucible of American Custom Culture for both cars and motorcycles, the home of the Barris Brothers, Von Dutch, and Arlen Ness. Why would he stay in a town that bi-coastal sophisticates might consider a nowhere place in a nowhere state? Wouldn't it have been easier to become America's largest motorcycle aftermarket retailer in a place where there is more talent, better resources, more fluid capital?

The aforementioned editorial in the *Cedar Rapids Gazette* goes on to provide an answer, at least in part, when it states, "These small towns are not, in this day and age, the hick towns of the United States. With the modern methods of communication and travel, they are 'in the know' with their city cousins." When this was written in 1962, it might have sounded like wishful thinking; somewhat unconvincing. But, if so, it was accurately prophetic. The belief that business in America will thrive only in Los Angeles, Chicago, New York, or some other major city is outmoded. With an efficient national postal service, a vast transportation system, electronic communication, and digital technology that can move vast amounts of data instantaneously, any small town can become the home of a business juggernaut. To ask how J&P Cycles achieved what it did in quiet, little Anamosa, one must also ask how Lands' End sprang from Dodgeville, Wisconsin, a town with a thousand less people than Anamosa; or how L.L. Bean became a $1.47 billion business in Freeport, Maine, with a population of only 800. It is the same reason we see a huge international manufacturer like Honda choose a town like

Marysville, in the heart of Ohio farm country, to build its first American factory, rather than Detroit or Cleveland where there is an established pool of auto workers.

Based on instant communication and efficient transportation, the new American business model places more emphasis on work ethic than on traditional urban business locations. J&P Cycles is the first and most successful example of this business model played out in the retail sector of the American motorcycle industry. Like Lands' End or L.L. Bean, J&P Cycles built a nexus of selection, quality, and extraordinary customer service to create a new American business model that supersedes the convenience of proximity. But it is a business model that will not work without the presence of all three of these features, and each of these features requires hard work and tireless attention to detail. The willingness to work is what many small towns and opportunity-hungry regions can provide. What a town like Anamosa—or Dodgeville or Freeport or Marysville—may have lacked in vision, energy, and civic ambition, it more than makes up for in work ethic. Some will tell you that the legendary Midwestern work ethic doesn't exist; that there are good and bad workers everywhere. But you won't convince Iowans of this. They believe there is a superior work ethic in the Midwest, and in believing it, they make it so. At J&P Cycles, work ethic is not only converted into basic sweat equity, it is played out as well in a pride of performance that is translated into superior customer service and attention to detail, the cornerstones of the company's success.

John and Jill Parham don't just expect hard work, they model it. Trafferd Anderson, a Certified Purchasing Manager who has been with the company for nine years, asserts, "John and Jill are people who will roll their sleeves up and get it done. They expect this of their employees, and they expect them to always rise to the occasion, whatever it requires. But they demand nothing of employees that they don't demand of themselves." As Anderson sees it, the products he is responsible for buying are only incidental to the real business of the company. He explains, "We don't sell motorcycle parts. We sell customer service. That is what we've always been about, and that is what we will always be about." Furthermore, Anderson believes that going the extra mile creates a literal bond with customers that assures future sales and greater loyalty to the J&P brand. To this point, he argues, "This is unlike any other environment I have worked in. Our people are not buying a product, they are buying a lifestyle. Because of this, our customers want to buy from someone they believe understands them, and to serve them well and meet their expectations, we must understand them." Charlie Becker, the director of Camp Courageous, a charity supported by J&P Cycles, would concur. He says, "Work ethic is what leads to accomplishment. I see in John and Jill that dedication to hard work because they love their business, their customers, and what they are doing, and they have instilled this behavior within the culture of their business." Rob DeSotel, who joined the company in 1992, believes that quality work is more than just working hard at the same task, day in and day out. He believes creativity and flexibility are inherent in a good work ethic, stating, "Working at J&P is exciting,

J&P employees believe the Midwestern work ethic is real, and that they embody it. Above is the J&P call center, fielding up to 4,000 customer enquiries a day.

Below: Products are picked, packed, and shipped from the J&P warehouse at the rate of up to 4,000 orders per day.

For J&P's Employee Appreciation Day, the managers put on costumes and serve food to the staff. (Ed Youngblood photo)

Below: J&P employees work together and play together, as depicted by the senior staff at Employee Appreciation Day 2007. (Ed Youngblood photo)

tiring, frustrating, all in one day. Things change so quickly, you have to be flexible, and that's what makes it exciting. We have people who would do anything for the customers, and they are more than prepared to confront the challenges that call for a new or different solution." He adds, "Employees here have a positive attitude toward their customers, their community, and about helping others."

Former employees agree. Harry Bunker worked as a customer service technician at J&P Cycles from 2002 through 2006, and is now with Full Blast Engineering, a high-performance engine development company in Sioux Falls, South Dakota. Bunker states, "There is such a thing as a Midwestern work ethic, it still works, and John and Jill model it every day. They could be sitting on a beach somewhere letting others run the company, but they come to work every day." He adds, "Quality performance is contagious. You may be tired, but you feel good at the end of the day. You feel good about yourself and the company you are working for." And Bunker would agree that good treatment of customers is implicit in a good work ethic, stating, "J&P never stops stressing the importance of customer service. Good customer service takes time and training and money, but keeping a current customer happy is a lot cheaper than bringing in new customers, especially if word-of-mouth is working against you. That doesn't happen at J&P. Brand reputation is critically important, and customer service is the key."

Making the grade at J&P Cycles isn't easy. But John and Jill don't think of personnel as a commodity, like many corporations today. They want the J&P crew to function like a family, and this means they must be able to adapt to the culture and pull their weight. Those who are happy with the J&P way of doing things after the first year usually go on to become long-term employees. Paul Gomez, who has been in the motorcycle industry since he was 18, and has worked for three J&P suppliers, came to the company as a product merchandising manager in 2002. He says, "J&P is a company that will offer you an opportunity, but you have to earn it." He elaborates, "J&P is not a place that just expects work and nothing more. The culture includes work, community, fun, and play among the workforce. We are expected to understand we are a huge family and everything each of us does effects about 300 other people. Being mindful of this is just part of treating others—customers or colleagues—the way we would like to be treated." The environment that Gomez describes is reinforced with appreciation dinners within departments and cash prizes for employees who come forward with ideas that benefit the company and the workforce as a whole. Every April there is a company-wide appreciation luncheon where department managers dress up in costumes and serve lunch to their employees. To add to the fun, John and Jill's executive staffs conspire to select their costumes, which are always a surprise on the day of the luncheon. One year John and Jill dressed as American Gothic. Another year, John was dressed as a bowling pin and Jill as a bowling ball. Certainly, no one missed the amusing symbolism in that.

The conspicuous work ethic at J&P does not go unnoticed among its suppliers. George Munger, who met John while he was an employee of Custom Chrome in 1987, and is now with Küryakyn, says, "John has more drive than any three people I know. People who go to work for him and make the grade adopt that same kind of drive. Part of it is the Midwestern work ethic, but just being around John seems to increase a person's desire to work harder and do more." Ben Kudon, with Rivera Primo, Inc., a supplier of clutches and drivetrain components, says, "Hard work is what makes anyone successful, and J&P Cycles is the evidence that proves it. John and Jill started with nothing, and they worked their little butts off. They still do, as do all of the people in their company." John Vaughan-Chaldy, owner of Baron Custom Accessories, a supplier of metric cruiser parts, recalls, "The first time I went to Anamosa, Trafferd was giving me the tour, and I noticed that everyone walked with purpose. There was no one standing around or acting like they didn't know what to do next. Everyone was on the move, like they knew exactly where they were going and what they needed to do. I could sense a lot of pride and good feeling, and this gave me a good feeling too. I immediately knew this was a company I wanted my brand and my products to be affiliated with."

Of course, a discussion of the Midwestern work ethic to justify J&P's location in Anamosa is analysis in retrospect. It may be true, but it was never something that John Parham included in some early business plan. The forces that kept most of his business ventures in Anamosa were probably more personal and emotional than business-related or analytical. It will be recalled that early in 1974, before he was married, John quit a job he liked because he was afraid a transfer would require him to leave Anamosa and Jill. His younger brother Mark offers insight into John's values when he says, "I don't think it ever crossed John's mind to leave Anamosa." And many years later, when a friend in the motorcycle industry, marveling at the international success of J&P Cycles, asked John why he had stayed in Anamosa, John replied, simply, "I met a girl and fell in love. Besides," he added, "Anamosa is a nice place to raise a family."

☙

In announcing a profit of more than $10 billion at its 2007 shareholder's meeting, Wal-Mart's CEO declared, "But we can do better!" Today, the way some American corporations have learned to do better is by doing worse with their human resources. To satisfy shareholders, further discount their prices, or improve the bottom line, they scrimp on salaries, workplace conditions, and employee benefits. This has never been the case at J&P Cycles. The company has become the largest private employer in Jones County, and with addition of more than 60 people at the new Destination Daytona store, full J&P payroll has

For Employee Appreciation Day 2007, John and Jill dressed as bowling pin and bowling ball.

Below: John and Jill in 2005.

Jill Parham's rendition of "American Gothic:" the Iowa work ethic in American biker style. (Ed Youngblood photo)

Below: A line art drawing of the famous "American Gothic" by Grant Wood used in Pumpkinfest promotions each year.

probably surpassed that of the Anamosa state prison. J&P employees receive health, dental, and vision insurance with the company providing a large contribution to the premium. In addition, employees receive long- and short-term disability coverage, and an optional life insurance program has been added to the menu of coverage. J&P also sponsors a wellness program by paying for employees' memberships at the local community center, and there is tuition reimbursement for continuing education relevant to job performance and skills. J&P Cycles sponsors a 401K plan as well. Suzy Gilkerson, a human resource assistant, says, "When we ask people during the prospective employee interview process why they have applied at J&P, the most common answer we get is, 'I've heard it is a great place to work.'" Doug Hessing, J&P's longest-serving employee, declares, "I don't know of another company that takes care of its people like this one," and Janet Thomas, a customer service representative who has been with J&P for 15 years, points to the little fringes like employee appreciation luncheons and cash awards for good ideas, and says, "They treat their employees well, the same as they treat their customers. It all fits together. You cannot expect your employees to treat customers right if you don't treat your employees right. They know that and have a lot of benefits in place to keep a happy workforce." Contrary to the trends in many American corporations, Heidi Meeks, an administrative assistant who has been with the company for 11 years, reports, "As J&P has gotten bigger, the employee benefits have improved." At J&P Cycles, there is no discrepancy between how the company treats its employees and how it treats its customers. In changing the paradigm for retail marketing in the motorcycle industry, John and Jill believe that the higher costs of quality customer service and quality employee benefits will bring self-fulfilling results of more business and better profits.

☙

In addition to a couple who have changed the American motorcycle industry, the little town of Anamosa can boast a Civil War hero (Col. William Shaw), a novelist (Lawrence Schoonover), a Miss Iowa (Sara Corpstein), an Iowa Homecoming Queen (Saira Morgan), and an American Farmer of the Year (Nathan Kaufman). However, its most famous human product is the acclaimed painter Grant Wood, born in Anamosa in 1891. Wood moved with his family at the age of 10 to nearby Cedar Rapids where he became an artist and teacher who, after studying the Impressionists in Europe during the 1920s, returned to Iowa as a leading proponent of Regionalism, the school of art and literature that found its inspiration and subject matter in the small towns and rural life of the American Midwest. Wood was regarded a philosopher-artist, and as a co-founder and teacher at the Stone City Art Colony, just northwest of Anamosa, he helped produce a crop of young artists whose murals graced the public buildings erected during the Depression by the Work Progress Administration. With jealousy, other artists complained of the abundance of "little Woods" in the field, which only gives credence to his enormous influence. After his communal experiment at Stone City, Wood went on to teach painting at the University of Iowa's School of Art. Upon his death in 1942, he was buried in the family plot in Anamosa.

Wood's most famous painting is American Gothic. Through this iconic work, he did perhaps more than any other single artist to imprint the concepts of traditional American agrarian values and the legendary Midwestern work ethic. Wood wanted to depict the traditional roles of men and women, she in her domestic smock and he with a pitchfork. Implied in the image of the couple is the value of teamwork and shared labor. In the background is a house of the "Carpenter Gothic" style, the model for which actually exists in Eldon, a town on the Des Moines River where Wood visited with friends, in southeastern Iowa. Wood entered the painting in a competition at the Art Institute of Chicago, winning $300 and a bronze medal. In addition, the Institute bought the painting, and this is where it remains today.

The memorable and highly unusual American Gothic captured peoples' imaginations from the outset, and was published in many Midwestern newspapers when results of the Art Institute competition were announced. When it was published in the *Cedar Rapids Gazette*, it elicited a very negative reaction from readers who felt that Wood was depicting Iowans as uncultured yokels and humorless bible-thumpers. One farm wife threatened to bite Wood's ear off! However, the painting received critical acclaim, and as the Great Depression deepened, it came to be seen as a favorable depiction of the steadfast American pioneer spirit and dedication to hard work through which the nation has prevailed. Over time, it has become arguably the most famous American painting, rivaling Da Vinci's Mona Lisa or his Last Supper for international recognition. Yet despite the reverence it has earned, there remains a whimsical quality that has caused it to be parodied time and again by artists, photographers, and cartoonists, perhaps more than any other work of art in history. It has proven especially rich fodder for the visual medium of television, spoofed and imitated by shows as diverse as Desperate Housewives, Green Acres, The Simpsons, Saturday Night Live, and The Rocky and Bullwinkle Show.

Another example of this playful obsession with American Gothic took place in Cedar Rapids, IA in 2001. Acquiring 34 copies of fiberglass mannequins caricaturing the couple in the painting, the Cedar Rapids Convention & Visitors Bureau asked artists to decorate them in any creative way they saw fit. These were sponsored by various businesses, and after their unveiling at a Grant Wood celebration, they were positioned on sidewalks around the city for the next year. Jill Parham was one of the artists who exercised her interpretation of American Gothic by dressing the couple in biker gear, complete with leathers and bandanas. Instead of a pitchfork, the man holds a wrench in his hand. Playing on "vroom, vroom," the media's hackneyed portrayal of the sound of motorcycles that people either love or hate, Jill named her depiction Vroom!mates. Today, Vroom!mates stands in the foyer of the National Motorcycle Museum in Anamosa, where it greets guests who invariably react with a laugh or a smile, and usually a click of their digital cameras. Whether Jill intended it on a conscious level or not, Vroom!mates articulates the qualities of partnership and shared interest that have resulted in the huge success of J&P Cycles, just as Wood's American

John and Jill in the showroom at J&P Cycles.

Below: Participating in the motorcycle rodeo at the J&P Cycles Open House in 1997.

John and Jill, winter in Iowa, 2004 at the site of their upcoming building expansion.

Below: While J&P employees work hard, they also take plenty of time for relaxation and fun. In Sturgis 2000 John and several J&P employees formed the J&P Cohiba tribe. Enjoying drinks and cigars after a long day of working at the rally. Left to right: (top) George Barnard, Jeff Carstensen, Jon Thompson, Dirk Downing, Shawn Stone. (Bottom): John and Paul Capodonno.

Gothic suggests the Midwestern qualities of hard work and shared labor that are equally responsible for the success of the company. In both literal and spiritual ways, John and Jill Parham are the "Vroom!mates."

Undoubtedly, traditional gender-based roles in America have changed since the nineteenth century, which was the era Grant Wood intended to depict in American Gothic, but the shared labor of a partnership, bound by commitment and mutual affection, remains a powerful force that can often be greater than the sum of its parts. Anyone who has observed John and Jill's adventure, since it began in the early-1970s, while they were still high school sweethearts, will readily opine, without disrespect to either party, that the success of J&P Cycles would never have happened without the business partnership that grew out of their marriage. It began with Jill's commitment to support John's pursuit of his dream, which at first took the form of her providing a reliable source of income while he looked for a path to success in the motorcycle industry. But the synergy that led to that success emerged only when Jill became an integral part of the dream, when she came to work at J&P Cycles. Focusing on a common cause, they were able to learn how to most effectively apply their very different talents and personalities in ways that would achieve spectacular results. A success like J&P Cycles is rare enough, but for it to have been achieved by a pair who kept a marriage and a business together through good times and bad is an even more rare achievement that does not go unnoticed by friends, admirers, and associates of the Parhams.

George Barnard, who has spent countless hours manning J&P's display booths and mobile showrooms, both in North America and Europe, says, " John's strong suit is his vision and his work ethic. He is always working, and he never stops thinking about finding better ways to do things. He has a knack for seeing what needs to be done to improve the company. He sees what's important and he can spot the trends. Jill's strong suit is people. She is an uncanny judge of character, and can spot a bullshitter in a minute. She is highly organized and keeps the company staffed with good people." Barnard adds, "Industry people have told John he would never make it in Anamosa. But Iowa has a great work ethic, and I don't think John can even imagine having made it anywhere else." Jeff Carstensen, who came to J&P when there were less than a dozen employees, and knows John and Jill as well as anyone, would concur with Barnard. Carstensen says, "John is quiet and sometimes hard to read, and he can be very demanding. He expects others to work as hard as he does. Jill is outspoken and can read people. She is an excellent judge of character. John does not always have this skill, and he too often takes people at face value. He can become frustrated when people don't understand his vision or where he wants the company to go, but Jill is always there to interpret. Together, they are super people to work for, especially if you understand how they work together." Dennis Walters, who handles commercial property development for John

Parham Enterprises, says, "John's strengths are his great vision and his knowledge of the motorcycle market, inside and out. He is a rather introspective person and does not often quit thinking about work. Jill is a detail person while John is not. She is very personable and has the ability to set work aside when she wants to. Together, they can make it all work."

Nicole Ridge, who started with the company in 1994 and is in charge of J&P's communications and advertising, explains the differences in their personalities. About John she explains, "John is very intelligent. He is kind of quiet because he is always thinking or listening. But in a conversation he can put anyone at ease. He has a good sense of humor, which comes out when he is relaxed, but this is something most people don't see." About Jill, she says, "You can tell what Jill is thinking easier than John. She is very straightforward. She knows what she wants and is not afraid to tell people what she wants. She is vocal and opinionated. With her outgoing nature, she can fit in with any situation." Ridge adds, "They balance each other well. They are both smart and they are both go-getters." Ted Sands, who works for Performance Machine, one of J&P's suppliers, has a similar view. He states, "John is pretty quiet. He seems like a serious guy, but he is friendly and humble. He can talk to anyone. Jill is outgoing, fun, friendly, and funny. They complement each other." Bob McClean, former president of the Antique Motorcycle Club of America, adds, "It's a good deal when one person is not under the gun for everything. We should all be so lucky as to have the kind of partnership that John and Jill have." John Vaughan-Chaldy, a customizer and supplier of metric cruiser accessories, says, "Jill has a very warm side. She is kind and friendly, but she does not beat around the bush or tolerate nonsense. She is very direct and does not waste time. John is child-like in his love of motorcycles and their history, and this fascination is what has led to his success in the industry."

Jill's brother, Doug Hessing, who has been with J&P Cycles since 1987, reports, "John is always looking for something new and a better way to do things. Jill attends to the details and makes sure we don't get ahead of our capabilities." Comparing and contrasting the two, Charlie Becker, whose Camp Courageous is a beneficiary of J&P's charitable work, says, "John is reserved and Jill is outgoing. They know how each other think and they understand their business with the same point of view, but they contribute to it with totally different skill sets." Harry Bunker, who once worked for J&P Cycles, says, "John knows where the industry is going and has his finger on the pulse. He leads the way, but Jill is there to take care of the details and the day-to-day. He is the forward thinker, the point man, and the figurehead, but Jill is always right behind him to make sure the company is on the right track." Mike Buettner, the former CFO of the Motorsport Aftermarket Group, puts it

Above and below: Through all the good times and bad, and the countless changes, John and Jill have worked together to build a strong company and a strong family. And, after all this time their love for each, and motorcycles, has not only continued, but grown.
1990 Photo - Mike Farabaugh.
2008 Photo - Michael Lichter

a little more graphically: "John has the dreams and Jill is the voice of reason, and sometimes she puts the boot up John's butt when it needs to be." John's swap meet and motorcycle collector friend Lonnie Isam, a former drag racing champion, puts the relationship in colorful mechanical terms, stating, "John is a set of drag pipes and Jill is the baffles." Jim Long, a vendor and longtime friend who has helped John run his swap meets, agrees, "Jill has the female personality traits that keep things grounded. When times were tough and John had to take big risks, she was always there. There were times when she might rag on him, but at those times she was usually right." R.T. Shaw, at whose home John and Jill used to stay in Sturgis, says, "John is a hard charger, and Jill makes him slow down and think about what he is doing. They are both hard workers, and fair and honest business people."

Most observers of the company see the two as essential halves of the whole, with each equally important to the success of J&P Cycles. Longtime friend Mike Corbin states, "Everyone knows John, but Jill is definitely 50 percent of the operation. John is the idea guy and the widget guy. He is the best product champion in the industry. Jill is the business head who can see how it all ties together financially." Harley-Davidson mega-dealer Bruce Rossmeyer, whose Destination Daytona in Ormond Beach is the site of J&P's new Florida store, says, "John and Jill are the right and left arms of J&P Cycles. It needs both of them to do what it does." Paul Gomez, who has been in the motorcycle aftermarket since 1982 and has been one of J&P's product selection experts since 2002, says, "It is unique to see a husband and wife work together like this. They have mutual respect for what the other does. Together, they are poetry in motion." Publisher Buzz Kanter, a longtime friend of the Parhams who comes from a family of publishers, says, "I believe strongly in a family business. Most don't work, but this one does."

Clearly, John and Jill are more than partners in marriage. For 30 years they have been the "vroommates" who propelled J&P Cycles to the spectacularly successful company it has become, embodying the values of hard work and shared labor inherent in American Gothic.

Jill, Zach, and John, summer 2008. (Michael Lichter photo)

Chapter Fourteen: Anamosa and the Field of Dreams

In April 1989, at a time when John Parham's resources were extended into four corporations, and J&P Cycles was growing, but not profitably, the motion picture "Field of Dreams" was released. Based on the novel "Shoeless Joe," by W.P. Kinsella, it is the story of a man who, threatened by financial disaster, chooses to follow his dream against all logic and the advice of his community. The film is about baseball, and was filmed on a set built on a farm in Dyersville, Iowa, less than an hour's drive north of Anamosa. As a story about financial risk and the pursuit of one's vision in the face of seemingly insurmountable odds, it has become one of John Parham's favorite motion pictures. For him, it has taken on the proportions of a scriptural parable involving personal struggle, lonely determination, and ultimate victory, and he finds mythical significance in the fact that the "field of dreams" which still exists today as a popular tourist attraction, is so close to Anamosa.

"Field of Dreams," starring Kevin Costner, Amy Madigan, and James Earl Jones, and featuring Burt Lancaster in one of the last dramatic roles of his career and Ray Liotta in his first, was an extremely popular motion picture. It earned

At the High Performance Motorcycle Show in Bad Salzuflen, Germany in 1989, John Parham saw a banner that translated: "Your dream is already in progress." (George Barnard photo)

J&P Cycles receives President's award at annual Chamber of Commerce dinner

ANAMOSA — Anamosa Chamber of Commerce's annual dinner January 22 took a different twist with awards this year. For the first time in recent history, the Chamber recognized businesses for their contribution to the Anamosa community. For the past several years, the Chamber had recognized local volunteers and named a Citizen of the Year.

The Chamber board decided to recognize businesses this year because, they said, the Chamber is a business organization.

Tammy Wiese, outgoing president of the Anamosa Chamber of Commerce presented John and Jill Parham the first President's Award at the Chamber's annual dinner January 22. Parhams are the owners of J&P Cycles in Anamosa, were instrumental in the relocation of the National Motorcycle Museum and Hall of Fame to Anamosa from Sturgis,

Parhams recognized for community involvement

J&P Cycles was the first company to be honored with the Anamosa Chamber of Commerce President's Award when this special recognition was created in 2003.

Below: J&P is a regular sponsor of the Anamosa Pumpkin Festival, and more than once John and Jill have been named its Grand Marshals.

Oscar, Grammy, and Writers Guild nominations, and won top awards in the best "foreign language" film category in three foreign countries, including Japan. It brought into popular use the phrase, "If you build it, they will come." In fact, the phrase used in both Kinsella's novel and the movie was, "If you build it, he will come," but the sentiment is the same. What Costner's character is supposed to build is a baseball diamond, for which he plows under a money crop. And he has no clue why he has done it except that a mysterious, disembodied voice has told him to. His act is one of utter faith, taken against all reason.

Ironically, Ray and Annie Kinsella (named after the hero of W.P. Kinsella's autobiographical novel) become married in the movie in 1974, the same year as John and Jill Parham. And Annie, played by Madigan, is a Jill-like character in that she fully supports her husband's dream, even when there seems to be no sanity behind it. When adherence to the dream finally threatens their home and she urges him to return to saner pursuits, even then she will not withdraw her full and loving support. It is easy to understand why John Parham likes this film, and why the concept of a field of dreams has so much meaning for him. The phrase, "If you build it, they will come" takes on real-world significance when one thinks of the success of J&P Cycles, and specifically in the context of the 80,000 people a year who patronize its original Anamosa store, and over 35,000 people pouring through its new Destination Daytona Super Store during the week of its grand opening, or the fact that the National Motorcycle Museum has made little Anamosa an international destination.

In the movie, the voice that speaks to Costner gives him a second mysterious challenge when he has fulfilled the first, and then a third. While Costner's character never understands how these instructions are supposed to benefit him, in the end he realizes that his reward has come in the ways his actions have enriched the lives of others, even to the extent of providing redemption for deceased people whom history has already cast as losers. Undoubtedly, when John Parham was 25 and risking everything he had to build J&P Cycles, his dream did not include building a $75 million company, or providing a livelihood for 300 people, or being president of a nationally-acclaimed museum. More likely, he just wanted to get by and make a decent living doing what he loved, which was riding and building motorcycles. But just as Costner's field of dreams produces wide-ranging benefits for others beyond his expectations, the same can be said for the largesse that has resulted from the fulfillment of John Parham's dream.

From Parham's real-world field of dreams, his hometown of Anamosa has become a primary beneficiary. As success has made John and Jill more able to support and serve, they have turned their attention toward the needs of their town and other institutions in eastern Iowa, and it is likely that over time they will bring more growth and improvement to the community than it has seen since it briefly became a wealthy center for limestone production in the late 19th century. For example, in addition to the wealth that Parham has brought to the community through salaries and tourism dollars, he has initiated the kind of commercial development that the town let pass it by in the 1980s. A 50-acre commercial park has been platted on Route 151 just south of J&P Cycles. In the plans are restaurants, retail, office buildings, and a hotel. Dennis Walters, the director of real estate for John Parham Enterprises, explains, "The front door lots will be commercially driven. We are in negotiations with a national hotel chain and several restaurants, two of which are motorcycle-themed restaurants. John has provided the land for the development, and will have equity in some of the commercial businesses." He adds, "While Anamosa suffers from the image of a sleepy, underdeveloped area, it is likely that this project will trigger the kind of growth and renewal that John caused in Sturgis." Vic Hamre, CEO of Anamosa's Citizens Bank and a member of the Anamosa Economic Development Board, explains, "We had a struggle getting a commercial park going because the community did not have the money to buy land. John did, and has gotten us over that hurdle. This will be a big contribution to the community." Hamre adds, "In so many cases, a local successful person forgets where he came from. So many abandon their communities and move on to more glamorous opportunities. John has stayed in the community that nurtured him. He chose to stay and reinvest, and this is rare for a community of this size."

The Parhams have also given back to their community by hosting students from Wartburg College. In May, 2008, Jill and J&P's senior staff conducted a tour of the Anamosa facility and shared their ideas, knowledge, and expertise with a class that visited J&P Cycles, Harley-Davidson, and other companies in the motorcycle industry as case studies of different business models. Wartburg business professor Gloria Campbell, who helped organize the program with alumnus Ozzie Schofield, said, "At J&P the students saw a business that is constantly looking forward, and they learned a respect for entrepreneurship." She continues, "I think they also learned that money is not how the Parhams measure success. They are in it for the pride of building a business that serves its customers and its community." Schofield, a 1963 Wartburg graduate, a successful insurance executive, and an enthusiastic motorcyclist, says, "At J&P the students saw a modern and technically tied-together business. It does not matter that the company is in a very small town. They learned that if you have good values and take advantage of the best technology, communication, and infrastructure, you can create a success anywhere." Campbell adds, "J&P helped make it an extremely success program. The students couldn't quit asking questions. They did not want to see it come to an end."

The National Motorcycle Museum, recognized by Iowa Department of Tourism as the Attraction of the Year in 2001 for cities with less than 10,000 population, contributes significantly to the local economy by bringing visitors that very likely would not have otherwise stopped in Anamosa. Combined with the

Every year J&P Cycles hosts a poker run to raise money for Camp Courageous of Iowa, John and Jill's favorite charity.

Below: Jill and her staff taught Wartburg College business students how J&P keeps the world on two wheels.

An annual golf tournament for its partners in the motorcycle industry (above) and a silent auction for its customers (below) are just two of the ways J&P Cycles supports organizations like Camp Courageous of Iowa and the National Motorcycle Museum.

J&P Cycles open house, it accounts for visitation by more than 18,000 motorcycle enthusiasts a year, amounting to four times the population of Anamosa. It is estimated that these day-trippers contribute more than five-million dollars to the local economy through spending at restaurants, bars, antique shops, and service stations. In evaluating this contribution to the local economy, one must consider that very few museums even come close to paying operational costs through admission fees, and even fewer turn a profit. Typical of most, the National Motorcycle Museum is not a profit center; rather John Parham has to subsidize it to keep it open. Patty Manuel, president of the Jones County Economic Development Committee, says, "I enjoy driving up and down Main Street and seeing far more motorcycles than cars, and you will see tags from all over the nation. John has definitely helped put Anamosa on the map." She adds, "John also serves on the Anamosa Economic Development Board, so he is in a good position to understand the local economic needs, which he can address directly, or indirectly, as a planner and policy-maker."

K.C. Kiner, the executive director of the Anamosa Chamber of Commerce, states, "J&P Cycles, and John and Jill as individuals, can be counted on to support practically every function of the Chamber. For example, Jill serves as a Chamber Ambassador, whose role is to welcome new businesses to the community. They are consistent sponsors of the Pumpkinfest, and in 2008 will be our Grand Marshals. This is the city's biggest festival, drawing growers from all surrounding states and from as far away as Colorado." Kiner adds that the festival, which attracts 20,000 people and a hundred vendors, has produced the world's second-largest pumpkin, weighing in at 1,668 pounds. "In addition," Kiner says, "John and Jill helped with the renovation of Main Street and support the Grant Wood Festival, which brings 30 to 50 artists to town for a show." Doug Ricklefs, a friend of John's dating back to high school, who has become a real estate developer in the area, and who was chairman of the Library Fund Raising Committee, explains, "Jill was a significant fund-raiser on the committee, and she and John made a major direct contribution to the project." He adds, "Jill serves on the Ambulance Board, the Parhams have contributed to the hospital, and J&P is the sponsor of fireworks at the county fair."

Sean Williams, Director at the Jones Regional Medical Center and a member of the Anamosa Rotary Club, says, "John and Jill Parham are an anchor in the community. It is inspiring to see how they manage their business and how they find so many ways to help." As an example, Williams points to the fact that the Parhams give Rotary free preferred exhibit space at the J&P Cycles open house where the club raises funds by selling ice cream. He adds, "What they do they do right." Donna Condry, who manages human resources at the Medical Center and is a fellow Chamber of Commerce Ambassador with Jill, says, "Jill was instrumental in lighting the downtown for Christmas, and the tourism their events bring to Anamosa during the summer is very important." The Reverend David Bracht-Wagner, who is former minister of the Anamosa United Methodist Church, says, "John and Jill donated a van to the church, and Jill has served on a committee that oversees the Jones County Food Pantry." In addition, J&P Cycles has sponsored a number of the local baseball teams, and the company sells POW-MIA T-shirts through its catalog, proceeds of which have raised over $9,500 for the local AMVETS chapter. Matt Ahrens states, "The Parhams model charitable service just as they model work on the job. Jill puts on her gloves and gets right out there and leads a group of employees to clean up the roadside along the highway."

Perhaps the favorite charity for the Parhams is Camp Courageous of Iowa, a unique institution near Anamosa that provides learning and recreational opportunities for the physically disabled. The facility, which is open year-round, serves 5,000 special-needs campers a year, and is supported entirely by donations. J&P Cycles promotes an annual poker run that brings out 200 to 300 motorcyclists, with all proceeds going to the Camp. Jeff Carstensen, who handles the layout and planning for the event, says, "It is a big deal. All the little towns in the area want to know if they will be on the route, because it is a bonanza for local restaurants and gas stations. People call me and want their business to be the site for a check point." In addition, on the day prior to its annual open house, J&P hosts a charity golf tournament for all of the motorcycle industry personnel who are in town. Hector Menendez, a representative for Daytona Twin Tech, laughs and says, "I learned a long time ago that I need to bring extra cash. I always leave this golf outing with my wallet about $400 lighter." J&P also sponsors an employee contribution day. Combined, its functions raise as much as $14,000 a year for Camp Courageous, and over time the company and its employees have contributed over $64,000. Charlie Becker, the Camp Director, says, "The Parhams and J&P are major supporters, but they are always so low key about it. Their actions always speak much louder than their words."

Those who have known John and Jill through the more than 30 years they have pursued their dream often comment on how little they have been changed by success since their days as humble

John Parham lives his dream, riding a custom motorcycle with the J&P Cycles big rig mobile showroom that helps keep the world on two wheels.

Below: The J&P Cycles Poker Run for Camp Courageous stops at the camp each year to visit with some of the kids they are helping.

John and Jill present their annual contribution to Charlie Becker, director of Camp Courageous, in 2007.

Below: John and Jill at the 2007 J&P Open House.

swap meeters, trying to buy, sell, and trade their way to a better life. Ed Ahlf, who met them at the very first swap meet they organized in Monticello in 1977, says, "John is a pretty common guy. He does not put on airs." Charlie Becker concurs, stating, "John and Jill are just salt of the earth people." Dick Betchkal, who acquired several of J&P Promotions' Midwestern shows when John began to phase out of the business, says, "If John has a big ego, he certainly doesn't show it. He is the real deal." Pat Burross, who has worked with the Parhams since she went to work at Chrome Specialties in 1985, states, "John and Jill have never changed over the years, and their customers feel that." Jeff Decker says, "John has become the single most important person in Anamosa, but he is as humble as he ever was. He has not turned into a corporate person who puts himself above others." Rocky Halter, a supplier of vintage Indian parts who met John at a swap meet in 1986, says about him, "He is the same person he was when I first met him. Now he is running a multi-million dollar business, but he is the same unassuming guy." Dave Ohrt, another swap meet friend and restorer of classic motorcycles, agrees, stating, "He doesn't think he is above anybody. He will hang with the people he has always been with." Ron Payne, who used to help John fix his BSA when he was in high school, says, "John and Jill have never lost touch with their roots. I can go out and sit down and talk to John today much as I did 30 years ago. John and Jill are just John and Jill." Ted Sands, who conducts technical training for Performance Machine, states, "Despite everything he has achieved, John is still a very friendly and humble guy." Rally organizer Charlie St. Clair asserts, "If John has made an enemy, I don't know him." He adds, "If anyone ever spoke ill about John Parham, I would have to look with great suspicion upon that person."

ᏡᏒ

In 1998, John Parham and George Barnard attended the High Performance Motorcycle Show in Bad Salzuflen, Germany. There they saw an exhibit of beautiful choppers under a big banner that said, "Dein Traum ist schon in Arbeit!" which can be translated as "Your dream is already in progress." Indeed, by 1998, John Parham was well into the fulfillment of his dream, far more than he once believed possible. And, like the story of "Field of Dreams," his dream had begun to enrich the lives of others, both in the American motorcycle industry and the community of Anamosa. In 2007, on the occasion of the grand opening of J&P's beautiful Destination Daytona store, Charlie St. Clair, an avid biker, a longtime friend of John's, and the organizer of the legendary Laconia Rally, said, **"The Field of Dreams isn't really in Dyersville. That's just a movie set. The real Field of Dreams is down the road in Anamosa."**

At one point in the movie "Field of Dreams," Shoeless Joe Jackson, a deceased baseball player who has been brought from the past into the present, asks Ray Kinsella, "Is this heaven?" and Kinsella replies, "No, this is Iowa." One can debate whether the real Field of Dreams is in Dyersville or Anamosa, but for John Parham it does not matter. For him, the belief in the idea is what gives it reality. In his case, that reality long ago took on the mission of...

Keeping The World on 2 Wheels®

Appendix A: J&P Time Line

1954 – On August 13, Jill Hessing is born in Anamosa, Iowa. On September 14, John Parham is born in Harlan, Iowa.

1956 – John Parham, age 2, moves to Anamosa, Iowa with his family.

1971 – On January 11, John Parham meets Jill at a dance at Monticello.

1972 – Jill graduates from high school, goes to work at Energy Manufacturing in Monticello.

1973 – John graduates from high school, goes to work at Pamida in Anamosa, and attends Kirkwood Community College.

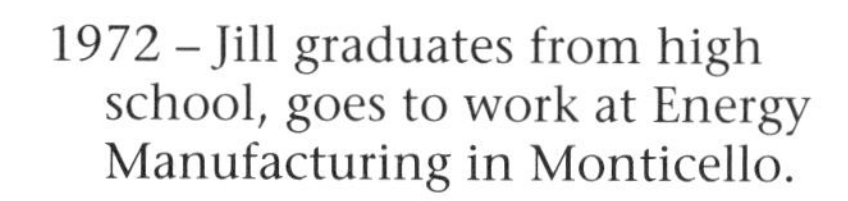

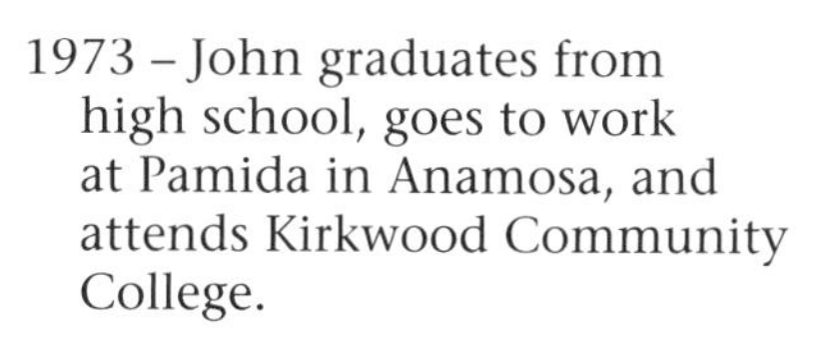

1974 – John and Jill are married on September 14, his 20th birthday.

1975 – John quits Pamida rather than accept a transfer to another city. He opens up D&J Cycles with former high school biology teacher Don Brown. He maintains a day job as a foreman at Doehr Electric, a manufacturer of electric motors.

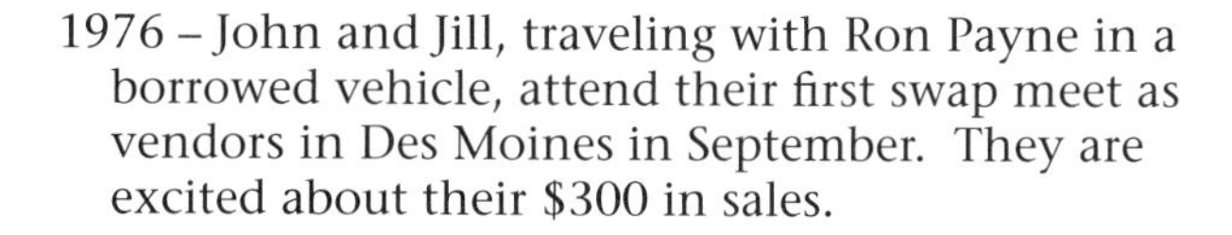

1976 – John and Jill, traveling with Ron Payne in a borrowed vehicle, attend their first swap meet as vendors in Des Moines in September. They are excited about their $300 in sales.

1977 – In January, John and Jill attend a swap meet at the Minneapolis Armory. They make nearly $5,000 in sales, and play Pink Floyd's "Money" all the way home. Later that year they organize their first swap meet at the fairgrounds in Monticello, with Doug Hessing and Sue and Ralph Shaw.

1979 – John and Jill buy their first house, on Hickory Street in Anamosa. John sells his Honda chopper for $2,700 to make the down payment. Also, he buys his first collectible motorcycle, a 1955 Harley-Davidson Panhead. John and Don Brown split up D&J Cycles. John starts J&P Cycles out of a building with a dirt floor.

1981 – John opens a video arcade in Anamosa in addition to running J&P Cycles while holding down a full-time job.

1982 – The video arcade in Anamosa does well, so John starts a regional video game distribution and service business in eastern Iowa, partnering with accountant Don Archer. John gets laid off from his job and decides to focus exclusively on his own business opportunities.

1984 – As home video games improve and become more popular, John and Jill's video game supply business begins to decline. They take a $25,000 loss and get out. By now they are organizing 12 and attending 25 motorcycle swap meets a year. On May 18, J&P Cycles burns. The building is a total loss and the inventory is under-insured by $35,000. On July 23, Zachary John Parham is born. John acquires permanent home for J&P Cycles on Highway 151 just north of Anamosa.

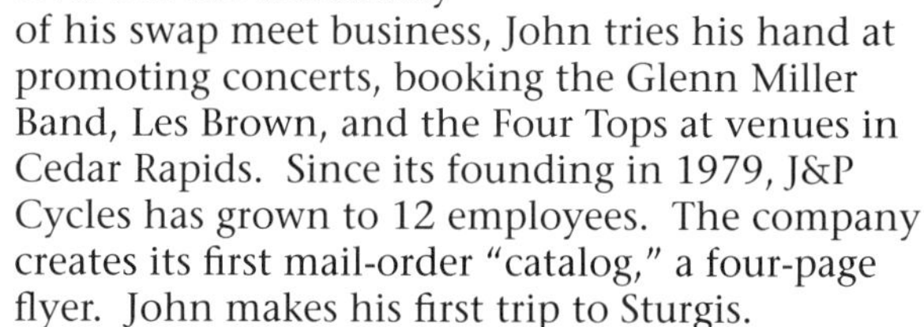

1985 – John organizes his first show at Chicago's McCormick Place, a venue that he will eventually turn into the world's largest indoor motorcycle swap meet and bike show. To level out the seasonality of his swap meet business, John tries his hand at promoting concerts, booking the Glenn Miller Band, Les Brown, and the Four Tops at venues in Cedar Rapids. Since its founding in 1979, J&P Cycles has grown to 12 employees. The company creates its first mail-order "catalog," a four-page flyer. John makes his first trip to Sturgis.

1987 – Jill leaves Energy Manufacturing and takes a job with Keltech Information Services in Cedar Rapids. The J&P catalog grows to 24 pages. John and Jill almost end up homeless in a complicated foreclosure move by a local banker, and to meet payroll, John must sell his beloved 1955 Harley-Davidson Panhead.

1988 – Jill's brother, Doug Hessing, joins J&P full-time. The National Motorcycle Museum is founded in Sturgis, South Dakota, with John as a board member and a supporter. J&P Promotions hosts vintage dirt track races at the AMCA meet in Davenport, Iowa. The popular races will be managed by J&P for the ensuing 13 years.

1989 – In July, J&P Promotions is set up as a separate for-profit corporation. The modern J&P Cycles logo is introduced, and John creates a new corporation called Zacharia Advertising and Publications, named after his son Zachary. John is able to buy back his 1955 Panhead.

1990 – On the occasion of the 50th anniversary of the Black Hills Classic, J&P Cycles opens a store front for seasonal sales in Sturgis, sharing space with the National Motorcycle Museum. Since 1985, J&P Cycles has doubled its employees from 12 to 23. The company surpasses $1 million in sales and loses money in the process. J&P Promotions organizes its first all-Harley motorcycle drag race.

1991 – Jill goes to work full-time for J&P Cycles. The J&P catalog grows to 96 pages. A store front for seasonal sales is opened in Daytona Beach on the occasion of the 50th anniversary of the Daytona 200. J&P Promotions creates the AHDRA Western Swing, a series of five drag races from Houston to Los Angeles.

1992 – John meets accountant and financial adviser Ron Helle. John and Jill spend the year improving J&P Cycles' infrastructure and internal business controls.

1993 – J&P Promotions creates the Custom Chrome, Inc. Super Series consisting of major bike shows from St. Paul to Harrisburg. John attends the European Super Rally in Italy, starting a program to distribute J&P's catalog in Europe.

1994 – J&P does $2.6 million in sales.

1995 – Since 1990, J&P Cycles doubles its employees from 23 to 50. Sales are $4.09 million. Ground is broken for a 20,000 square foot expansion. John

Parham Enterprises now holds four companies: J&P Cycles, J&P Promotions, Nostalgic Toy Creations, and Zacharia Advertising and Publications.

1996 – J&P puts the whole of its catalogs on the Internet and puts its first big truck on the road to attend rallies throughout the United States. Sales improve by more than 50 percent over 1995 to $6.48 million.

1997 – J&P Cycles becomes a benefactor for Camp Courageous, conducting annual fund-raising poker run and golf tournament for the charity. J&P Cycles breaks ground for a 12,000 square-foot permanent store on Lazelle Street in Sturgis. J&P Promotions promotes its last motorcycle drag race.

1998 – J&P's new purpose-built retail store at Sturgis is opened and dedicated during the 1998 Rally.

1999 – J&P Cycles celebrates its 20th anniversary. Its product catalog now numbers 692 pages. Ground is broken for a 50,000 square foot expansion in Anamosa. J&P Cycles is named in Top 100 Dealers by *Dealernews*. Turning his focus to the growing retail business, John sells his flagship shows, Madison, St. Paul, and Chicago to R&B Promotions.

2000 – Since 1995, J&P Cycles has increased its employment by over 150 percent, from 50 to 132. The J&P Harley catalog has grown to 800 pages, and a new vintage Harley catalog is launched. J&P is named a Top 100 Dealer for the second year in a row. The National Motorcycle Museum in Sturgis becomes insolvent; John moves it to Anamosa to rescue the project. J&P Promotions promotes its final vintage dirt track race at Davenport.

2001 – The National Motorcycle Museum and Hall of Fame holds its grand opening in Anamosa and J&P Cycles launches a vintage Harley-Davidson parts and accessory catalog. Memphis Shades names J&P Cycles its Retailer of the Year. A new mobile showroom is put on the road featuring a 31-foot tractor with staff apartment and a 40-foot trailer. J&P is named a Top 100 Dealer for the third time. J&P becomes part of the Motorsport Aftermarket Group, formed specifically to invest in leading companies in the motorcycle industry.

2003 – J&P Cycles receives the first President's Award from the Anamosa Chamber of Commerce, is featured on "Corbin's Ride On" on Speed Vision, and is named a Top 100 Dealer for the fifth time. A 300-page Metric Catalog is launched. The famous Captain America chopper from the movie "Easy Rider," now owned by John Parham, is exhibited at Harley-Davidson's 100th Anniversary where Peter Fonda signs papers attesting to its authenticity. Zachary graduates from high school.

2004 – By its 25th anniversary, J&P's Harley catalog has grown to 932 pages; the Metric catalog is 432 pages. On June 26 over 8,500 attend the company's 25th anniversary open house. *Dealernews* names J&P Cycles a Top 100 Dealer for the sixth consecutive year, and the nation's Best Independent Dealership. J&P opens a separate 26-person call center in Daytona Beach, Florida. In October the National Motorcycle Museum Hall of Fame and the Motorcycle Hall of Fame merge their Hall of Fame programs, though the museums remain separate and autonomous. John Parham joins the board of the Motorcycle Hall of Fame Museum. In December, John's mother, Anna, passes away from pulmonary fibrosis.

2005 – Since 2000, J&P Cycles has again more than doubled the number of people hired, from 132 to 279 employees. *Dealernews* names J&P a Top 100 Dealer for the seventh year in a row. J&P's Sturgis retail presence now covers a full city block. John and his friend David Ohrt stage a vintage dirt track race for the History Channel.

2006 – Another 15,000 feet are added to the J&P Cycles facility, bringing to total size to 165,000 square feet. Ground is broken for a new store at Ormond Beach, Florida. J&P launches a sport bike product line and catalog and the company is named a *Dealernews* Top 100 Dealer for the eighth consecutive year. John is inducted into the Sturgis Motorcycle Hall of Fame. J&P Cycles sponsors the J&P Cycles Express, a speed racing streamliner, and sets a national record in its engine class of 178.85 mph at the Bonneville Salt Flats.

2007 – Zachary Parham graduates magna cum laude from Wartburg College with a degree in business and accounting. He joins the J&P Cycles staff. A custom motorcycle Zach built is featured in the Wartburg College magazine and in *Easyriders*. In October J&P Cycles celebrates the grand opening of its multi-million Destination Daytona SuperStore in Ormond Beach, Florida. J&P is named Best Independent Dealer in the Nation for a second time and John, Jill, and J&P Cycles become the cover story for the August issue of *Dealernews*. The J&P catalogs now include Harley-Davidson, 1192 pages; Metric Motorcycles, 496 pages; Vintage Harley, 336 pages; and Sport Bike, 132 pages. More than a million catalogs a year are printed and distributed. John Parham Enterprises breaks ground for a 50-acre commercial park on Highway 151 in Anamosa, Iowa with an additional 40 acres available for expansion. With over 285 employees, 58 of which are in the new Florida store, J&P Cycles becomes the largest private employer in Jones County, Iowa.

2008 – J&P Cycles has its largest open house ever with 15,000 people. Zachary Parham and Brianna Johnson are married on July 12. J&P raises a record $14,500 for Camp Courageous. John and Jill are Grand Marshals for the Pumpkinfest in October.

2009 – J&P Celebrates 30 years in business! Join us for our 30th Anniversary Open House June 27 & 28, 2009!

About the Author

Ed Youngblood, an active motorcyclist for fifty years, worked for the American Motorcyclist Association for 28 years and served 19 years as its President and CEO. He served for 20 years on the Management Council of the International Motorcycle Federation, based in Geneva, Switzerland, and still holds the title of Honorary Deputy President with that organization.

Youngblood is a member of the Motorcycle Hall of Fame and serves on the boards of several not-for-profit organizations, including the Antique Motorcycle Club of America Foundation and Ohio Motorcyclists for Children, a charitable organization that plans motorcycle events to raise funds for children at risk.

He holds a Master of Arts Degree from Ohio University and has authored six books on American motorcycle history. In addition to "Keeping the World on Two Wheels," he has written "John Penton and the Off-Road Motorcycle Revolution," "Mann of his Time," a biography of Dick Mann, "Take it to The Limit," a biography of Dave Mungenast, "Heroes of Harley-Davidson" and "A Century of Indian." His articles about motorcycle history have appeared in *Racer X Illustrated, The Antique Motorcycle, Thunder Press, Classic Bike Rider, American Motorcyclist,* and other periodicals.

Since 1999 he has managed Motohistory, a company for the publication of historical information about motorcycling and the motorcycle industry in both digital and print media. He has curated exhibits about motorcycles for The Ohio State University, the Columbus College of Art and Design, the Orlando Museum of Art, the Wonders Museum at Memphis, the Motorcycle Hall of Fame Museum, the Saratoga Automobile Museum, and the Guggenheim Museum.